Pension Mathematics for Actuaries

by Arthur W. Anderson

Second Edition

ACTEX Publications • Winsted, Connecticut

1st printing — February 1985
2nd printing — September 1985
2nd edition — January 1990
2nd edition, 2nd printing — November 1991
2nd edition, 3rd printing — May 1992

Printed in the United States of America

Cover Design by MUF

Library of Congress Cataloging-in-Publication Data
Anderson, Arthur W., 1941 -
Pension mathematics for actuaries

Includes index.
1. Insurance, Life -- Mathematics. 2. Old age pensions -- Mathematics. I. Title.
HG8782.A497 1985 332.2'52'0151 85-11231

ISBN 0-936031-10-7

Contents

Chapter 1

Introduction

The student trained in the mathematics of life contingencies may understandably wonder whether there is in pension mathematics something fundamentally new, or whether it is just a particular application of what he has already learned. When he encounters the "accrued liability", for example, he will notice its resemblance to a net level-premium reserve for a life-insurance policy. A "normal cost" will look much like a net premium. But these similarities will be seen to be only superficial: pension mathematics is a distinct actuarial specialty, different from life-insurance mathematics in many ways.

One such difference has to do with the size of the groups normally dealt with. When the life-insurance actuary prices an annuity policy he works from the hypothesis that there will be enough purchasers of the policy that he can ignore statistical fluctuations; he often has the luxury of allowing hefty margins for error. In a pension plan covering a hundred employees, by contrast, statistical fluctuation is more important than the law of averages: the actuary knows his estimates will be off the mark; the question is how to deal with the inevitable difference between expected and actual results. Ironically, the pension actuary must plan ahead for his own "error".

A second difference arises from the pension actuary's lack of control over many critical variables. A life actuary could not sanction, for example, an individual annuity policy whose face amount varied with the salary of the policyholder, or which allowed the annuitant unrestricted control over the commencement date of the annuity. The pension actuary, on the other hand, must often deal with plans which allow choice of retirement date, whose benefits depend on final earnings before retirement, and under which benefits may be forfeited if an employee leaves employment too soon. Predicting the unpredictable is part of his daily work.

There is also a difference in attitude toward "conservatism". In the case of the life actuary, conservatism means erring on the side of the insurance company. Redressing equity between policyholders, or between policyholders and stockholders, is for him a secondary task which, for mutual companies at least, can be handled by careful distribution of surplus. The pension actuary's assignment is to assess the cost of a particular plan — error on either the high or the low side being equally undesirable. Too high a pension expense can cause taxes to be raised (if the employer is a government) or profits reduced (if the employer is a private business). Too low a cost may be the ruination of the plan itself. In his attempt to weigh the sometimes conflicting interests of employer, employees, the public, and the long-term fiscal health of the plan, the pension actuary must be very sure of where he stands, and why.

Therefore, in this book we shall be concerned not only with the specialized mathematics of pensions, but also with the development of actuarial judgment. To be a competent pension actuary you must know much more than, say, how to do a valuation using the entry-age-normal cost method on a typical pension plan. You must, in this example, know (a) why you are using the entry-age-normal method, which means (b) you must know what other methods there are and how they differ, and (c) you must know how to go about choosing assumptions, taking into account (d) the size of the plan (does it cover one employee? 1,000? 100,000?). Also (e) you have to know how to deal with non-pension benefits which may be a part of the plan, and you must look into (f) the value of assets and future cash flow and (g) stability of annual cost. You must also have a firm understanding of how your results may be affected by (h) future events — a layoff, a plan improvement, or a turn in the economy. In short, you have to possess both *knowledge* and *perspective.* Acquisition of these cannot take place overnight, but the process is speeded up considerably if you start off with a solid foundation in the theory behind the practice. The purpose of this book is to help you build that foundation.

Whenever one attempts to teach a complicated subject to beginners, there is the question of where and how to begin, since every aspect of the subject is related to every other. One way to proceed — which we shall avoid — is that of the formal mathematical treatise, in which each term is completely defined when it is introduced, and in which theorem and proof alternate to form a purely *deductive* exposition. This approach is very sure-footed from a logical standpoint and is particularly satisfying to the person who knows where the path is leading; but it is difficult for the beginner who, especially if he is a typical student actuary, is trying to learn directly from a book.

The approach we shall use instead is *inductive* and evolutionary. We shall first discuss each new topic in a simplified setting so that we can move quickly through the important points; later we shall return to sharpen up hazy definitions and add embellishments. Thus, as you study this book, you will find youself following the same steps as if you were learning the subject on the job. First you will tackle simple ideas at the apprentice level, and later take on sophisticated concepts at the master level.

Learning is a cooperative endeavor between the student (you) and the teacher (this book). You will be required to bear your fair share of the burden. The wide outside margins on each page are intended for your own notes as you read the book. Since the author regards the thread of logic equally as important as the results reached, you should use the margins to mark the turning points of each discussion. This will allow you to look back quickly to see the logical path by which any result is reached. Many important points have been pre-annotated by the author, as you will see.

While your purpose in reading this book may be to pass a particular examination, you will find the book ill suited as a "cram" manual. The book presupposes that you want to master the material completely, and actually to *understand* pension mathematics. The book is divided into six chapters (after this one), and each chapter into relatively short sections. At the end of each section you will find exercises which help you to review and expand your knowledge. As you proceed you will find continual back-referencing of material previously discussed, so as to reinforce the logical coherence of the subject.

The exercises are of several types. Some ask you to complete or check a mathematical development in the text. Others are numerical examples, which are indispensable adjuncts to an otherwise abstract algebraic discussion. Many ask you to develop related material on your own (with suitable hints); these cover important topics using the same logical approach as the text. Finally, several exercises serve to expand your intellectual horizons; these may direct your attention to deeper mathematical or philosophical questions which lie outside the scope of this text, or to material in related fields. The wisest course is to work each exercise in a permanent notebook, because results of exercises are relied upon extensively in the text and you may find it difficult to remember the details of a solution after the passage of weeks or months.

As you study this book, allow plenty of time for the material to sink in. The book is intended to be studied sequentially — starting at the beginning — and if you try to skip lightly over difficult topics you will find yourself getting bogged down in the later material. Do *not* be tempted when you are asked to derive a particular formula, for example, merely to accept that the formula must be correct and move on: There are subtle points which you will see readily if you try to derive the formula yourself, but which you will certainly miss if you do not.

While this book is addressed to beginners in *pension* mathematics, it is designed for students who have a firm grounding in basic actuarial mathematics, particularly life contingencies. The discussion also presumes a reasonable education in general college-level mathematics (calculus, probability, statistics, etc.) as well as familiarity with the international actuarial notation.

Like other technical fields, pension mathematics has its own jargon, which has grown up rather haphazardly over the decades. As a result, there are often several terms for the same quantity or concept. For example, what we shall in this book call the "accrued liability" has gone under such names as "past service liability", "past service cost", "supplemental liability", "prior sevice cost", "supplemental present value", and so on. Many of these terms were used mainly by non-actuaries or were attempts by actuaries to impose new, non-idiomatic terms to achieve uniformity. In this case the author uses the term "accrued liability" because it is the one most often encountered in practice.

The latest move toward rationalizing pension terminology in North America is the adoption by six major actuarial groups of the report of the Joint Committee on Pension Terminology (JCPT), in July 1981. For the most part, the JCPT terminology coincides with traditional pension terminology in the United States, although a few new terms were introduced. The hope of the organizations is that the new terminology will take root where previous standardization attempts have failed. At the time of writing, however, there are some differences between real-life actuarial usage and the recommendations of the Joint Committee. For example, the actuarial cost method known generally to U.S. actuaries as the "frozen-initial-liability" method is renamed the "frozen-entry-age" method by the Report. For the most part this book follows the recommendations of the Joint Committee; the few significant differences will be noted.

Each country has its own laws, regulations, and customs affecting pension plans; to practice as a pension actuary in your own country you have to be familiar with them. For example, to practice in the United States you must know all about the "funding standard account". In this book, however, we shall avoid a direct discussion of any of these purely national matters, in favor of concentrating on the central question of *how to determine the cost of a pension plan.* Once you know that, the details of laws and regulations affecting your practice will present no problem. Although the text will undoubtedly reflect the fact that the author is a citizen of the United States and practices in that country, this book is intended for an international audience. If the reader will be so kind as to look beyond the obvious Americanisms (spelling, terminology, etc.) he will find the underlying language of the book to be that of logic and mathematics, which translates easily into any language or dialect.

Chapter 2

Actuarial Cost Methods

2.1 *Why and Wherefore*

Cost methods apply to pension plans, so we cannot begin to understand what a cost method is, how it works, or why we need to have one, without saying a little about pension plans in general. Although the term "pension plan" is applied to a bewildering variety of retirement and deferred-compensation schemes, we shall use the term *pension plan* in a very restrictive sense: any arrangement for providing monthly payments to a person for life beginning at a stated age, where the amount of the payment is determined by formula (rather than, for example, by the amount of money accumulated in an account). Thus, an arrangement whereby every employee reaching age 65 receives a pension of $10 per month for each year of service with the employer, is a pension plan, as is an arrangement which provides a pension of 50% of final salary. In other words, we are dealing with "defined-benefit" plans and shall have little to do with "money-purchase" or "defined-contribution" plans, which provide for the deposit of a certain percentage of pay into an account for each employee each year, and where benefits are based on the balance in the account at retirement.

Pension plans are often festooned with ancillary benefits: survivor's pensions, lump-sum death benefits, disability benefits, and the like — but we shall not concern ourselves with these for the moment. Whatever else it may do, a pension plan always provides a *life annuity* to each participant who retires from employment (and who has satisfied the age and service requirements of the plan).

An employer who sets up a pension plan thereby commits himself to the expenditure of sums of money in future years. If he decides simply to pay the pensions as they fall due — i.e., if he uses the "pay-as-you-go" cost method — then over the next 40 or 50 years his annual expenditures will show a pattern something like that of Figure 2.1.1.

For the first several years (region A of the curve) his expenditures will rise only moderately, because at first no one will be receiving a pension and very likely the pensions which are paid early will be smaller than those ultimately payable, because the pensions are usually based on length of service, and often compensation as well. During this initial period the employer enjoys the most pleasant years of pension sponsorship: He gets credit from the employees for having established a fine new plan, but the plan consists primarily of promises at this stage so his cash outlay is still small.

But when the passage of time brings the employer to region B of the curve, the plan starts to pinch. Employees keep retiring on bigger and bigger pensions, and those who are already retired are not dying at a sufficiently rapid rate to offset the new additions to the pension rolls. During this stage of pension plan growth annual outlays begin to rise steeply — outstripping the rise in covered payroll even if the employer stays in business at normal employment levels. This stage of growth is the most trying period for a pay-as-you-go pension plan, and is in fact the stage of growth of many of our governmental plans in the United States — Social Security in particular. During this stage the plan has not changed. There is no improvement in the benefit formula. But the cost is nevertheless snowballing, so the employer must pay ever increasing sums of money each year with no plan improvements to show for it.

Figure 2.1.1
Typical Pattern of Benefit Payments from a Pension Plan

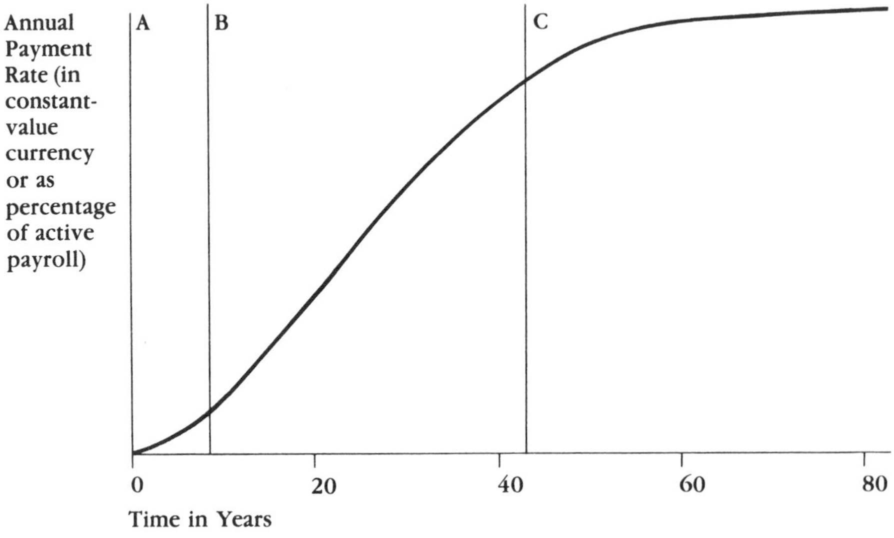

At last, if the plan has survived the passage through region B, the cost begins to stabilize, more or less, as shown in region C of the curve of Figure 2.1.1. The danger is that the cost will stabilize at a level too high for the employer to bear. A pay-as-you-go pension plan depends on a thriving group of active employees to generate, either through taxes or through profit-making endeavor, sufficient revenues to pay the pensions. To make matters worse, the period of stability is often followed by a period of decline in the fortunes of the plan sponsor, leading to a decline in the number of active employees, and in this case there is an even worse period following region C: The cost measured against the number of active employees or total active payroll explodes upward and the plan soon thereafter collapses.

The painful lesson which has been learned over and over again in the last century by various types of employers — first private employers, and later public employers — is that the cost of a pension plan must be recognized during the *working lifetimes* of the employees who are ultimately going to receive pensions, preferably by actually funding amounts sufficient to provide completely for each employee's life annuity at the time of retirement. When pension plans are funded in this manner, the safety of pensions which are being paid to those already retired is assured, and cannot be jeopardized by fluctuations in employment levels among active employees or by the financial collapse of the employer himself. So well has this lesson been learned, that in the United States and Canada, and indeed in almost every modern industrialized country, it is generally not legal for a private employer to establish a pension plan which is not properly funded. Public plans, on the other hand, are sometimes still funded on a pay-as-you-go basis, but hardly anybody believes this is a sound state of affairs. (It is a political problem of huge proportions, however, when your predecessors have enjoyed the high praise and low cost of region A, while bequeathing to you the leapfrogging costs and no glory of region B, and to know that you have the unpalatable choice of either (a) raising your contributions right away to a level intermediate between your point on the curve and the ultimate level of region C, or (b) simply letting things ride along as they are and shipping the problem downstream to your successors.)

This is where actuaries come into the picture, because the outflow of benefit payouts over time is subject to life and other contingencies, and because the inflow of contributions is occuring at a different time and in a different pattern, so that the time value of money is an important consideration. The actuary can, by making assumptions about rates of return on the pension fund, ages at retirement, rates of turnover and mortality, etc., assign to each fiscal year a portion of the present value of future benefit payments in such a way as generally to accrue costs over the working lifetimes of employees. Any scheme for making such an assignment of costs is called an *actuarial cost method* — which we shall henceforth refer to simply as a "cost method." There are many such cost methods in common use, each with a different philosophical foundation. We shall examine the most popular of these in the next pages — starting always from the philosophical underpinnings of each, and proceeding to a general description.

The application of a cost method to a particular plan in order to compute its cost is called an *actuarial valuation.* The same term applies to the process of determining the liabilities of an insurance company, but a pension-plan valuation differs from an insurance-company valuation in many ways — some obvious and others quite subtle — which will reveal themselves as our discussion unfolds. The pension valuation may involve the computation of "liabilities" and the valuation of assets, but its primary purpose is to determine annual cost.

2.2 *Unit Credit*

Assuming that each employee is entitled to retire at age y with an annual pension (payable monthly) equal to $B(y)$, a properly funded plan should have accumulated for each employee when he reaches age y an amount sufficient to fund his pension, i.e., an amount equal to $B(y)\ddot{a}_y^{(12)}$. This requirement is the first logical premise of the unit credit cost method (as well as a number of other methods as we shall see).

Now the benefit $B(y)$ does not arise suddenly at age y, but is earned or "accrued" in a more or less continuous fashion during the employee's active years of service. Thus, when the employee is hired, say at age w, his accrued benefit $B(w)$ is exactly zero; at age y when he retires it is equal to its ultimate value $B(y)$; and at any point inbetween, at age x, it has some intermediate value $B(x)$, which we call his *accrued benefit.*

At any age x, earlier than y, the present value of employee j's accrued benefit is equal to $B^j(x)\,\ddot{a}_{y_j}^{(12)}\dfrac{D_{y_j}}{D_{x_j}}$. Note that the factor D_y/D_x is computed using a table of q_x's which represents probabilities of termination of employment before age y from all causes — not just from mortality, but also resignation, discharge, disablement, etc. This table of q's is called a *service table* — a term parallel to but more general than *"mortality table"*.

So, if we had assets on hand at all times equal to $\sum_{\mathbf{A}_t} B^j(x)\,\ddot{a}_y^{(12)}\dfrac{D_y}{D_x}$ (we shall henceforth omit the subscript j from age subscripts to reduce clutter) then no matter what the distribution of ages was among the group $\mathbf{A}_t$ of active employees at time t, we should be assured of having sufficient funds to be able to withdraw $B^j(y)\,\ddot{a}_y^{(12)}$ as each employee reached age y — even if all employees were the same age and all retired at once. (Of course, we might not actually withdraw money to purchase an annuity, but the philosophy is the same no matter what medium of funding is used. It will make our discussion easier if we assume that retired lives are removed from both the asset and liability columns of our pension plan. We shall put them back later on, but for now we shall send retirees packing with sufficient assets to purchase their lifetime pensions.)

This observation is the source of the second premise of the unit-credit cost method, which distinguishes it from all others: The ideal fund balance, or desired amount of assets, on hand at any given time t is equal to $\sum_{\mathbf{A}_t} B^j(x)\,\ddot{a}_y^{(12)}\frac{D_y}{D_x}$, where $\mathbf{A}_t$ denotes the set of active employees at time t (remember, we have assumed we don't have any retired employees in our plan). This ideal fund balance is called the *accrued liability:*

$$\textit{(Accrued liability)}_t = AL_t = \sum_{\mathbf{A}_t} B^j(x)\,\ddot{a}_y^{(12)}\frac{D_y}{D_x}. \tag{2.2.1}$$

In other words, under the unit credit cost method the accrued liability is defined as the *present value of accrued benefits.* This definition distinguishes it from all other cost methods, and carries with it, by implication, a complete definition of what pension cost should be ascribed to any given year, as we shall now see.

Let us digress for a moment to remark our peculiar use of the word "liability" to denote a desired level of *assets.* This oddity, which has caused no end of confusion among accountants, arises from life-insurance terminology. In ordinary financial accounting, a business records each transaction twice — once on each side of the balance sheet — and its "liabilities" are therefore (roughly speaking) the sum of amounts actually owed to someone else. In life-insurance accounting, by contrast, premiums received are not recorded on both sides of the ledger, but only as assets — liabilities being determined by a sort of inventory, the annual actuarial valuation. To a life-insurance company, a "liability" is an actuarially determined amount which has first claim on the invested *assets* of the company. It is not, strictly speaking, an amount owed to anyone — although it will be if the reserve basis proves true — it is the amount of *assets* to be set aside for whatever the actual claims turn out to be. In the same way, the accrued liabilty of a pension plan represents a claim on plan assets.

From year to year the accrued liability changes, not only because the ages of the active participants increase, but also because the composition of the active group itself changes. To keep things simple, we shall assume that there are no new entrants into the plan; we shall put them in their own separate pension fund for the moment, and recall them later when we have need of them. Then, the active group can never grow but can only shrink during the year. Denote by $\mathbf{T}$ the set of all employees who terminate employment between time t and time $t+1$ and by $\mathbf{R}$ the set of employees during the year who reach age y, so we can write:

$$\mathbf{A}_{t+1} = \mathbf{A}_t - \mathbf{T} - \mathbf{R}. \tag{2.2.2}$$

We now construct the following purely algebraic argument to show the relationship between the accrued liability at time t and the accrued liability at time $t+1$ (using the results of exercise 2.2.1):

$$(Accrued\ liability)_{t+1} \equiv AL_{t+1} = \sum_{\mathbf{A}_{t+1}} B^j(x+1)\,\ddot{a}_y^{(12)}\,\frac{D_y}{D_{x+1}}$$

$$= \sum_{\mathbf{A}_t} B^j(x+1)\,\ddot{a}_y^{(12)}\,\frac{D_y}{D_{x+1}} - \sum_{\mathbf{T}+\mathbf{R}} B^j(x+1)\,\ddot{a}_y^{(12)}\,\frac{D_y}{D_{x+1}}$$

$$= \sum_{\mathbf{A}_t} B^j(x+1)\Big[\frac{D_y}{D_x}(1+i) + q_x\frac{D_y}{D_{x+1}}\Big]\ddot{a}_y^{(12)} - \sum_{\mathbf{T}+\mathbf{R}} B^j(x+1)\,\ddot{a}_y^{(12)}\,\frac{D_y}{D_{x+1}}$$

$$= \sum_{\mathbf{A}_t}\Big[B^j(x) + \Delta B^j\Big]\,\ddot{a}_y^{(12)}\,\frac{D_y}{D_x}(1+i) + \sum_{\mathbf{A}_t} q_x B^j(x+1)\,\ddot{a}_y^{(12)}\,\frac{D_y}{D_{x+1}}$$

$$- \sum_{\mathbf{T}+\mathbf{R}} B^j(x+1)\,\ddot{a}_y^{(12)}\,\frac{D_y}{D_{x+1}}$$

. . . where ΔB^j is the increase in j's accrued benefit during the year. This means that

$$AL_{t+1} = \Big[AL_t + \sum_{\mathbf{A}_t}\Delta B^j\,\ddot{a}_y^{(12)}\,\frac{D_y}{D_x}\Big](1+i)$$

$$- \Big[\sum_{\mathbf{T}} B^j(x+1)\,\ddot{a}_y^{(12)}\,\frac{D_y}{D_{x+1}} - \sum_{\mathbf{A}_t} q_x B^j(x+1)\,\ddot{a}_y^{(12)}\,\frac{D_y}{D_{x+1}}\Big]$$

$$- \sum_{\mathbf{R}} B^j(x+1)\,\ddot{a}_y^{(12)}\,\frac{D_y}{D_{x+1}}\,. \tag{2.2.3}$$

Don't forget that D_y/D_x was computed using a table of q's which represent the probability at each age of withdrawing from the active group — not just the probability of dying. In other words, the D_x's are taken from our *service table.*

Now look at the second bracketed term of equation (2.2.3). If actual experience during the year is in direct accord with assumed experience, this term will be zero. That is to say, the expected release of liability on account of termination of employment before age y from all causes except retirement (the second summation) will exactly offset the actual amount of accrued liability released on account of employees who actually did terminate, i.e., who were members of the set **T**. Also, if actual experience is in accord with assumed, the ideal fund balance, AL_t will have grown to $AL_t(1+i)$ minus $\sum_{\mathbf{R}} B^j(x+1)\,\ddot{a}_y^{(12)}\,\frac{D_y}{D_{x+1}}$ withdrawn for purchase of annuities. Therefore, if the assumptions work out, an amount equal to

$$NC_t = \sum_{\mathbf{A}_t}\Delta B^j\,\ddot{a}_y^{(12)}\,\frac{D_y}{D_x} = \sum_{\mathbf{A}_t} NC_t^j \tag{2.2.4}$$

will have to be added at the beginning of the year in order to raise the desired fund balance to its proper level at time $t+1$. This amount is called the *normal cost* of the plan, because it is the cost of keeping the pension fund at the desired level if the assumptions work out and if fund assets equal the accrued liability — i.e., the cost under "normal" circumstances. This normal cost is the present value of the increase in accrued benefits between time t and time $t+1$, and is a single sum assumed to be paid at time t. (In fact, the normal cost is never paid at time t because the valuation is not finished as of that date, and by the time you get your data together and complete the calculations, you are many weeks at best into the next year.)

The normal cost is not a proper reflection of the full cost of the plan except in this ideal setting: i.e., except where the fund balance is exactly equal to the accrued liability and where the assumptions are exactly borne out in reality. In real life, (a) actual experience is not exactly in accord with assumptions during a given year, and (b) the fund balance is not equal to the accrued liability — either because when the plan was started past service benefits were granted and the accrued liability started right off at some non-zero value, or because the plan has experienced good fortune (relative to assumptions) over the years so that there are assets in the fund in excess of the accrued liability (or bad experience has produced an accrued liability in excess of assets). Therefore, although the central component of the pension cost is the normal cost, there must also be adjustments in the cost to allow for these variations from the ideal.

Let us now assume that the fund balance is equal to F_t at time t, abandoning our previous assumption that the fund is exactly equal to AL_t. During the year between time t and $t+1$ the fund balance will increase by some amount (I) attributable to investment return and by contributions to the fund (C), and will be diminished by amounts (P) withdrawn to "purchase" pensions:

$$F_{t+1} = F_t + I + C - P. \tag{2.2.5}$$

The difference $AL_t - F_t$ between the accrued liability and the fund balance at time t is called the *unfunded accrued liability*. A negative unfunded accrued liability is often called a *surplus*, but we shall use the term "unfunded accrued liability" or simply "unfunded" to refer to this quantity whether it is positive or negative.

We now subtract equation (2.2.5) from equation (2.2.3) in order to derive a relationship between the unfunded accrued liability at time t and its value at time $t+1$:

$$\textit{(Unfunded accrued liability)}_{t+1} \equiv UAL_{t+1} = AL_{t+1} - F_{t+1}$$

$$= (AL_t + NC_t)(1+i) - \Big[\sum_{\mathbf{T}} B^j(x+1)\ddot{a}_y^{(12)}\frac{D_y}{D_{x+1}} - \sum_{\mathbf{A}_t} q_x B^j(x+1)\ddot{a}_y^{(12)}\frac{D_y}{D_{x+1}}\Big]$$

$$- \sum_{\mathbf{R}} B^j(x+1)\ddot{a}_y^{(12)}\frac{D_y}{D_{x+1}} - (F_t + I + C - P)$$

or,

$$UAL_{t+1} = UAL_t(1+i) - \left[I - iF_t\right] + \left[NC_t(1+i) - C\right]$$

$$- \left[\sum_{\mathbf{T}} B^j(x+1)\ddot{a}_y^{(12)} \frac{D_y}{D_{x+1}} - \sum_{\mathbf{A}_t} q_x B^j(x+1)\ddot{a}_y^{(12)} \frac{D_y}{D_{x+1}}\right]$$

$$- \left[\sum_{\mathbf{R}} B^j(x+1)\ddot{a}_y^{(12)} \frac{D_y}{D_{x+1}} - P\right]. \tag{2.2.6}$$

We should like to be able to say that all terms but the first in equation (2.2.6) would be zero if all assumptions worked out and if contributions actually were equal to the normal cost, but a bit of adjustment is needed to maneuver the equation into suitable form. Let I_C represent interest on the actual contributions at the assumed rate i from the date they are actually made to year-end. For example, if the contribution were made in a single deposit at the beginning of the year

$$I_C = iC,$$

and if the contribution were made in a single sum half-way through the year

$$I_C = \left[(1+i)^{1/2} - 1\right]C,$$

etc. Define a similar term I_P for pension purchases. Then we can write

$$UAL_{t+1} = UAL_t(1+i) - \left[I - iF_t - I_C + I_P\right] - \left[C + I_C - NC_t(1+i)\right]$$

$$- \left[\sum_{\mathbf{T}} B^j(x+1)\ddot{a}_y^{(12)} \frac{D_y}{D_{x+1}} - \sum_{\mathbf{A}_t} q_x B^j(x+1)\ddot{a}_y^{(12)} \frac{D_y}{D_{x+1}}\right]$$

$$- \left[\sum_{\mathbf{R}} B^j(x+1)\ddot{a}_y^{(12)} \frac{D_y}{D_{x+1}} - P - I_P\right]. \tag{2.2.7}$$

Now look at equation (2.2.7) and note that if the actual rate of interest earned during the year were i, then the second term would equal zero, and that if the actual accrued liability released by those who actually terminated during the year before age y worked out exactly as planned, then the fourth term would be exactly zero as well. Likewise, the fifth term would be zero if the amounts withdrawn for retirement were exactly those anticipated.

The unfunded measures the deviation of the actual fund balance F_t from its ideal value AL_t, and the sum of the second, fourth, and fifth terms represents the change in unfunded due to deviations of actual from expected *experience* (as opposed to amount of contributions). We have a name for the sum of these three terms: It is called the *actuarial gain,* and is defined as follows:

$$Gain = (UAL_t + NC_t)(1+i) - C - I_c - UAL_{t+1}. \tag{2.2.8}$$

Of course, we could just as well have defined the gain as the sum of the second, fourth, and fifth terms of equation (2.2.7), but these terms are more difficult to compute. Historically, the gain has always been defined by (2.2.8). ("Gain and loss analysis", however, involves the direct computation of the components of the gain using terms similar to the second, fourth, and fifth terms of equation (2.2.7). A "loss" is just a negative gain.)

Finally, looking at the third term of (2.2.7), you can see that the unfunded is not expected to decrease unless the actual contribution to the fund exceeds the normal cost with interest from the beginning of the year to the date of deposit. Any additional contribution, in excess of the normal cost and interest, goes to *amortize* the unfunded. The minimum funding standards prescribed by law in the U.S. and Canada, as well as the maximum limitation on deductible contributions in the U.S. prescribe bottom and top limits, respectively, on the amount which may be added to the normal cost each year to amortize the unfunded.

Summary

Under the unit-credit method the pension cost in the year t to $t+1$ is equal to

(1) the normal cost;

plus (2) amortization of the unfunded accrued liability;

minus (3) amortization of the gain (except in the first year of operation); where

- the *unfunded accrued liability* is equal to the present value of accrued benefits less assets;
- the *normal cost* is equal to the present value of the increase in accrued benefit during the year, and
- the *gain* is equal to last year's unfunded plus the normal cost with a year's interest, minus contributions with interest, minus the new unfunded.

Note that the current unfunded includes prior gains, so you may either (a) continue amortizing the initial unfunded at a rate established when the plan started and amortize each successive gain separately, or (b) recompute the amortization each year based on the *current* unfunded.

Exercises

2.2.1 Show that
$$\frac{D_y}{D_{x+1}} = \frac{D_y}{D_x}(1+i) + q_x \frac{D_y}{D_{x+1}}. \tag{2.2.9}$$

2.2.2 (a) Look at equation (2.2.4) and notice that the normal cost is the sum of individual normal costs equal to
$$NC_t^j = \Delta B^j(x)\ddot{a}_y^{(12)}\frac{D_y}{D_x}.$$
Differentiate this equation with respect to x and get
$$\frac{1}{NC_c^j}\frac{d}{dx}NC_t^j = \frac{d}{dx}(log\, NC_t^j) = \frac{d}{dx}\Big(log\, \Delta B^j(x)\Big) + \mu_x + \delta. \tag{2.2.10}$$

(b) Suppose that the pension plan is such that a unit of pension is credited each year in the amount of 1% of that year's salary, and the salaries increase at annual rate r. Show that
$$\frac{d}{dx}(log\, NC_t^j) = \mu_x + \delta + log\,(1+r). \tag{2.2.11}$$

(c) Now consider the ratio $\dfrac{NC_t^j}{S_t^j}$ — j's normal cost expressed as a fraction of his salary — and show that
$$\frac{d}{dx}\Big[log\Big(\frac{NC_t^j}{S_t^j}\Big)\Big] = \mu_x + \delta. \tag{2.2.12}$$

(d) Conclude that if there are no preretirement decrements other than mortality and if mortality follows Gompertz' law ($\mu_x = ae^{bx}$) then $\dfrac{d}{dx}\Big[log\Big(\dfrac{NC_t^j}{S_t^j}\Big)\Big] = ae^{bx} + \delta$, which implies that the individual normal cost increases more than exponentially, *as a percentage of pay.*

2.2.3 Show that for an individual the accrued liability is equal to the actuarial present value of prior normal costs:
$$AL_t^j = \sum_{k=0}^{t-1} NC_k^j \frac{D_{w+k}}{D_x}. \tag{2.2.13}$$

2.2.4 Note that in deriving equation (2.2.3), we required only that the accrued liability equal the present value of accrued benefits at time t and again at time $t+1$, but not necessarily in-between. Suppose we had adopted the more stringent standard that at any age z $(x \le z \le x+1)$ the accrued liability for employee j be defined as

$$\overline{AL}^j_{t+z-x} = B^j(z)\, \ddot{a}_y^{(12)} \frac{D_y}{D_z}. \tag{2.2.14}$$

Then, for any age z and for an arbitrarily small time increment h, we should have to require also that

$$\overline{AL}^j_{t+z-x+h} = B^j(z+h)\, \ddot{a}_y^{(12)} \frac{D_y}{D_{z+h}}. \tag{2.2.15}$$

Show that this line of reasoning leads to the expression

$$\frac{d}{dt}\overline{AL}^j_t = \overline{NC}^j_t + (\mu_x + \delta)\overline{AL}^j_t, \tag{2.2.16}$$

where

$$\overline{NC}^j_t = \frac{d}{dx} B^j(x)\, \ddot{a}_y^{(12)} \frac{D_y}{D_x}. \tag{2.2.17}$$

Give a verbal interpretation of these equations (2.2.16) and (2.2.17).

2.2.5 Show algebraically that if assumptions work out exactly and if ΔB is constant for each employee over his entire career,

$$AL_{t+1} = (AL_t + NC_t)(1+i) - P - I_P \tag{2.2.18}$$

and

$$NC_{t+1} = NC_t(1+i). \tag{2.2.19}$$

Note that equation (2.2.18) shows how the accrued liability may be viewed as an ideal fund balance.

2.3 *Entry Age Normal*

In exercises 2.2.2 and 2.2.5 we saw that under the unit-credit method individual normal costs tend to rise more rapidly than salary, when the benefit is based on salary. This means that in general the normal cost for the plan as a whole will do likewise, except to the extent that new entrants into the group (because they are young and perhaps low-paid) lower the average normal cost. Thus, it is possible to maintain a cost which is level as a percentage of payroll using the unit-credit method, but such a state is generally unstable, in that if new hiring should slacken off the average age of the group would rise and the normal cost would revert to its basic tendency to increase more rapidly than payroll.

You will recall that the unit-credit method was built upon the premise that the accrued liability should equal the present value of accrued benefits at all times during an employee's career, right up until retirement. From this premise the definitions of normal cost and actuarial gain followed directly as corollaries. The fact that the normal cost had this generally undesirable characteristic — that it tended to increase more rapidly than pay — was therefore a result of the way the method was constructed. It would be possible, however, to eliminate that bad feature by defining the normal cost directly and letting the accrued liability be the corollary item, and that is the approach we take in constructing the *entry-age-normal* method.

In the simplest case, where the benefit is expressed in dollars unrelated to salary, the normal cost under the entry-age-normal method is defined as a level annual contribution such that the present value of all future normal costs at age w (the entry age, which for purposes of this chapter will be the same as age at hire) is exactly equal to the present value of future benefits at w. I.e.,

$$B^j(y)\ddot{a}_y^{(12)}\frac{D_y}{D_w} = NC^j\frac{N_w - N_y}{D_w}$$

...where NC^j is the normal cost on behalf of employee j. Then

$$NC_t = \sum_{A_t} NC^j = \sum_{A_t} B^j(y)\ddot{a}_y^{(12)}\frac{D_y}{N_w - N_y}, \tag{2.3.1}$$

where, of course, the factor $D_y/N_w - N_y$ is based on the service table. Thus, under the entry-age-normal method as under the unit-credit the total normal cost is simply the sum of a lot of individual normal costs.

Note that this definition overcomes the problem of exponentially increasing normal costs, and that as long as $B^j(y)$, the projected benefit does not change, the normal cost remains constant for each individual during his whole career. (In actual practice, $B^j(y)$ is re-estimated each year, and to the extent it goes up the normal cost goes up — but only in proportion to the increase in $B^j(y)$, because the factor $D_y/(N_w - N_y)$ is not dependent on the present age x.)

You showed in exercise (2.2.3) that the accrued liability under the unit-credit method was the present value of prior normal costs. This result was a consequence of the definition of accrued liability, but for the entry age normal method we make this the *definition* of accrued liability. We define the accrued liability for employee j as the present value of his prior normal costs:

$$AL_t = \sum_{A_t} NC^j \frac{N_w - N_x}{D_x} = \sum_{A_t} B^j(y)\ddot{a}_y^{(12)} \frac{D_y}{D_x} \frac{N_w - N_x}{N_w - N_y}. \tag{2.3.2}$$

This is equivalent (by exercise 2.3.1) to

$$AL_t = \sum_{A_t} B^j(y)\ddot{a}_y^{(12)} \frac{D_y}{D_x} - \sum_{A_t} NC^j \frac{N_x - N_y}{D_x}, \tag{2.3.3}$$

or, in words: the accrued liability equals the present value of future benefits minus the present value of future normal costs. This is the formal definition of accrued liability under the entry-age-normal method. (If we tried to define the accrued liability formally as the present value of prior normal costs we should have to explain to everyone why it was that we were not able to take the actual normal costs computed over the years and accumulate them in some fashion in order to arrive at the accrued liability. The prospective definition makes everything much easier to explain, but pension actuaries must realize the equivalence of the two definitions.)

Let us use the symbol AL_t^j to represent the accrued liability on behalf of employee j at time t (age x), so that $AL_t = \sum_{A_t} AL_t^j$. Then, if we recall equation (2.2.2) we can write

$$AL_{t+1} = \sum_{A_t} AL_{t+1}^j - \sum_{T+R} AL_{t+1}^j. \tag{2.3.4}$$

We can also write

$$AL_{t+1}^j = B_{t+1}^j(y)\ddot{a}_y^{(12)} \frac{D_y}{D_{x+1}} \frac{N_w - N_{x+1}}{N_w - N_y}, \tag{2.3.5}$$

where we have appended the subscript $t+1$ to $B(y)$ so as to remind ourselves that this projected benefit may not be the same as it was at time t, because we estimate the projected benefit at retirement anew each year. From now on we shall also omit the argument (y), because under the entry-age-normal method we are always projecting the benefit to age y. Also, denote by ΔB^j the change in j's projected benefit between time t and $t+1$ (i.e., $\Delta B^j = B_{t+1}^j(y) - B_t^j(y)$; (note that this is not the same definition as was used in section 2.2!). Then

$$AL^j_{t+1} = B^j_t \ddot{a}_y^{(12)} \frac{D_y}{D_{x+1}} \frac{N_w - N_{x+1}}{N_w - N_y} + \Delta B^j \ddot{a}_y^{(12)} \frac{D_y}{D_{x+1}} \frac{N_w - N_{x+1}}{N_w - N_y}$$

$$= B^j_t \ddot{a}_y^{(12)} \frac{D_y}{N_w - N_y} \Big[\Big(\frac{N_w - N_x}{D_x} + 1 \Big)(1+i) + q_x \frac{N_w - N_{x+1}}{D_{x+1}} \Big]$$

$$+ \Delta B^j \ddot{a}_y^{(12)} \frac{D_y}{D_{x+1}} \frac{N_w - N_{x+1}}{N_w - N_y},$$

or,

$$AL^j_{t+1} = (AL^j_t + NC^j_t)(1+i) + q_x B^j_t \ddot{a}_y^{(12)} \frac{D_y}{D_{x+1}} \frac{N_w - N_{x+1}}{N_w - N_y}$$

$$+ \Delta B^j \ddot{a}_y^{(12)} \frac{D_y}{D_{x+1}} \frac{N_w - N_{x+1}}{N_w - N_y} \tag{2.3.6}$$

. . . where we have made use of the result of exercise 2.3.2 and appended the subscript t to NC^j to remind us that it is computed using $B_t(y)$. Now if we plug (2.3.6) into (2.3.4), and use equation (2.3.5) on sets **T** and **R**, we get

$$AL_{t+1} = (AL_t + NC_t)(1+i) + \sum_{\mathbf{A}_t} q_x B^j_t \ddot{a}_y^{(12)} \frac{D_y}{D_{x+1}} \frac{N_w - N_{x+1}}{N_w - N_y}$$

$$+ \sum_{\mathbf{A}_t} \Delta B^j \ddot{a}_y^{(12)} \frac{D_y}{D_{x+1}} \frac{N_w - N_{x+1}}{N_w - N_y}$$

$$- \sum_{\mathbf{T}+\mathbf{R}} (B^j_t + \Delta B^j) \ddot{a}_y^{(12)} \frac{D_y}{D_{x+1}} \frac{N_w - N_{x+1}}{N_w - N_y}. \tag{2.3.7}$$

There is still something funny about equation (2.3.7) though, because we have used the term ΔB^j on sets **T** and **R**, which is not quite proper. Remember that we defined ΔB^j as the difference in projected benefits between times t and $t+1$. But the members of sets **T** and **R** were those who terminated or retired during the year, and there are no projected benefits at time $t+1$ for them! This fact, however, gives us the latitude to define ΔB^j however we like for these sets of employees, so we shall make things easy for ourselves by defining $\Delta B^j = 0$ for employees in sets **T** and **R**. This means that the second summation of (2.3.7) is, in effect, taken over the set $\mathbf{A}_t - \mathbf{R} - \mathbf{T} = \mathbf{A}_{t+1}$ so we can write

$$AL_{t+1} = (AL_t + NC_t)(1+i) + \sum_{\mathbf{A}_{t+1}} \Delta B^j \ddot{a}_y^{(12)} \frac{D_y}{D_{x+1}} \frac{N_w - N_{x+1}}{N_w - N_y}$$

$$+ \sum_{\mathbf{A}_t} q_x \widetilde{AL}^j_{t+1} - \sum_{\mathbf{T}+\mathbf{R}} \widetilde{AL}^j_{t+1} \tag{2.3.8}$$

. . . where $\widetilde{AL}^j_{t+1}$ means j's accrued liability at time $t+1$ computed as though his projected benefit at time t, B^j_t, remained unchanged — i.e., as though ΔB^j equaled zero.

As with the unit-credit method, we define the ***unfunded accrued liability*** as $AL_t - F_t$. Then we can relate two successive years' unfundeds as follows, by subtracting (2.2.5) from (2.3.8):

$$\begin{aligned} UAL_{t+1} &= AL_{t+1} - F_{t+1} \\ &= AL_t(1+i) - F_t - I + NC_t(1+i) - C \\ &+ \sum_{A_{t+1}} \Delta B^j \ddot{a}_y^{(12)} \frac{D_y}{D_{x+1}} \frac{N_w - N_{x+1}}{N_w - N_y} + \sum_{A_t} q_x \widetilde{AL}^j_{t+1} \\ &- \sum_{T} \widetilde{AL}^j_{t+1} - \sum_{R} \widetilde{AL}^j_{t+1} + P. \end{aligned} \tag{2.3.9}$$

As in section 2.2, we must neutralize the effect of the timing of contributions and benefit withdrawals by reintroducing I_C (interest on contributions from date of deposit to year-end) and I_P (interest on pension "purchases" from date of withdrawal to year-end) — and thereby get the relationship (2.3.9) into proper form:

$$\begin{aligned} UAL_{t+1} &= UAL_t(1+i) - \left[I - iF_t - I_C + I_P\right] \\ &- \left[C + I_C - NC_t(1+i)\right] + \sum_{A_{t+1}} \Delta B^j \ddot{a}_y^{(12)} \frac{D_y}{D_{x+1}} \frac{N_w - N_{x+1}}{N_w - N_y} \\ &- \left[\sum_{T} \widetilde{AL}^j_{t+1} - \sum_{A_t} q_x \widetilde{AL}^j_{t+1}\right] \\ &- \left[\sum_{R} \widetilde{AL}^j_{t+1} - P - I_P\right] \end{aligned} \tag{2.3.10}$$

. . . which is reminiscent of equation (2.2.7).

Now look at (2.3.10) and note that if everything had gone according to plan during the year, the second term would be exactly zero because I, the actual interest credited to the fund, would equal interest at rate i on last year's balance and on contributions and benefit payments. The fourth term would be zero, because last year's projected benefit would be the same as this year's. The fifth term would be zero because actual releases of accrued liability on account of terminations would be equal to those expected. And the last term would be zero because actual withdrawals for purchases of annuities would equal reserves on hand for that purpose. This means that all of these terms reflect only variations of actual experience from expected, and we can therefore add them together and call the sum the *actuarial gain,* so that (2.3.10) becomes

$$UAL_{t+1} = (UAL_t + NC_t)(1 + i) - (C + I_C) - Gain \qquad (2.3.11)$$

or, equivalently

$$Gain = (UAL_t + NC_t)(1 + i) - (C + I_C) - UAL_{t+1} \qquad (2.3.12)$$

This is truly a remarkable result! Although we have constructed a new cost method on premises totally different from the unit-credit method, we have nevertheless arrived at the same expression for the actuarial gain. It is important to remember, however, that the *quantities* represented are entirely different because the unfundeds are not the same and the normal costs are different.

Pension actuaries refer to the quantity $(UAL_t + NC_t)(1 + i) - (C + I_C)$ as the *expected unfunded accrued liability* and thus say that the gain equals the expected unfunded minus the actual unfunded — a nice easy way to remember the formula. It makes sense to call these terms the "expected unfunded" because, as we have seen, if all experience followed assumptions, the gain terms in equation (2.3.10) would all be zero.

Now we have all the ingredients to cook up our assessment of the "cost" of our pension plan under the entry-age-normal method.

Summary

Under the entry-age-normal cost method the total cost for the year equals the normal cost *plus* amortization of the unfunded *minus* amortization of the gain, where

- the *normal cost* is the level annual contribution from entry age to assumed retirement age which is sufficient to fund the *projected* benefit at retirement;
- the *unfunded accrued liability* is the present value of future benefits minus the present value of future normal costs minus assets; and
- the *gain* is the expected unfunded accrued liability minus the actual.

Exercises

2.3.1 Show that the retrospective definition of accrued liability, equation (2.3.2), is identical to the prospective (2.3.3).

2.3.2 Prove that

$$\frac{N_w - N_{x+1}}{D_{x+1}} = \left(\frac{N_w - N_x}{D_x} + 1\right)(1+i) + q_x \frac{N_w - N_{x+1}}{D_{x+1}} . \tag{2.3.13}$$

2.3.3 (a) It is customary to define the normal cost under any cost method as an amount payable in a single annual installment at the beginning of each year. There is nothing sacred about this, however: we could just as well define it as an annual amount payable continuously, i.e., under the entry-age-normal method:

$$\overline{NC}^j = B^j \ddot{a}_y^{(12)} \frac{D_y}{\bar{N}_w - \bar{N}_y} .$$

Then, the individual accrued liability would be — what? (Use the same logical development as section 2.3).

(b) What is the derivative of this continuous-normal-cost accrued liability with respect to attained age x?

$$\left[\text{Answer: } \frac{d}{dx}\overline{AL}_t^j = \overline{NC}^j + (\mu_x + \delta)\overline{AL}_t^j\right]$$

(c) Compare your answer to (b) with equation (2.2.16). At entry age w, when the accrued benefit is zero, what are the rates of increase in the accrued liabilities under the unit-credit and entry-age-normal methods, respectively? Assume that the benefit $B^j(x)$ accrues uniformly over employee j's period of service; then prove algebraically that at age w the entry-age-normal accrued liability is increasing at a rate faster than that of the unit-credit.

(d) Draw a rough graph showing accrued liability on the vertical axis and age on the horizontal axis. Draw a curve for the entry-age-normal accrued liability and another for the unit-credit. At which point(s) do the curves intersect? If a large proportion of employees terminated during the year (more than expected), under which method would the actuarial gain be larger? Under which method would you expect to build up a larger fund?

2.4 *More Entry Age Normal*

When the pension benefit itself is based on salary, the entry-age-normal method is usually used in conjunction with a salary-increase assumption. Often the assumption is simply that salaries will increase at rate r per year. But sometimes more sophisticated assumptions are employed, under which different rates of salary increase are used for different ages or for different lengths of employment. In the general case, we have a set of salary indices s_x such that if S_t^j is an employee's rate of pay at time t (age x) then $S_t^j \dfrac{s_{x+g}}{s_x}$ is his assumed salary at age $x+g$ — where g can be *either positive or negative*. For example, if salaries are assumed to increase at a constant rate r then s_x = (arbitrary constant) $\times$ $(1+r)^x$ and the salary at age $x+g$ is assumed to be $S_t^j \dfrac{(1+r)^{x+g}}{(1+r)^x} = S_t^j(1+r)^g$. Such a set of salary indices is called a *salary scale.*

When salaries are assumed to increase, the normal cost under the entry-age-normal method is defined, not as a level dollar amount payable each year, but as a level percentage of salary, as follows: First, note that if S_t^j is the salary at age x (time t) then the salary at age w is $S_t^j \dfrac{s_w}{s_x}$. Now we want the normal cost to be a constant fraction, U_t^j, of salary for each year of age. This means that when we set the present value of future benefits at age w equal to the present value of future normal costs at age w we get:

$$U_t^j \cdot S_t^j \frac{s_w}{s_x} \sum_{z=w}^{y-1} \frac{s_z}{s_w} \frac{D_z}{D_w} = B_t^j \, \ddot{a}_y^{(12)} \frac{D_y}{D_w} \quad . \tag{2.4.1}$$

From this we see that the individual normal cost at age x is simply equal to current salary times the fraction U_t^j :

$$NC_t^j = U_t^j S_t^j \quad . \tag{2.4.2}$$

Note that each employee has his own, distinct normal-cost rate U_t^j, and that this rate is proportional to the projected benefit B_t^j.

It will be convenient to define some new commutation functions incorporating the salary indices:

$${}^sD_x \equiv s_x D_x \ \ and \ \ {}^sN_x \equiv \sum_{z=x}^{\infty} {}^sD_z \quad . \tag{2.4.3}$$

Using these functions we can now rewrite (2.4.1) as

$$U_t^j S_t^j \frac{s_w}{s_x} \frac{{}^sN_w - {}^sN_y}{{}^sD_w} = B_t^j \, \ddot{a}_y^{(12)} \frac{D_y}{D_w} \quad , \tag{2.4.4}$$

from which it follows that

$$NC_t^j = \underbrace{B_t^j \ddot{a}_y^{(12)} \frac{D_y}{D_w} \frac{{}^sD_w}{{}^sN_w - {}^sN_y}}_{\text{hypothetical normal cost at age } w} \cdot \frac{s_x}{s_w} . \tag{2.4.5}$$

Note that now the normal cost depends upon the attained age x, unlike the normal cost in section 2.3. The percentage U_t^j is designed to be constant, but the salary to which it is applied is assumed to increase, so the normal cost increases likewise.

When using a salary-increase assumption with entry-age-normal, we define the accrued liability in the same way as before, namely, as the present value of future benefits minus the present value of future normal costs:

$$AL_t^j = B_t^j \ddot{a}_y^{(12)} \frac{D_y}{D_x} - NC_t^j \frac{{}^sN_x - {}^sN_y}{{}^sD_x} = B_t^j \ddot{a}_y^{(12)} \frac{D_y}{D_x} \left(\frac{{}^sN_w - {}^sN_x}{{}^sN_w - {}^sN_y} \right) , \tag{2.4.6}$$

which corresponds to (2.3.2). From this we can derive (using the result of exercise 2.4.5):

$$AL_{t+1}^j = (AL_t^j + NC_t^j)(1+i) + q_x \widetilde{AL}_{t+1}^j + \Delta B^j \ddot{a}_y^{(12)} \frac{D_y}{D_{x+1}}$$

$$- \Delta B^j \left(\ddot{a}_y^{(12)} \frac{D_y}{D_w} \frac{{}^sD_w}{{}^sN_w - {}^sN_y} \right) \frac{s_{x+1}}{s_w} \cdot \frac{{}^sN_{x+1} - {}^sN_y}{{}^sD_{x+1}} . \tag{2.4.7}$$

Note that the last two terms in (2.4.7) represent the change in present value of future benefits and present value of future normal costs, respectively, owing to the change ΔB^j in projected benefit at retirement.

Now we can add up the individual accrued liabilities and normal costs in the manner of section 2.3, then follow the standard procedure of subtracting equation (2.2.5), and wind up with the relationship between the unfunded accrued liabilities in two successive years:

$$UAL_{t+1} \equiv AL_{t+1} - F_{t+1} = UAL_t(1+i) - \left[C + I_C - NC_t(1+i) \right]$$

$$- \left[I - iF_t - I_C + I_P \right] + \sum_{A_{t+1}} \Delta B^j \ddot{a}_y^{(12)} \left(\frac{D_y}{D_{x+1}} - \frac{D_y}{D_w} \frac{{}^sD_w}{{}^sN_w - {}^sN_y} \cdot \frac{s_{x+1}}{s_w} \frac{{}^sN_{x+1} - {}^sN_y}{{}^sD_{x+1}} \right)$$

$$- \left[\sum_{T} \widetilde{AL}_{t+1}^j - \sum_{A_t} q_x \widetilde{AL}_{t+1}^j \right] - \left[\sum_{R} \widetilde{AL}_{t+1}^j - P - I_P \right] , \tag{2.4.8}$$

Not surprisingly, we have arranged the equation so that the third through the sixth terms will be zero if actual experience is in accord with expected. Consequently we call the sum of all these (with a negative sign in front) the actuarial gain, and find that the actuarial gain in this case too can be defined by (2.3.12).

Exercises

2.4.1 If salaries are assumed to increase at rate r, and interest is assumed at rate i, show that ${}^sN_x$ is proportional to N_x computed using an interest rate equal to $\dfrac{1+i}{1+r} - 1$.

2.4.2 Show mathematically that if the projected benefit $B(y)$ does not depend on salary, then the normal cost (EAN method) at entry age w is *lowered* if we introduce a salary increase assumption.

2.4.3 Now assume that the benefit $B(y)$ is proportional to the rate of salary at age y and that salaries increase at annual rate $r > 0$. Then show that for an employee just hired (i.e., for whom $x = w$)

$$ {}^sNC^j_w > NC^j $$

where ${}^sNC^j_w$ is the normal cost at age w including the salary-increase assumption, and NC^j is the normal cost with no salary-increase assumption. Since both series of normal costs are to fund the same benefit, can the initial relationships hold up throughout j's career?

2.4.4 Suppose we fund the benefit described in exercise 2.4.3 with no salary-increase assumption, but j's salary actually does increase at annual rate$_\rho$. What will happen to j's normal cost as he approaches age y? What will happen to his accrued liability?

2.4.5 Prove that for $x < y$

$$ \frac{S_{x+1}}{S_x}\,\frac{{}^sN_{x+1} - {}^sN_y}{{}^sD_{x+1}} = \left[\frac{{}^sN_x - {}^sN_y}{{}^sD_x} - 1\right](1+i) + q_x\,\frac{S_{x+1}}{S_x}\,\frac{{}^sN_{x+1} - {}^sN_y}{{}^sD_{x+1}}\ . \qquad (2.4.9) $$

2.4.6 Following the line of argument of section 2.3 show in detail how we got from equation (2.4.6) to (2.4.8), and demonstrate that the gain can be defined by (2.3.12).

2.4.7 Does the rule that the accrued liability equals the present value of future benefits less the present value of future normal costs distinguish the entry-age-normal from the unit-credit cost method? If not, what does? (Remember to use mathematical *demonstrations* instead of mere verbal *impressions.*)

2.4.8 What is the meaning of the fourth term on the right-hand side of equation (2.4.8)? Rewrite this term using $\widetilde{AL}_{t+1}$.

2.5 *Individual Level Premium*

Both the unit-credit and the entry-age-normal cost methods were constructed on the premise that the *desired* amount of assets at age y was the present value of the pension at that age. The desired level of assets at any earlier age was called the accrued liability. And indeed if the actual fund assets are equal to the accrued liability — i.e., if there is no unfunded — the desired amount of assets will be on hand as each employee retires, regardless of the actual pattern in time of those retirements (given, of course, that the actuarial assumptions work out). Even if there *is* an unfunded accrued liability, as long as it is amortized over a reasonable period, there will be no solvency problem, because the present value of future benefits still will equal the present value of future contributions to the fund. But this says nothing about the *short run.* It is possible to have the present value of future benefits equal the present value of future contributions and still have the fund go negative for a period of time! This possibility must be addressed when there is an unfunded.

In many plans, perhaps most larger corporate pension plans, the problem is mitigated by not having to withdraw a lump sum at retirement to purchase an annuity, because the plan pays pensions month-by-month directly from the fund. This eases liquidity requirements considerably, and in most such situations the question of solvency never arises even where there is an unfunded accrued liability.

On the other hand, many plans routinely allow pensions to be converted into lump sums at retirement, and others are funded with insurance contracts which require that a single-premium annuity be purchased at retirement. What we need for situations like these, where short-run liquidity is a problem, is a cost method which not only accumulates the proper amount at retirement, but also guarantees solvency at all times by virtue of never having an unfunded accrued liability (except perhaps incidentally because of actuarial losses). One approach to the problem would be to use the entry-age-normal method with entry age defined not as the age at hire, but the age on the effective date of the plan (using age at hire only for those hired after the effective date).

Then there would be no initial unfunded accrued liability; the problem is that if a substantial proportion of the accrued liability were attributable to a single individual (as, for example, in a plan covering only a doctor and his nurse) the plan could realize substantial losses on account of salary increases in excess of those anticipated (see the fourth term of equation (2.4.8)). These losses on account of salary increases amount to the accumulated value of the deficiency in prior normal costs from having underestimated the benefit at retirement, and thus can snowball as a principal individual gets closer to retirement.

A cost method which addresses both of these concerns is the ***individual-level-premium*** method. It funds each person's projected benefit with "level premiums" over his years of actual participation in the plan, and it starts with a zero unfunded.

The individual-level-premium method begins in the first year of operation of the plan with a normal cost computed in the same way as under the entry-age-normal method using an entry age of x, the age attained on the effective date of the plan. That is, it requires that the normal cost be a level amount payable from attained age through retirement age which will provide the necessary funds to "purchase" the benefit:

$$NC_t^j \frac{N_x - N_y}{D_x} = B_t^j(y)\ddot{a}_y^{(12)} \frac{D_y}{D_x}, \tag{2.5.1}$$

or,

$$NC_t^j = B_t^j(y)\ddot{a}_y^{(12)} \frac{D_y}{N_x - N_y}. \tag{2.5.2}$$

These are the same as we used in section 2.3 (equation (2.3.1)). The difference comes next year (at time 1, assuming that the plan is established at time 0). When we re-estimate $B^j(y)$, we do *not* let the normal cost be defined by

$$B_{t+1}^j(y)\ddot{a}_y^{(12)} \frac{D_y}{N_x - N_y} = NC_t^j + \Delta B^j \ddot{a}_y^{(12)} \frac{D_y}{N_x - N_y}, \tag{2.5.3}$$

as we would under entry-age-normal. Instead, we let the normal cost be equal to the normal cost computed at time 0 plus an increment computed as a new level payment sufficient to fund the increase in benefit $(\Delta B)_1^j$ from the new attained age:

$$NC_1^j = NC_0^j + (\Delta B)_1^j \ddot{a}_y^{(12)} \frac{D_y}{N_{x+1} - N_y}. \tag{2.5.4}$$

Note that the individual-level-premium method has the same first premise as both the unit-credit and entry-age-normal, namely, that the quantity $B^j(y)\ddot{a}_y^{(12)}$ will be accumulated for each individual at retirement. Under the unit-credit method we defined the accrued liability and let the normal cost fall out, but here, as with entry-age-normal, we have defined the normal cost and it remains now to see what the accrued liability is.

At the effective date of the plan (time 0) the accrued liability is equal to zero identically, by definition of normal cost. But at time $t = 1$ the accrued liability must equal the present value of future benefits minus the present value of future normal costs:

$$AL_1^j = \left[B_0^j + (\Delta B)_1^j\right] \ddot{a}_y^{(12)} \frac{D_y}{D_{x+1}} - \left[B_0^j \ddot{a}_y^{(12)} \frac{D_y}{N_x - N_y}\right.$$

$$\left. + (\Delta B)_1^j \ddot{a}_y^{(12)} \frac{D_y}{N_{x+1} - N_y}\right] \frac{N_{x+1} - N_y}{D_{x+1}} ; \tag{2.5.5}$$

where we have dropped the argument (y) from B_t^j to reduce clutter and $(\Delta B)_1^j \equiv B_1^j - B_0^j$. Equation (2.5.5) boils down to

$$AL_1^j = NC_0^j \frac{D_x}{D_{x+1}} . \tag{2.5.6}$$

At time $t = 2$ we add another increment to the normal cost equal to

$$(\Delta NC)_2^j = \underbrace{(B_2^j - B_1^j)}_{(\Delta B)_2^j} \frac{D_y \ddot{a}_y^{(12)}}{N_{x+2} - N_y}$$

and get

$$NC_2^j = NC_0^j + \Delta NC_1^j + \Delta NC_2^j . \tag{2.5.7}$$

Again, the accrued liability is defined as the present value of future benefits minus the present value of future normal costs:

$$AL_2^j = \left[B_0^j + (\Delta B)_1^j + (\Delta B)_2^j\right] \ddot{a}_y^{(12)} \frac{D_y}{D_{x+2}}$$

$$- \left[NC_0^j + (\Delta NC)_1^j + (\Delta NC)_2^j\right] \frac{N_{x+2} - N_y}{D_{x+2}}$$

$$= (AL_1^j + NC_1^j) \frac{D_{x+1}}{D_{x+2}} . \tag{2.5.8}$$

Therefore, arguing by induction, we can see that for any time $t > 0$

$$AL_{t+1}^j = (AL_t^j + NC_t^j)\frac{D_{x+t}}{D_{x+t+1}} . \tag{2.5.9}$$

The accrued liability proper is then the sum of the individual accrued liabilities, so that at any time $t+1$ we can write

$$\begin{aligned} AL_{t+1} &= \sum_{\mathbf{A}_{t+1}} AL_{t+1}^j = \sum_{\mathbf{A}_t}(AL_t^j + NC_t^j)\frac{D_{x+t}}{D_{x+t+1}} - \sum_{\mathbf{T+R}} AL_{t+1}^j \\ &= \sum_{\mathbf{A}_t}(AL_t^j + NC_t^j)(1+i) + \sum_{\mathbf{A}_t} q_{x+t} AL_{t+1}^j - \sum_{\mathbf{T+R}} AL_{t+1}^j , \end{aligned} \tag{2.5.10}$$

which can be expressed as

$$AL_{t+1} = (AL_t + NC_t)(1+i) - \left[\sum_{\mathbf{T}} AL_{t+1}^j - \sum_{\mathbf{A}_t} q_{x+t} AL_{t+1}^j\right] - \sum_{\mathbf{R}} AL_{t+1}^j , \tag{2.5.11}$$

from which we can subtract equation (2.2.5) to get

$$\begin{aligned} UAL_{t+1} &= UAL_t(1+i) - \left[I - iF_t - I_C + I_P\right] - \left[C + I_C - NC_t(1+i)\right] \\ &\quad - \left[\sum_{\mathbf{T}} AL_{t+1}^j - \sum_{\mathbf{A}_t} q_{x+t} AL_{t+1}^j\right] - \left[\sum_{\mathbf{R}} AL_{t+1}^j - P - I_P\right] . \end{aligned} \tag{2.5.12}$$

You will not be surprised that we are going to add up the second, fourth, and fifth terms of (2.5.12) and call them the "actuarial gain." An important feature of this gain is the absence of a term representing the loss due to salary increases and/or benefit increases greater than expected (compare this with equation (2.3.10), for example). The reason is that all losses due to salary increases — in which we include increases in projected benefit greater than expected, because these are normally due to greater-than-expected salary increases — have been pushed up into the normal cost. We then see that the actuarial gain can be expressed as

$$Gain = (UAL_t + NC_t)(1+i) - C - I_C - UAL_{t+1} , \tag{2.5.13}$$

which is the familiar form. Only the definitions of unfunded and normal cost have been changed!

It is also possible to use the ILP method with a salary-increase assumption in a manner similar to that outlined in section 2.4. In the first year of operation (time 0) we compute the individual normal cost as

$$NC_0^j = B_0^j \ddot{a}_y^{(12)} \frac{D_y}{D_x} \frac{{}^sD_x}{{}^sN_x - {}^sN_y} . \tag{2.5.14}$$

As with entry-age-normal, (2.5.14) implies that j's salary increases each year by the factor s_{x+1}/s_x. This means that the incremental normal cost computed in the following year is an increment over and above the ***natural increase*** in the normal cost due to the use of a salary scale:

$$(\Delta NC)_1^j = (\Delta B)_1^j \ddot{a}_y^{(12)} \frac{D_y}{D_{x+1}} \frac{{}^sD_{x+1}}{{}^sN_{x+1} - {}^sN_y}, \tag{2.5.15}$$

where $(\Delta B)_1^j$, as before, is the change in projected pension. The normal cost at time 1 is, therefore,

$$NC_1^j = NC_0^j \frac{s_{x+1}}{s_x} + (\Delta NC)_1^j. \tag{2.5.16}$$

The accrued liability at time 1 for an individual who is still active can then be determined as the present value of future benefits minus the present value of future normal costs:

$$\begin{aligned} AL_1^j &= (B_0^j + \Delta B_1^j)\, \ddot{a}_y^{(12)} \frac{D_y}{D_{x+1}} - \left[NC_0^j \frac{s_{x+1}}{s_x} + (\Delta NC)_1^j\right] \frac{{}^sN_{x+1} - {}^sN_y}{{}^sD_{x+1}} \\ &= B_0^j \ddot{a}_y^{(12)} \frac{D_y}{D_{x+1}} - B_0^j \ddot{a}_y^{(12)} \frac{D_y}{D_x} \frac{{}^sD_x}{{}^sN_x - {}^sN_y} \cdot \frac{s_{x+1}}{s_x} \left(\frac{{}^sN_x - {}^sN_y}{{}^sD_{x+1}} - \frac{{}^sD_x}{{}^sD_{x+1}}\right) \\ &= NC_0^j \frac{D_x}{D_{x+1}}. \end{aligned} \tag{2.5.17}$$

This leads directly to the general relation expressed by equation (2.5.9) — just as though we had no salary-increase assumption. By the same argument we get the same expression for the gain (equation (2.5.13)).

Thus, we see that the individual-level-premium method resembles entry-age-normal with entry age defined as the age at hire or age at the effective date (whichever is greater). The difference is that under ILP we take a normally large component of the actuarial gain — a component which is normally negative — out of the accrued liability and spread it into future normal costs. Under entry-age-normal, this portion of the gain was simply amortized in the manner of other gains — i.e., over a period which may or may not have been longer than the future working lifetime of a particular individual.

Summary

Under the individual-level-premium cost method the cost of the plan for any particular year is equal to

- the normal cost

minus • amortization of the previous years' gains;

where the normal cost for an individual is computed as a "level premium" from attained age at participation in the plan, supplemented by incremental normal costs computed at later attained ages sufficient to fund any increases in projected pension.

(Note that there can be an unfunded accrued liability at any time after the first year, but it is entirely the result of actuarial losses, which are in the course of being amortized as prescribed above.)

Exercises

2.5.1 Show that equation (2.5.5) leads to equation (2.5.6).

2.5.2 Verify equation (2.5.10).

2.5.3 Verify equation (2.5.16).

2.5.4 Derive the following general formula for the normal cost at time $t \geq 0$:

$$NC_t^j = \frac{PVFB_t^j - AL_t^j}{PVFS_t^j} S_t^j \ . \tag{2.5.18}$$

Explain why this equation would be easier to use in practice than equations (2.5.14) and (2.5.15). What does each of the terms stand for?

2.6 *Frozen Initial Liability*

In the previous sections we have looked at two cost methods, unit-credit and entry-age-normal, which generate a pension cost for a given year equal to the sum of the three components, normal cost, amortization of initial unfunded, and amortization of gains. The third method, individual-level-premium, eliminated the amortization of the unfunded and produced a cost equal to the sum of just two components, normal cost and gain amortization. We now come to the discussion of a fourth method, *frozen-initial-liability**, which expresses the cost as the sum of the normal cost and the amortization of the initial unfunded, but which gets rid of the actuarial gain! Remember, though, that we use the term "gain" to mean an unexpected decrease in the unfunded accrued liability (see, for example, equation (2.3.12)). People sometimes speak of "actuarial gains" in the looser sense of unexpected good experience. Obviously, any cost method must have some mechanism for reflecting deviations of actual experience from expected, and the frozen-initial-liability method is no exception.

We saw in exercise 2.4.7 that under both the entry-age-normal and unit-credit cost methods the accrued liability was equal to the present value of future benefits less the present value of future normal costs, although under the unit-credit method we never computed present value of future benefits directly. Under the individual-level-premium method, too, we defined

$$AL_t = \sum_{\mathbf{A}_t} AL_t^j = \sum_{\mathbf{A}_t} PVFB_t^j - \sum_{\mathbf{A}_t} PVFNC_t^j \,. \tag{2.6.1}$$

For a given plan and a given set of assumptions, the present value of future benefits is the same no matter what cost method is used. Therefore, we are free to invent a new cost method by defining accrued liability and normal cost in any way we please, as long as these definitions are consistent with equation (2.6.1) — i.e., the accrued liability and normal cost must "pivot" around the present value of future benefits. If we have a lower accrued liability, we must have a higher normal cost, and vice versa.

Under the three cost methods already studied in this chapter, the accrued liability was computed separately for each individual and then summed to produce the total accrued liability. Under the frozen-initial-liability method, however, we do not directly compute an accrued liability separately for each individual. Let us for the moment, in order to introduce the method properly, not specify how to compute the accrued liability at time t — let us just assume that we have one and that as usual it is a benchmark which represents the desired fund balance at any given time. Then we can write

$$AL_t = \sum_{\mathbf{A}_t} PVFB_t^j - PVFNC_t \,,$$

or,

$$PVFNC_t = \sum_{\mathbf{A}_t} PVFB_t^j - AL_t \,, \tag{2.6.2}$$

where $PVFNC_t$ represents the present value of future normal costs at time t.

Equation (2.6.2) is not peculiar to the frozen-initial-liability cost method, but is a general relationship which must govern all cost methods. The task of any particular method is to define a normal cost in such a way as to "pay off" the $PVFNC$. In the methods we have looked at previously, this was done by defining a normal cost for each individual and therefore, by implication, a

---

*In the JCPT Report this cost method has been renamed the "frozen-entry-age" method.

present value of future normal costs for each individual:

$$PVFNC_t^j = NC_t^j \frac{N_x - N_y}{D_x} .$$

These were then summed up to get

$$PVFNC_t = \sum_{\mathbf{A}_t} PVFNC_t^j = \sum_{\mathbf{A}_t} NC_t^j \frac{N_x - N_y}{D_x} .$$

Under the frozen-initial-liability method, however, we take a completely different approach. We assume that the normal cost is a level dollar amount, and that it is the *same dollar amount* for each active employee, so that if we call the total normal cost NC_t we *define* the normal cost for any individual to be $NC_t^j = \frac{1}{n_t} NC_t$ where n_t is the number of persons in $\mathbf{A}_t$. Then we can express the present value of future normal costs as

$$PVFNC_t = NC_t \cdot \frac{1}{n_t} \sum_{\mathbf{A}_t} \frac{N_x - N_y}{D_x} . \tag{2.6.3}$$

or, equivalently,

$$NC_t = \frac{PVFNC_t}{\frac{1}{n_t} \sum_{\mathbf{A}_t} \frac{N_x - N_y}{D_x}} = \left(\frac{\sum_{\mathbf{A}_t} PVFB_t^j - AL_t}{\sum_{\mathbf{A}_t} \frac{N_x - N_y}{D_x}} \right) \cdot n_t . \tag{2.6.4}$$

Note that the large parenthetical term in equation (2.6.4) is the normal cost per active employee, which we shall refer to as U_t (standing for unit normal cost). In other words, we say that $U_t = \frac{1}{n_t} NC_t$.

Equation (2.6.4) is a partial definition of the normal cost under the frozen-initial-liability method; it is not a *complete* definition because we have still not said what AL_t stands for. Actually, we know that AL_t stands for accrued liability, it is just that we have not decided yet how to compute it. Nevertheless, since it does stand for accrued liability we can *assume* that equation (2.2.8) and equation (2.3.12) apply to this accrued liability as well; i.e., we can declare that

$$AL_{t+1} - F_{t+1} = (AL_t - F_t + NC_t)(1 + i) - C - I_C - Gain , \tag{2.6.5}$$

where "Gain" has yet to be defined. For now let us just consider "Gain" to be a catch-all term to make up for any inadequacies in our declaration of equation (2.6.5).

We now set about to work out an expression for U_{t+1} from equations (2.6.4) and (2.6.5). From exercise 2.6.1 we get the result

$$PVFNC_{t+1} = \sum_{\mathbf{A}_{t+1}} PVFB_{t+1}^{j} - AL_{t+1}$$

$$= PVFB_t(1+i) - \Big[\sum_{\mathbf{T}} \widetilde{PVFB}_{t+1}^{j} - \sum_{\mathbf{A}_t} q_x \widetilde{PVFB}_{t+1}^{j}\Big]$$

$$- \sum_{\mathbf{R}} \widetilde{PVFB}_{t+1}^{j} + \sum_{\mathbf{A}_{t+1}} \Delta B^j \ddot{a}_y^{(12)} \frac{D_y}{D_{x+1}} - AL_{t+1}\,, \tag{2.6.6}$$

where the tildes indicate values computed as though the increase ΔB^j in j's projected benefit between times t and $t+1$ is equal to zero. Also, from exercise 2.6.2 we get the relationship

$$\sum_{\mathbf{A}_{t+1}} \frac{N_{x+1} - N_y}{D_{x+1}} = \sum_{\mathbf{A}_t} \Big(\frac{N_x - N_y}{D_x} - 1\Big)(1+i) - \Big[\sum_{\mathbf{T}} \frac{N_{x+1} - N_y}{D_{x+1}} - \sum_{\mathbf{A}_t} q_x \frac{N_{x+1} - N_y}{D_{x+1}}\Big]$$

$$- \sum_{\mathbf{R}} \frac{N_{x+1} - N_y}{D_{x+1}}\,. \tag{2.6.7}$$

If we now divide equation (2.6.6) by equation (2.6.7), we get an expression of the form

$$U_{t+1} = \frac{\textit{Numerator}_t + \Delta \textit{Numerator}}{\textit{Denominator}_t + \Delta \textit{Denominator}}\,. \tag{2.6.8}$$

Now note that for any numbers N, ΔN, D, and ΔD the following algebraic identity can be stated (exercise 2.6.3):

$$\frac{N + \Delta N}{D + \Delta D} = \frac{N}{D} + \frac{1}{D + \Delta D}\Big(\Delta N - \frac{N}{D}\Delta D\Big)\,. \tag{2.6.9}$$

Using this relationship we can combine equations (2.6.6), (2.6.7), and (2.6.9) to get a relationship between U_{t+1} and U_t (exercise 2.6.4):

$$U_{t+1} = U_t - \frac{1}{\sum_{\mathbf{A}_{t+1}} \frac{N_{x+1} - N_y}{D_{x+1}}} \Big\{\Big[I - iF_t - I_C + I_P\Big]$$

$$+ \Big[\sum_{\mathbf{T}} \Big(\widetilde{PVFB}_{t+1}^{j} - U_t \frac{N_{x+1} - N_y}{D_{x+1}}\Big) - \sum_{\mathbf{A}_t} q_x \Big(\widetilde{PVFB}_{t+1}^{j} - U_t \frac{N_{x+1} - N_y}{D_{x+1}}\Big)\Big]$$

$$- \Big[\sum_{\mathbf{A}_{t+1}} \Delta B^j \ddot{a}_y^{(12)} \frac{D_y}{D_{x+1}}\Big] + \Big[\sum_{\mathbf{R}} \widetilde{PVFB}_{t+1}^{j} - P - I_P\Big] - Gain\Big\}\,. \tag{2.6.10}$$

Now you will recall that we defined U_t to be the *level* normal cost applicable to each active employee (equation (2.6.3)), so we would like U_{t+1} to be equal to U_t if actual experience during the year is in accord with our assumptions. Look at equation (2.6.10) and note that if actual experience were the same as expected, all the terms inside the braces would be zero, except possibly the catch-all term "Gain", which we have not yet defined. Note also that "Gain" has a negative sign, which looks wrong because the other gain terms are positive. Therefore, it is easy to see that *we must define "Gain" to be exactly zero.* Then we can restate equation (2.6.5) as

$$UAL_{t+1} = (UAL_t + NC_t)(1+i) - C - I_C \, . \tag{2.6.11}$$

This tells us the relationship between two successive years' unfundeds, so if we know what the value of the unfunded is at time 0 we can compute it for any subsequent year using equation (2.6.11), with the normal cost defined by equation (2.6.4).

The normal cost, in any year except the first, is therefore computed in the following four steps:

(1) update the unfunded using equation (2.6.11) to get UAL_t;

(2) look up the fund balance F_t;

(3) compute $PVFB_t = \sum_{A_t} B_t^j \, \ddot{a}_y^{(12)} \frac{D_y}{D_x}$ and the present value of future working years $PVFY_t = \sum_{A_t} \frac{N_x - N_y}{D_x}$;

(4) compute the normal cost by the formula

$$NC_t = \frac{PVFB_t - F_t - UAL_t}{PVFY_t} \cdot n_t \, . \tag{2.6.12}$$

Now we have completely defined the frozen-initial-liability cost method, except that we have not said how to initialize the unfunded at time $t = 0$, the first year of operation. We shall now do so. ***Under the frozen-initial-liability method the unfunded accrued liability at time 0 is computed under the entry-age-normal cost method.***

The definition of the initial unfunded accrued liability is quite arbitrary. We could have set it equal to zero or any numerical value whatever without impairing the operation of the cost method, because under this method we simply take whatever portion of the present value of future benefits that is left after subtracting the accrued liability (the unfunded plus the fund balance) and spread it over the average future working lifetime of the active participants. This amount which is spread includes any "gains" due to the deviation of actual from expected experience.

Sometimes this cost method is used with the initial unfunded computed on the unit-credit method rather than the entry-age-normal. When the unfunded is initialized under the unit-credit method, this cost method is referred to as the *attained-age-normal* method.*

Summary

The cost of a pension plan under the frozen-initial-liability cost method (or the attained-age-normal method) is the sum of

(1) the normal cost, plus

(2) amortization of the unfunded accrued liability;

where

- the normal cost is defined by equation (2.6.12)

and

- the unfunded is defined in the first year the same as under the entry-age-normal method (unit-credit for attained-age-normal) and is thereafter carried forward using equation (2.6.11).

Any deviation of actual from expected experience causes a change in the unit normal cost (see equation (2.6.10)).

Exercises

2.6.1 Taking $PVFB_t^j = B_t^j \ddot{a}_y^{(12)} \frac{D_y}{D_x}$ and $PVFB_t = \sum_{\mathbf{A}_t} PVFB_t^j$, derive equation (2.6.6).

2.6.2 Derive equation (2.6.7).

2.6.3 Prove equation (2.6.9).

2.6.4 Combine equation (2.6.6) with equation (2.6.7) and (2.6.9) to get equation (2.6.10). (Hint: for members of set **R**, $x + 1 = y$.) Note the sign of the term "Gain" in equation (2.6.10); shouldn't it be " + " instead of " − "? Is there a logical error here?

*In the JCPT Report this has been renamed the "frozen-attained-age" method.

2.6.5 Is the normal cost under the frozen-initial-liability method such that for *each person* an amount equal to $B(y)\,\ddot{a}_y^{(12)}$ will be accumulated at age y? (Answer: No. What is the reason?)

2.6.6 In equation (2.6.10) we saw some terms of the form $PVFB_t^j - U_t \dfrac{N_x - N_y}{D_x}$ which could be interpreted as individual "ac- "accrued liabilities" for each person. Could such an "accrued liability" be negative for a given employee? If so, what would that mean?

2.6.7 Show that for the FIL method we have, instead of equation (2.2.18),

$$AL_{t+1} = (AL_t + NC_t)(1+i) - \left[P + I_P\right] + \left[I - iF_t - I_C + I_P\right]. \tag{2.6.13}$$

Why the extra term?

2.7 *New Entrants*

Throughout the discussion so far, beginning in section 2.2, we have been deliberately ignoring new entrants into the group of active employees covered by our pension plan (see, for example, equation (2.2.2)). This omission did not hinder our understanding of the unit-credit, entry-age-normal, and individual-level-premium cost methods because under those methods accrued liabilities were calculated separately for each individual and were defined as zero for persons just entering the plan. This meant that the size of the gain in any particular year would have been unaffected if we had included new entrants because, as we went from time t to time $t+1$, there would have been no additional unfunded due to new entrants. As far as the normal cost under these three methods is concerned, we have been assuming that each year's new entrants would be covered under a separate plan, but again that made no difference to the logic of our discussion because the total costs for all these plans — both the original plan that we have been looking at, and the new ones set up each year for each year's new entrants — would be the same as if all were included under a single plan: Normal costs and accrued liabilities are computed separately for each person, then summed to get the result.

Such was not the case, however, with the frozen-initial-liability method (and its cousin attained-age normal), because under these methods the present value of future normal costs was spread over the average future working lifetime of all active participants at time t, and again at time $t+1$. This average lifetime was $\dfrac{1}{n_t}\sum_{A_t}\dfrac{N_x - N_y}{D_x}$ at time t, and $\dfrac{1}{n_{t+1}}\sum_{A_{t+1}}\dfrac{N_{x+1} - N_y}{D_{x+1}}$ at time $t+1$, so the composition of the group — which portion was old participants and which portion new entrants — affected the value of the normal cost, because it affected the period over which the present value of future normal costs got spread. We must therefore not ignore new entrants in our discussion of the FIL and AAN cost methods. We shall undertake in this section to generalize our discussion of all the cost methods by bringing new entrants into the picture.

Let us denote by **N** the set of new entrants during the year t to $t+1$. Then we can write a more general version of equation (2.2.2):

$$\mathbf{A}_{t+1} = \mathbf{A}_t - \mathbf{T} - \mathbf{R} + \mathbf{N} . \tag{2.7.1}$$

Now let us see how this modification affects the discussions of each of the cost methods studied so far.

Under the *unit-credit* method, a new entrant will arrive at time $t+1$ with a nonzero accrued liability only to the extent that he has an accrued benefit at that point — which will depend on the precise terms of the plan (how service is credited, etc.). However, even if the accrued benefit at time $t+1$ is zero we should have added a term $\sum_{\mathbf{N}} B^j(x+1)\, \ddot{a}_y^{(12)} \dfrac{D_y}{D_{x+1}}$ (taking x to mean age at time t even for new entrants!) to equation (2.2.3), which related AL_t and AL_{t+1}. Because set **N** is distinct from set $\mathbf{A}_t$, NC_t as defined by equation (2.2.4) remains valid. The same term should also be added to the right-hand side of equation (2.2.7) (which related UAL_t and UAL_{t+1}), and this would have the effect of reducing the gain (equation (2.2.8)) by a like amount. Thus, to the extent that persons appear on the census rolls of the plan at time $t+1$ with a nonzero accrued benefit, the gain will be reduced by the present value of such accrued benefits. Otherwise, the discussion of section 2.2 remains valid even with new entrants taken into account.

Under the *entry-age-normal* method, the entry age w is exactly equal to $x+1$, the age at time $t+1$, and the accrued liability is therefore identically zero at time $t+1$ for new entrants (see, for example, equation (2.3.5) with w set equal to $x+1$). This means that the definition and amount of the gain is unaffected, and the only impact on the cost computed at time $t+1$ is to add individual normal costs for new entrants to the total. The fourth term of equation (2.3.10) (which relates UAL_t and UAL_{t+1}) however should show a summation over the set $\mathbf{A}_{t+1} - \mathbf{N}$, rather than the entire set $\mathbf{A}_{t+1}$ (note that $\mathbf{A}_{t+1} - \mathbf{N} = \mathbf{A}_t \cap \mathbf{A}_{t+1}$); likewise, for the corresponding term of equation (2.4.8) (which relates UAL_t and UAL_{t+1} when a salary scale is used). Otherwise, the operation of the entry-age-normal cost method is unaffected by new entrants.

Under the *individual-level-premium* method new entrants do not affect the gain either, because as with entry-age-normal the accrued liability of new entrants is always zero. The new entrants do increase the normal cost at time $t+1$, though, by the sum of their "individual level premiums."

Under the *frozen-initial-liability* method the addition of new entrants requires major modifications to the argument:

(1) To equation (2.6.6) (for $PVFNC_{t+1}$) we must add the term $\sum_{\mathbf{N}} B^j \ddot{a}_y^{(12)} \frac{D_y}{D_{x+1}}$ and change the fourth term to $\sum_{\mathbf{A}_t \cap \mathbf{A}_{t+1}} \Delta B^j \ddot{a}_y^{(12)} \frac{D_y}{D_{x+1}}$ (because A_{t+1} includes $\mathbf{N}$).

(2) To equation (2.6.7) we must add the term $\sum_{\mathbf{N}} \frac{N_{x+1} - N_y}{D_{x+1}}$ to the righthand side.

(3) Equation (2.6.10) (which relates U_t to U_{t+1}) must then be modified to include the changes noted above and also must acquire another term within the braces equal to $-\sum_{\mathbf{N}} \left(B^j \ddot{a}_y^{(12)} \frac{D_y}{D_{x+1}} - U_t \frac{N_{x+1} - N_y}{D_{x+1}} \right)$. Note also that the summation in the third bracketed term within the braces is taken over the set $\mathbf{A}_t \cap \mathbf{A}_{t+1}$ rather than $\mathbf{A}_{t+1}$.

This last is an important change. It says that to the extent that the unit normal cost U_t, computed for the set $\mathbf{A}_t$ of active participants at time t, is not sufficient to fund the projected benefits of new entrants from their respective attained ages at time $t+1$, the new unit normal cost U_{t+1} will be *increased;* and vice versa.

As we saw in exercise 2.6.5, the unit normal cost U_t is sufficient *in aggregate* to fund the projected benefits over the average working lifetimes of all the employees in set $\mathbf{A}_t$ — but it is not sufficient, in general, to fund any particular individual benefit. U_t will be more than sufficient for younger employees, generally speaking, and less than sufficient for older employees, so to the extent that new hires are younger than average the term $\sum_{\mathbf{N}} \left(B^j \ddot{a}_y^{(12)} \frac{D_y}{D_{x+1}} - U_t \frac{N_{x+1} - N_y}{D_{x+1}} \right)$ will be negative, and thus will decrease U_{t+1} from what it would have been in the absence of new entrants. This is not always true, however: Depending on the distribution of ages and benefit amounts, new entrants can have a positive, negative, or zero effect on the change in U_t. But whatever their effect on U_t, the normal cost at time $t+1$ is equal to U_{t+1} multiplied by the number of employees in set $\mathbf{A}_{t+1}$, which includes $\mathbf{N}$, so the amount of normal cost will generally increase merely because of the addition of new entrants. It sometimes happens, however, that the decrease in *unit* normal cost on account of new entrants more than offsets the additional body count by which the unit normal cost is multiplied to get the total normal cost. All we can say absolutely is that new entrants have an effect on the cost of a plan determined under the frozen-initial-liability method different from that which they would have if they went into a separate plan.

Exercises

2.7.1 Re-write the following equations in entirety to reflect the addition of new entrants: (2.2.3), (2.2.4), (2.2.7), (2.3.10), (2.4.8), (2.6.6), (2.6.7), (2.6.10).

2.7.2 Show algebraically that under any cost method which defines the normal cost and accrued liability individually for each active participant, and which defines the gain in the usual manner (for example, equation (2.3.12)),

(a) new entrants between times t and $t+1$ will have no effect on the gain unless and to the extent that they come into the plan with a nonzero accrued liability; and

(b) the normal cost at $t+1$ can be separated into two mutally independent components for new entrants and the set $\mathbf{A}_t \cap \mathbf{A}_{t+1}$ of ongoing actives.

2.7.3 Show that the normal cost under the frozen-initial-liability method cannot be separated as in exercise 2.7.2, and that while the cost *can* be separated for ongoing actives and new entrants, the two components are dependent on each other.

2.8 *More Frozen Initial Liability*

As with the entry-age-normal and individual-level-premium methods, the frozen-initial-liability method operates differently when benefits are based on salary and a salary-increase assumption is used. Instead of expressing the normal cost as a level dollar amount for each employee, we express it as a level percentage of salary, U_t, for each employee: $NC_t^j = U_t S_t^j$, where S_t^j is j's annual rate of salary at time t. Then, instead of equation (2.6.3), we have:

$$PVFNC_t = \sum_{\mathbf{A}_t} U_t S_t^j \, \frac{{}^sN_x - {}^sN_y}{{}^sD_x} = U_t \sum_{\mathbf{A}_t} S_t^j \, \frac{{}^sN_x - {}^sN_y}{{}^sD_x} \,. \tag{2.8.1}$$

That is,

$$\begin{aligned} NC_t = U_t \sum_{\mathbf{A}_t} S_t^j &= \left(\frac{PVFNC_t}{\sum_{\mathbf{A}_t} S_t^j \, \frac{{}^sN_x - {}^sN_y}{{}^sD_x}} \right) \sum_{\mathbf{A}_t} S_t^j \\ &= \frac{PVFB_t - F_t - UAL_t}{PVFS_t} \sum_{\mathbf{A}_t} S_t^j \,, \end{aligned} \tag{2.8.2}$$

which corresponds to equation (2.6.12). The symbol $PVFS_t$ stands for the present value of future salaries at time t. As in section 2.6, UAL_t is derived from the prior year's value by equation (2.6.11).

These modifications mean that the counterpart of equation (2.6.10) is

$$
\begin{aligned}
U_{t+1} = U_t - \frac{1}{PVFS_{t+1}} \Big\{ & \big[I - iF_t - I_C + I_P \big] \\
& + \Big[\sum_{\mathbf{T}} (P\widetilde{VFB}^j_{t+1} - U_t P\widetilde{VFS}^j_{t+1}) - \sum_{\mathbf{A}_t} q_x (P\widetilde{VFB}^j_{t+1} - U_t P\widetilde{VFS}^j_{t+1}) \Big] \\
& + \Big[\sum_{\mathbf{R}} P\widetilde{VFB}^j_{t+1} - P - I_P \Big] \\
& + \Big[\sum_{\mathbf{A}_t \cap \mathbf{A}_{t+1}} (P\widetilde{VFB}^j_{t+1} - U_t P\widetilde{VFS}^j_{t+1}) - \sum_{\mathbf{A}_t \cap \mathbf{A}_{t+1}} (PVFB^j_{t+1} - U_t PVFS^j_{t+1}) \Big] \\
& + \Big[- \sum_{\mathbf{N}} (PVFB^j_{t+1} - U_t PVFS^j_{t+1}) \Big] \Big\},
\end{aligned}
\tag{2.8.3}
$$

where again $P\widetilde{VFB}^j_{t+1}$ indicates the present value of future benefits computed at time $t+1$ as though the change in projected benefit ΔB equals zero, and, likewise, $P\widetilde{FVS}^j_{t+1} = S^j_t \dfrac{s_{x+1}}{s_x} \dfrac{{}^sN_{x+1} - {}^sN_y}{{}^sD_{x+1}}$ and $PVFS^j_{t+1} = S^j_{t+1} \dfrac{{}^sN_{x+1} - {}^sN_y}{{}^sD_{x+1}}$. Here again, if you examine each of the terms of equation (2.8.3) carefully, you will see clearly how favorable experience tends to depress the unit normal cost and unfavorable experience tends to raise it.

Here, as in section 2.6, the unfunded accrued liability in the first year of operation (which we call time zero) is computed using the entry-age-normal cost method. Following the results obtained in section 2.4 this means we compute a normal cost as

$$
NC_0 = \sum_{\mathbf{A}_0} B \ddot{a}_y^{(12)} \frac{D_y}{D_w} \frac{{}^sD_w}{{}^sN_w - {}^sN_y} \frac{s_x}{s_w}, \tag{2.8.4}
$$

which can be expressed

$$
NC_0 = \sum_{\mathbf{A}_0} \frac{PVFBW^j_0}{PVFSW^j_0} S^j_0, \tag{2.8.5}
$$

where

$$
PVFBW^j_t = B^j_t \ddot{a}_y^{(12)} \frac{D_y}{D_w} \quad \text{and} \quad PVFSW^j_t = S^j_t \frac{s_w}{s_x} \frac{{}^sN_w - {}^sN_y}{{}^sD_w}.
$$

Then we get the entry-age-normal accrued liability by

$$AL_0 = \sum_{A_0} PVFB_0^j - \sum_{A_0} \frac{PVFBW_0^j}{PVFSW_0^j} S_0^j \frac{{}^sN_x - {}^sN_y}{{}^sD_x}$$

$$= \sum_{A_0} \left(PVFB - \frac{PVFBW}{PVFSW} PVFS \right), \tag{2.8.6}$$

where we have dropped the superscript j and subscript 0 to reduce clutter. Now at time zero there is no fund (i.e., $F_0 = 0$) so the unfunded is the entire accrued liability. That means when we compute the normal cost under the frozen-initial-liability method we get (from equation (2.6.12))

$$NC_0 = \frac{\sum_{A_0} PVFB_0^j - UAL_0}{\sum_{A_0} PVFS_0^j} \sum_{A_0} S_0^j$$

$$= \frac{\sum PVFB - \sum \left(PVFB - \frac{PVFBW}{PVFSW} PVFS \right)}{\sum PVFS} \sum S$$

$$= \frac{\sum \left(\frac{PVFBW}{PVFSW} PVFS \right)}{\sum PVFS} \sum S. \tag{2.8.7}$$

Here we face a small dilemma. The normal cost computed under the entry-age-normal method (equation (2.8.5)) produced an accrued liability (2.8.6) which, when plugged into the FIL normal-cost formula (2.6.12), yielded a new normal cost (2.8.7) which was different from the original one (2.8.5). Which is the *real* normal cost at time zero? The answer: the one defined by (2.6.12), because we assumed that equation would hold when we developed equation (2.6.10) and its counterpart (2.8.3) — which demonstrate that the frozen-initial-liability method "works" (i.e., that it adjusts properly for the deviation of actual experience from expected). On the other hand, there is usually not much difference between the two in dollars, and the world would certainly not come to an end if you were to use (2.8.5) instead of (2.6.12), or its equivalent in this case, (2.8.2).

The nicest way out of the dilemma, however, is afforded by using the so-called *aggregate entry-age-normal* cost method to compute the initial accrued liability. Under this method, instead of equation (2.8.5) we use

$$NC_0 = \frac{\sum_{A_0} PVFBW_0^j}{\sum_{A_0} PVFSW_0^j} \sum_{A_0} S_0^j. \tag{2.8.8}$$

The two are similar, but in the first we took the sum of quotients, while in the second the quotient of sums. Note that

$$NC_0 = U_0 \sum S_0^j$$

where $U_0 = \sum PVFBW_0^j \,/\, \sum \text{PVFSW}_0^j$.

The accrued liability under this new cost method is then

$$\begin{aligned} \text{AL}_0 &= \sum_{A_0} PVFB_0^j - \sum_{A_0} U_0 S_0^j \frac{{}^sN_x - {}^sN_y}{{}^sD_x} \\ &= \sum_{A_0} PVFB_0^j - U_0 \sum_{A_0} PVFS_0^j . \end{aligned} \tag{2.8.9}$$

Solving for U_0, we get

$$U_0 = \frac{\sum_{A_0} PVFB_0^j - AL_0}{\sum_{A_0} PVFS_0^j};$$

and, therefore,

$$NC_0 = U_0 \sum S_0^j = \frac{\sum PVFB_0^j - UAL_0 - F_0}{\sum PVFS_0^j} \sum S_0^j , \tag{2.8.10}$$

which is the same as that obtained under the frozen-initial-liability method! So if we use the aggregate entry-age-normal in conjunction with the FIL method, we avoid any ambiguity owing to the calculation of two normal costs on the same valuation date.

It should be noted that with FIL's cousin, attained-age-normal, we never get the problem of two normal costs, because we simply compute the accrued liability at time zero as the present value of accrued benefits on that date. With the unit-credit method, you do not have to compute the normal cost in order to get the accrued liability as you do under entry-age-normal.

Exercises

2.8.1 In going from equation (2.6.10) to equation (2.8.3), what became of the term involving ΔB?

2.8.2 Starting from the definition of the FIL normal cost (equation (2.6.12)) and the set relationship (equation (2.7.1)), prove that equation (2.8.3) is correct (use a line of argument analogous to that of section 2.6).

2.8.3 If the FIL method is used in conjunction with the aggregate EAN in the first year, and in the normal fashion the following year; and if the aggregate EAN calculation is also repeated in the second year; what is the difference between the unit normal costs under the two methods at time 1? Show that if $U_0 = U_1$ under FIL, the gain computed under aggregate EAN is not necessarily zero. Can the aggregate-EAN gain be computed using equation (2.3.11)? What if there are no new entrants? [Hint: proceed as follows:

(a) Express U_1 in terms of U_0 for both methods;

(b) Note that the two values of U_1 differ by a term arising from the recalculation of entry-age values at time 1 under EAN;

(c) See that if $U_0 = U_1$ under FIL, then the gain under aggregate EAN is not necessarily equal to zero;

(d) Note that if there are no new entrants, the extra term referred to in (b), above, is zero as long as assumptions are realized.]

2.8.4 Assume that the contribution C for the year t to $t+1$ is made at time $t+1$. Does the size of C have any effect on the size of NC_{t+1} under the FIL method? Prove your answer algebraically.

2.9 *Aggregate*

Having looked at a cost method (ILP) which dispenses — at least initially — with the unfunded accrued liability, and another (FIL) which dispenses with the gain, we come at last to the ultimate in simplicity: a cost method which dispenses with both the unfunded and the gain! Such is the *aggregate* cost method. Under this method the cost of the plan in any year is precisely equal to the normal cost, with no additional components representing amortization of gains or the initial unfunded.

Remember that under the frozen-initial-liability method (and the attained-age-normal method) we defined the unfunded accrued liability to be equal to the expected unfunded, thereby defining the gain to be zero. Under the aggregate method we step boldly forward and declare the unfunded to be *zero* at all times. This is just another way of saying that the accrued liability is always equal to the assets on hand:

$$AL_t = F_t .$$

(2.9.1)

As with FIL or AAN, under the aggregate method we define the normal cost to be the same amount, U_t, for each active employee:

$$NC_t = \sum_{\mathbf{A}_t} U_t = U_t n_t ,$$

(2.9.2)

where n_t stands for the number of employees in the set $\mathbf{A}_t$. Because the accrued liability must always equal the present value of future benefits less the present value of future normal costs, we have

$$AL_t = F_t = \sum_{\mathbf{A}_t} PVFB_t^j - U_t \sum_{\mathbf{A}_t} \frac{N_x - N_y}{D_x} .$$

(2.9.3)

This means that

$$U_t = \frac{PVFB_t - F_t}{PVFY_t} \quad \text{and} \quad NC_t = n_t U_t ,$$

(2.9.4)

where $PVFY_t = \sum_{\mathbf{A}_t} \frac{N_x - N_y}{D_x}$ (the present value of future working years).

The preceding discussion, of course, is valid only where there is no salary-increase assumption. Where we have a salary scale the expression equivalent to (2.9.4) is

$$U_t = \frac{PVFB_t - F_t}{PVFS_t} \quad \text{and} \quad NC_t = U_t \sum_{\mathbf{A}_t} S_t^j ,$$

(2.9.5)

where $PVFS_t = \sum_{\mathbf{A}_t} S_t^j \frac{{}^sN_x - {}^sN_y}{{}^sD_x}$ (the present value of future salaries). Equation (2.9.5) is the general definition of the normal cost, because if you have no salary-increase assumption you can simply set $s_x = 1$ for all ages and $S_t^j = 1$ for all employees, and get (2.9.4). In general, therefore, U_t is a uniform *level percentage of salary* for all active employees.

Using equation (2.6.6), as modified by the discussion in section 2.7, we can derive the relationship between $PVFNC_{t+1}$ and $PVFNC_t$ as follows (exercise 2.9.1):

$$PVFNC_{t+1} = PVFB_{t+1} - F_{t+1} = PVFNC_t(1+i) - \left[C + I_C\right]$$

$$- \left[I - iF_t - I_C + I_P\right] - \left[\sum_{\mathbf{R}} P\widetilde{VFB}^j_{t+1} - P - I_P\right]$$

$$+ \sum_{\mathbf{A}_t \cap \mathbf{A}_{t+1}} \Delta B^j \ddot{a}_y^{(12)} \frac{D_y}{D_{x+1}} + \sum_{\mathbf{N}} PVFB^j_{t+1}$$

$$- \left[\sum_{\mathbf{T}} P\widetilde{VFB}^j_{t+1} - \sum_{\mathbf{A}_t} q_x P\widetilde{VFB}^j_{t+1}\right]. \tag{2.9.6}$$

Likewise, from exercise 2.9.2 we get the result

$$PVFS_{t+1} = \sum_{\mathbf{A}_{t+1}} S^j_{t+1} \frac{{}^sN_{x+1} - {}^sN_y}{{}^sD_{x+1}}$$

$$= \left(PVFS_t - \sum_{\mathbf{A}_t} S^j_t\right)(1+i) + \sum_{\mathbf{A}_t} q_x P\widetilde{VFS}^j_{t+1} - \sum_{\mathbf{T}+\mathbf{R}} P\widetilde{VFS}^j_{t+1}$$

$$+ \sum_{\mathbf{A}_t \cap \mathbf{A}_{t+1}} (PVFS^j_{t+1} - P\widetilde{FVS}^j_{t+1}) + \sum_{\mathbf{N}} PVFS^j_{t+1}. \tag{2.9.7}$$

Pension actuaries call $\sum_{\mathbf{A}_t} S^j_t$ the "covered payroll" at time t. Now, remembering equation (2.6.9), we can get the relationship between the unit normal costs in two successive years (exercise 2.9.3):

$$U_{t+1} = \frac{PVFB_{t+1} - F_{t+1}}{PVFS_{t+1}} = U_t - \frac{1}{PVFS_{t+1}} \Big\{\left[I - iF_t - I_C + I_P\right]$$

$$+ \left[C + I_C - NC_t(1+i)\right] + \Big[\sum_{\mathbf{T}} (P\widetilde{VFB}^j_{t+1} - U_t P\widetilde{VFS}^j_{t+1})$$

$$- \sum_{\mathbf{A}_t} q_x (P\widetilde{VFB}^j_{t+1} - U_t P\widetilde{VFS}^j_{t+1})\Big] + \left[\sum_{\mathbf{R}} P\widetilde{VFB}^j_{t+1} - P - I_P\right]$$

$$+ \Big[- \sum_{\mathbf{A}_t \cap \mathbf{A}_{t+1}} (\Delta PVFB^j - U_t \Delta PVFS^j)\Big] + \Big[- \sum_{\mathbf{N}} (PVFB^j_{t+1} - U_t PVFS^j_{t+1})\Big]\Big\}, \tag{2.9.8}$$

where $\Delta PVFB^j = \Delta B \ddot{a}_y^{(12)} \dfrac{D_y}{D_{x+1}}$ and $\Delta PVFS^j = PVFS^j_{t+1} - P\widetilde{VFS}^j_{t+1}$.

Compare equation (2.9.8) to equation (2.8.3). The only difference is the addition of the term $\left[C + I_C - NC_t(1+i)\right]$ within braces. Under the FIL method, the unfunded absorbed any contribution in excess of the normal cost plus required interest, but here we have defined the unfunded to be zero so that the excess-contribution item is forced into the normal cost. This is a more important consequence than you might first imagine: aggregate is the only cost method so far discussed whose *normal cost* is affected by the amount contributed to the fund! The FIL normal cost is affected by the rate of investment return on the fund, but not the amount contributed to it (exercise 2.8.4).

With the aggregate as with the FIL and EAN cost methods, the terms within braces in equation (2.9.8) may be looked upon as "gains" (even though we need not define such a term in order to compute the cost of a plan). These "gains" are seen to be spread over the average present value of future salaries, because

$$NC_{t+1} = U_t \sum_{A_{t+1}} S_{t+1}^j - \frac{\sum_{A_{t+1}} S_{t+1}^j}{PVFS_{t+1}} \left[\text{"}Gains\text{"} \right], \tag{2.9.9}$$

which follows directly from equation (2.9.8)

Exercises

2.9.1 Derive equation (2.9.6).

2.9.2 Derive equation (2.9.7), using the definition

$$\widetilde{PVFS}_{t+1}^j = S_t^j \frac{s_{x+1}}{s_x} \frac{{}^sN_{x+1} - {}^sN_y}{{}^sD_{x+1}} .$$

2.9.3 Derive equation (2.9.8).

2.9.4 Suppose that we have been using the FIL cost method and at time t the unfunded is exactly zero.

(a) Will the aggregate normal cost exactly equal the FIL normal cost at time t?

(b) If no contribution is made for the year t to $t + 1$ what will be the difference between the normal cost under the FIL and aggregate methods at time $t + 1$?

(c) If the employer decides at time $t + 1$ to contribute (under the FIL method) an amount equal to the normal cost plus $UAL_{t+1}/\ddot{a}_{\overline{n}|}$ — i.e., to amortize the unfunded over an n-year period, what must be the value of $\ddot{a}_{\overline{n}|}$ in order that this total FIL contribution be equal to the aggregate normal cost at time $t + 1$ (assuming a nonzero unfunded at time $t + 1$ under the FIL method)?

2.9.5 Consider a pension plan providing a flat pension of \$1,000 per year to all employees at age 65. Let $\ddot{a}_{65}^{(12)} = 10$ and assume the following:

x	$\dfrac{N_x - N_{65}}{D_x}$	$\dfrac{D_{65}}{D_x}$
30	19	0.1
64	1	0.9

The plan covers two active employees at time zero: one aged 30 and the other aged 64.

(a) What is the normal cost under the aggregate cost method? (Answer: \$1000.)

(b) What is the normal cost under the individual-level-premium method? (Answer: \$9,053.)

(c) Is the aggregate method appropriate for such a situation?

2.10 *Pensioners*

In our discussion up to this point, we have been assuming that pensioners retire at age y and that a premium P is transferred to a separate fund which pays the life annuities. Now it is time to take a look at that pensioners' fund to see how it works.

If B^j is the annual pension benefit of pensioner j, then there can be no question that the desired fund balance, or accrued liability, for j at time t is $B^j \ddot{a}_x^{(12)}$, so that the total accrued liability must be

$$AL_t = \sum_{\mathbf{P}_t} B^j \ddot{a}_x^{(12)} , \tag{2.10.1}$$

where $\mathbf{P}_t$ is the set of all pensioners at time t. Remember that $\mathbf{R}$ is the set of all active employees reaching age y during the year and retiring. If we now let $\mathbf{D}$ be the set of all pensioners who die during the year, we can write

$$\mathbf{P}_{t+1} = \mathbf{P}_t + \mathbf{R} - \mathbf{D} . \tag{2.10.2}$$

The approximation

$$\ddot{a}_x^{(12)} \approx \ddot{a}_x - \frac{11}{24} \tag{2.10.3}$$

is practically universal in the pension world (see exercise 2.10.1), so annuity values at two successive ages are related by the equation

$$\ddot{a}_{x+1}^{(12)} = \ddot{a}_x^{(12)}(1+i) - \left(1 + \frac{13}{24}i - \frac{11}{24}q_x\right) + q_x\ddot{a}_{x+1}^{(12)} . \tag{2.10.4}$$

Note that in this pensioners' fund, as distinct from the active-life fund we have been looking at in previous sections, q_x represents only the probability of dying, because there is no other way to leave the group of pensioners.

If we now combine equations (2.10.1), (2.10.2), and (2.10.4) we can see how the accrued liability for pensioners grows from year to year:

$$\begin{aligned} AL_{t+1} &= \sum_{\mathbf{P}_{t+1}} B^j \ddot{a}_{x+1}^{(12)} = \sum_{\mathbf{P}_t} B^j \ddot{a}_{x+1}^{(12)} + \sum_{\mathbf{R}} B^j \ddot{a}_{x+1}^{(12)} - \sum_{\mathbf{D}} B^j \ddot{a}_{x+1}^{(12)} \\ &= \sum_{\mathbf{P}_t} B^j \left[\ddot{a}_x^{(12)}(1+i) - \left(1 + \frac{13}{24}i - \frac{11}{24}q_x \right) + q_x \ddot{a}_{x+1}^{(12)} \right] + \sum_{\mathbf{R}} B^j \ddot{a}_{x+1}^{(12)} - \sum_{\mathbf{D}} B^j \ddot{a}_{x+1}^{(12)} \\ &= AL_t(1+i) - \sum_{\mathbf{P}_t} B^j \left(1 + \frac{13}{24}i\right) + \sum_{\mathbf{R}} B^j \ddot{a}_{x+1}^{(12)} \\ &\quad - \left[\sum_{\mathbf{D}} B^j \ddot{a}_{x+1}^{(12)} - \sum_{\mathbf{P}_t} q_x B^j \left(\ddot{a}_{x+1}^{(12)} + \frac{11}{24} \right) \right]. \end{aligned} \tag{2.10.5}$$

The fund balance for pensioners follows the progression

$$F_{t+1} = F_t + I + P - B$$

or

$$F_{t+1} = F_t(1+i) + (I - I_P + I_B - iF_t) + (P + I_P) - (B + I_B) , \tag{2.10.6}$$

where P is the amount transferred from the active-life fund to "purchase" the pensions B^j for members of set **R**, and B represents the actual pension payments made from the fund.

If we now subtract (2.10.6) from (2.10.5) we can relate the unfunded accrued liabilities from year to year as follows:

$$UAL_{t+1} = AL_{t+1} - F_{t+1} = UAL_t(1+i) - \Big[I - iF_t - I_P + I_B\Big]$$

$$- \Big[\sum_{\mathbf{P}_t} B^j\Big(1 + \frac{13}{24}i - \frac{11}{24}q_x\Big) - B_{old} - I_{B_{old}}\Big]$$

$$- \Big[P + I_P - \sum_{\mathbf{R}} B^j \ddot{a}_{x+1}^{(12)} - B_{new} - I_{B_{new}}\Big]$$

$$- \Big[\sum_{\mathbf{D}} B^j \ddot{a}_{x+1}^{(12)} - \sum_{\mathbf{P}_t} q_x B^j \ddot{a}_{x+1}^{(12)}\Big]. \tag{2.10.7}$$

Note that the second term of equation (2.10.7) is zero if the fund earns interest at the assumed rate i. The third term is equal to zero if both the mortality and interest assumptions work out, because (within the limits of approximation) the term under the summation sign represents the benefits paid out to members of set $\mathbf{P}_t$. Note, too, that we have divided the total benefits B into two components, B_{old} (pensions paid to members of set $\mathbf{P}_t$) and B_{new} (pensions to members of set $\mathbf{R}$, who in general will have retired sometime during the year and received a few pension payments before the end of the year). Thus, if the assumptions work out, the fourth term is zero because $\mathbf{P}$ was computed to be equal to the reserve required to fund each pension at the time of transfer to the pensioners' fund — which reserve was computed to be equal to the benefits plus interest expected to be paid before year-end, plus the reserve at the end of the year, less interest on the premium. Finally, the fifth term is exactly zero if the assumptions work out because the actual reserve released will be equal to the expected release. Therefore, the sum of the bracketed terms is the actuarial gain:

$$Gain = UAL_t(1+i) - UAL_{t+1} . \tag{2.10.8}$$

Note that there is no normal cost in the computation of the gain for this group; and that if there were no unfunded accrued liability at time zero and the assumptions were correct then there would never be an unfunded (this follows directly from equation (2.10.8)). This means (exercise 2.10.2 and exercise 2.10.3) that we can simply add the accrued liability for pensioners to that of actives — or, equivalently, add it to the present value of future benefits if we are using aggregate or FIL — and, if we also add the funds together, still have the cost methods work as before.

If, on the other hand, we keep the pensioners in a separate fund, we must have some way of either (a) getting additional funds over and above the "premium" P, in case of actuarial losses, or (b) refunding to the active-life fund any actuarial gains. In the typical pension plan, pensioners are thrown into the same fund with actives, but in arrangements such as "deposit administration'' insurance contracts, pensions are actually purchased, and there are dividend mechanisms for adjusting the cost of the plan for gains or losses among pensioners. (These and other insurance contracts are described in section 5.4.)

Exercises

2.10.1 (a) Prove that

$$\ddot{a}_{x+1}^{(12)} = \ddot{a}_x^{(12)}(1+i) - \sum_{t=0}^{11} \frac{1}{12}\, {}_{t/12}p_x (1+i)^{1-t/12} + q_x \ddot{a}_{x+1}^{(12)} \,. \tag{2.10.9}$$

(b) Prove that if D_x is linearly interpolated, i.e.,

$$D_{x+t/12} = (1 - \frac{t}{12}) D_x + \frac{t}{12} D_{x+1} \,,$$

then equation (2.10.4) follows directly from (2.10.9).

(c) Show that if D_x is geometrically interpolated, i.e.,

$$\frac{D_{x+t/12}}{D_x} = \left(\frac{D_{x+1}}{D_x}\right)^{t/12} ,$$

then equation (2.10.9) becomes

$$\ddot{a}_{x+1}^{(12)} = \ddot{a}_x^{(12)}(1+i) - \ddot{s}_{\overline{1}|i'}^{(12)} + q_x(\ddot{a}_{x+1}^{(12)} + \ddot{s}_{\overline{1}|i'}^{(12)}) \,, \tag{2.10.10}$$

where the dummy interest rate $i' = (1+i)e^{\mu_x} - 1$. Can you express $\ddot{a}_x^{(12)}$ in terms of $\ddot{a}_x$ using this approximation? Compare equation (2.10.10) with (2.10.4).

2.10.2 Show that equation (2.3.12) still properly defines the gain for the unit-credit, entry-age-normal, and individual-level-premium cost methods, if we add the accrued liability for pensioners (along with their fund balance) to that of actives.

2.10.3 Show that under the aggregate or FIL methods, if the pensioners are added to the active fund, the present value of future normal costs is increased by the unfunded accrued liability for pensioners — and that, as a consequence, gains generated from mortality and interest in the pensioners' fund get spread over future working years of active employees in the same manner as other ''gains'' under these methods, i.e., that equation (2.9.9) still holds.

2.10.4 (a) Explain why there is only one cost method suitable for a pension fund which covers only pensioners. ("Suitable" is defined implicitly in section 1 of this chapter.)

(b) What is the normal cost under this cost method?

(c) Why, in the expression of the gain, equation (2.10.8), are there no terms involving the premiums P, corresponding to the contributions C in equation (2.3.12)?

2.10.5 Conclude that if a plan covers only pensioners then there is no normal cost, and the cost of the plan for any year is equal to an amortization payment on the unfunded (if any), less amortization of the gain.

2.11 *Pension Cost in Perspective*

We have not yet seen all the cost methods being used by pension actuaries. We have not even seen how to apply the cost methods we have looked at in any but the most rudimentary situations. Nevertheless, we need now to pause for a deep breath and get our bearings before proceeding to further complexities.

We have seen that in general (but not always in particular) a cost method produces a normal cost, an unfunded accrued liability, and a gain. This is not because we decided arbitrarily in advance that we would have these components, but because we set out to fund pensions during the active working lifetimes of the eventual pensioners. That motivation led us naturally to the discovery of normal costs, accrued liabilities, and gains. We have also seen that there is no universally "correct" cost method, but rather that different logical approaches to the problem of funding pensions during working lifetimes result in different cost methods. For example, under the unit-credit method, we defined the accrued liability to start with, whereas under entry-age-normal we started out by defining the normal cost. Under the aggregate methods (including frozen-initial-liability and attained-age-normal) we arbitrarily assigned each individual the same normal cost — with the result that pensions under these cost methods are fully funded at retirement only if there is a large number of participants (see, for example, exercise 2.9.5). All "proper" cost methods are characterized and unified by the proposition that pensions should be funded before they commence. Any approach to assigning pension costs which does not achieve this result is not, strictly speaking, an actuarial cost method. For example, the pay-as-you-go approach is not a "cost method" in our sense of the term.

Except under the aggregate method, computation of the normal cost, unfunded, and gain does not precisely determine the cost of a plan for a particular year, because the unfunded and gains may be amortized over various periods, and in various ways (such as a level dollar amount, a level percent of payroll, etc.).

With respect to the initial unfunded accrued liability — the one established at the inception of the plan — if this amount is not amortized, that is if the pension cost does not include an amount *in excess* of interest on this amount, then the cost method is not being applied properly, because full funding of the pensions before they commence will not occur. Where the initial unfunded is not amortized, the plan may remain solvent, but only to the extent that normal costs on behalf of new entrants to the plan each year go directly to pay for pensions of persons already retired. For any cost method to work properly the unfunded must, within some reasonable period of time, be reduced to zero. There can be no hard and fast rule as to the period over which the initial unfunded must be amortized: for example, it would not be wise to amortize it over a 30-year period if all participants were over age 50 and retirement were at age 65.

As to actuarial gains, in theory the amortization period should not matter very much, because if the assumptions have been chosen properly gains in one year will be offset by losses in other years, so that the net gain over a period of years will be close to zero. If the assumptions do not prove out, there will be a consistent pattern of gains or losses, and in this case the assumptions themselves should be changed — but that is a matter which is outside the scope of this chapter (we shall get into that in Chapter 6). With a small group of participants, the statistical fluctuations will be larger because, for example, only one person can die at a time and if the actuarial assumptions expect one eighth of a death in a given year, then there is bound to be either a gain or a loss — even if over time the assumption turns out to be correct. Larger plans will usually have more predictable experience from year to year, and for them an amortization period as short as one year (i.e., immediate adjustment for gains or losses) might be entirely in order.

We began the chapter by pointing out that a prime motivation for "actuarial" funding of pension plans is the avoidance of insolvency, but insolvency is not the only pitfall. Remember that a pension actuary's task is to determine the cost of a particular plan which is to be assigned to each year. If his only objective were to avoid insolvency then he would have to recommend extremely conservative assumptions, require one-year amortization of the initial unfunded, one-year amortization of actuarial losses, and no amortization of gains — which would result in a distorted picture of the true cost of the plan. Too high an assessment of pension cost is to be avoided equally as too low an assessment. For example, if a company is being reimbursed for its work under a cost-plus-expenses contract, the pension cost must be fairly determined, being neither too high nor too low. Likewise, income-tax authorities are concerned that not too much pension cost be claimed as a deduction from taxable income in a given year, while the owners of any profit-making business are interested in charging the proper pension expense so as to avoid either under- or overstating earnings.

Chapter 3

Contributory Plans

3.1 *Remarks*

Of course, every pension plan is contributory in the sense that someone must contribute to it, but in the world of employee benefits the term "contributory" means "employee-contributory". Under a contributory plan, each participating employee contributes annually an amount determined by formula — either a flat-dollar amount or some fraction of pay, almost never related to age or other factors. If the employee stays in the plan until retirement, his contributions are used together with those of the employer to fund his pension; but if he terminates employment before retirement for any reason (including death), these plans usually refund his contributions with interest at some stated rate.

Usually the form of pension under a contributory plan is not a straight life annuity, but contains some sort of refund or period-certain feature — but we shall ignore this fact for the moment. As we shall see later, the value of these death benefits is very small in relation to the value of the life annuity itself.

When a plan is contributory there are two major implications for the determination of the employer's cost:

(a) The employer does not have to contribute as much for the same benefit as he would if the plan were not contributory; and

(b) A new benefit, namely, the pre-retirement refund of employee contributions in case of termination, is added to the plan.

This all sounds quite simple, but in fact application of the cost methods studied in Chapter 2 to contributory plans is not a trivial matter. In this chapter we shall re-examine each of them and see how the contributory aspect modifies the results that we obtained in Chapter 2.

3.2 *Unit Credit*

To see how an actuarial valuation of a contributory plan is different in the simplest of circumstances, refer back to section 2.2, where we discussed a barebones plan with no pensioners or new entrants and no ancillary benefits. Suppose that the same plan were contributory, that C_t^j represents employee j's contributions in the year beginning at time t and ending at $t+1$. Let the accumulated prior contributions of employee j at time t be denoted by AC_t^j, which includes the sum of all contributions made together with interest at the stated rate i'.

Remember that under the unit-credit cost method we begin by defining the accrued liability as the present value of all accrued benefits. In section 2.2 the accrued benefit meant the accrued portion of the ultimate retirement benefit, but in our contributory version of the same plan the employee has also accrued a right to receive a refund of his accumulated contributions with interest. It is therefore proper that we add the present value of this refund to the accrued liability.

The present value of all future refunds of prior contributions at time t is

$$PVFR_t = \sum_{\mathbf{A}_t} \int_x^y {}_{z-x}p_x \, \mu_z \, v^{z-x} AC_t^j (1+i')^{z-x} dz \,, \tag{3.2.1}$$

which, if we make the simplifying assumption that $i = i'$, becomes

$$PVFR_t = \sum_{\mathbf{A}_t} AC_t^j \int_x^y {}_{z-x}p_x \, \mu_z \, dz = \sum_{\mathbf{A}_t} AC_t^j \, \frac{l_x - l_y}{l_x} \,. \tag{3.2.2}$$

Remember that l_x in this case is taken from the pre-retirement service table and therefore μ_x comprises not just the force of mortality but also the force of turnover and other causes of leaving the plan before retirement. $PVFR_t$ must be added to the accrued liability at time t.

The following year, at time $t+1$, we would have to add a similar amount

$$PVFR_{t+1} = \sum_{\mathbf{A}_{t+1}} AC_{t+1}^j \, \frac{l_{x+1} - l_y}{l_{x+1}} \,. \tag{3.2.3}$$

It is a peculiarity of contributory plans that interest is often not credited to employee contributions for the year in which they are made. The author is not sure how this got started or why it continues, but he suspects that it may be because employers deduct the contributions from employees' paychecks and are not always very prompt about remitting them to the pension fund. In such cases, the accumulated employee contributions with interest at rate i' grow from year to year as follows:

$$AC_{t+1}^j = AC_t^j(1+i') + C_t^j \; . \tag{3.2.4}$$

We shall simply assume that all employee contributions come in at the end of the year, which is not far from the truth in many situations. Incidentally, when the employee terminates, it is traditional to credit a portion of a year's interest from the beginning of the plan year to the date of termination.

We should now like to find out how $PVFR_{t+1}$ is related to $PVFR_t$, because these are additional accrued-liability amounts, and under the unit-credit cost method we determine the normal cost by analyzing the change in the accrued liability. If we incorporate equation (3.2.11) into equation (3.2.3) we can write

$$\begin{aligned} PVFR_{t+1} &= \sum_{A_{t+1}} AC_{t+1}^j \frac{l_{x+1} - l_y}{l_{x+1}} \\ &= \sum_{A_t}\left[AC_t^j(1+i) + C_t^j\right]\left[\frac{l_x - l_y}{l_x} + q_x\left(\frac{l_{x+1} - l_y}{l_{x+1}} - 1\right)\right] - \sum_{T} AC_{t+1}^j \frac{l_{x+1} - l_y}{l_{x+1}} \\ &= \left(PVFR_t + \sum_{A_t} vC_t^j \frac{l_x - l_y}{l_x}\right)(1+i) \\ &\quad - \left[\sum_{T} AC_{t+1}^j \frac{l_{x+1} - l_y}{l_{x+1}} - \sum_{A_t} q_x AC_{t+1}^j \frac{l_{x+1} - l_y}{l_{x+1}}\right] - \sum_{A_t} q_x AC_{t+1}^j \; . \end{aligned} \tag{3.2.5}$$

Because $PVFR_t$ is just an extra amount of accrued liability, the total accrued liability including the employee contributions and the refund feature may be found by simply adding equation (3.2.2) to equation (2.2.1), so that the accrued liability becomes

$$AL_t = \sum_{A_t}\left(AB_t^j \frac{D_y}{D_x} \ddot{a}_y^{(12)} + AC_t^j \frac{l_x - l_y}{l_x}\right), \tag{3.2.6}$$

where we have used AB_t^j to denote the accrued benefit at time t (rather than $B^j(x)$ as in Chapter 2).

Note that equations (3.2.5) and (2.2.3) are arranged in the same order: the new accrued liability equals (a) last year's accrued liability plus the normal cost plus interest, less (b) the gain from terminations, less (c) the expected benefit payments. In the case of the additional accrued liability $PVFR_t$, the "normal cost" is obviously $\sum_{A_t} vC_t^j \frac{l_x - l_y}{l_x}$. As the accrued liabilities from the two equations are to be added together, so must their "normal costs". Thus the *total normal cost* is

$$NC_t^{Total} = \sum_{A_t}\left(\Delta B^j \frac{D_y}{D_x} \ddot{a}_y^{(12)} + vC_t^j \frac{l_x - l_y}{l_x}\right). \tag{3.2.7}$$

The employees contribute $\sum_{A_t} C^j$ however, so the portion the employer has to pay, called the *employer normal cost,* is the total normal cost minus employee contributions:

$$NC_t = \sum_{A_t} \left(\Delta B^j \frac{D_y}{D_x} \ddot{a}_y^{(12)} - v C_t^j \frac{l_y}{l_x} \right). \tag{3.2.8}$$

From now on we shall use the term "normal cost" to mean the employer normal cost.

Continuing the logical development used in section 2.2, let us see how the definition of actuarial gain is affected by the presence of employee contributions. Equation (2.2.5) is still valid, except that the contributions C comprise both employer and employee contributions. Also, we have to add a term R to represent the refunds of employee contributions paid out during the year. So we can relate the year-end fund balances as follows:

$$F_{t+1} = F_t + I + \underbrace{C^{ER}}_{\textit{employer contributions}} + \underbrace{C^{EE}}_{\textit{employee contributions}} - P - R \tag{3.2.9}$$

The accrued liability (equation (3.2.6)) has been reconciled between two years in equations (2.2.3) and (3.2.5), so those two equations and equation (3.2.9) completely reconcile the unfunded between two years. If we cast out from that reconciliation all terms which are zero if actual experience equals expected we find (exercise 3.2.2) that the gain is still properly defined by

$$Gain = (UAL_t + NC_t)(1 + i) - C^{ER} - I_C - UAL_{t+1} \tag{3.2.10}$$

— where NC_t is defined by equation (3.2.8). Note that we still subtract only the employer contribution when determining the gain, which makes sense because NC_t is net of employee contributions. Also note that I_C is interest on employer contributions only.

In summary, when the plan is contributory we add to the accrued liability the present value of future refunds of employee contributions already contributed (not, in the case of unit-credit, considering any contributions after the valuation date) and we subtract from the normal cost the expected employee contribution for the coming year, adjusted for the fact that it is refundable if the employee terminates before retirement. And with these adjustments the actuarial gain is computed in the same way as for a non-contributory plan (except, of course, that the values of the unfunded and normal cost have been changed!).

Exercises

3.2.1 Show that for $x < y$

$$\frac{l_{x+1} - l_y}{l_{x+1}} = \frac{l_x - l_y}{l_x} + q_x\left(\frac{l_{x+1} - l_y}{l_{x+1}} - 1\right).$$

(3.2.11)

3.2.2 Combine equations (2.2.3), (3.2.5), and (3.2.9) to create an equation relating UAL_t to UAL_{t+1}. Identify all terms that are zero if actual experience follows expected and prove equation (3.2.10).

3.2.3 Suppose that i does not equal i'. Show that equation (3.2.1) then implies

$$PVFR_t^j = AC_t^j \frac{\bar{M}_x'' - \bar{M}_y''}{D_x''},$$

(3.2.12)

where the commutation functions are computed using an interest rate of $i'' = \dfrac{1+i}{1+i'} - 1$.

3.2.4 Show that for $x < y$

$$\frac{M_{x+1} - M_y}{D_{x+1}} = \frac{M_x - M_y}{D_x}(1 + i) + q_x\left(\frac{M_{x+1} - M_y}{D_{x+1}} - 1\right).$$

(3.2.13)

What is the corresponding relationship for the function $\dfrac{\bar{M}_x - \bar{M}_y}{D_x}$?

3.2.5 Develop an expression for $PVFR_{t+1}$ in terms of $PVFR_t$ similar to equation (3.2.5), but based on equation (3.2.12). Identify each term in your answer with its counterpart in equation (3.2.5). What adjustment to the noncontributory normal cost is implied by your result (i.e., what is your counterpart of equation (3.2.7))?

3.2.6 Simplify the result of exercise 3.2.5 by assuming that refunds are paid only at the end of the year instead of immediately upon termination of employment. Again, relate your result, term by term, with equation (3.2.5). What is the consequent definition of normal cost corresponding to equation (3.2.7)?

3.2.7 Comment on the relative simplicity of the approaches in exercises 3.2.5 and 3.2.6, respectively. If actual experience is in direct accord with expected, with all terminations of employment occurring midway through the year, what is the difference between the actuarial gains computed under each of the two methods, respectively?

3.2.8 Derive an expression for $PVFR_t$ assuming that refunds are made at year-end, but without the simplifying assumption that $i = i'$.

(a) Show how $PVFR_{t+1}$ relates to $PVFR_t$ and organize the terms of your equation the same as equations (3.2.5) and (2.3.3).

(b) Write an expression for NC_t (employer normal cost).

(c) Derive an expression for the gain. Is it the same as equation (3.2.10)?

3.3 *Entry Age Normal*

With entry-age-normal we begin always by defining the normal cost. Under a contributory plan we cannot equate the present value of future benefits at entry age w with the present value of future normal costs at w, because we must also take into account the present value of future employee contributions. The proper relationship is

PV of future pension benefits at w
plus PV of future refunds of employee contributions
equals
PV of future (employer) normal costs
plus PV of future employee contributions.

(3.3.1)

Let us examine this relationship in the simple setting of section 2.3. Suppose that the annual contribution demanded of participant j is C^j. Assuming no salary increases, this means that at age w, j would have contributed nothing (because he just entered the plan). At age $w+1$ his contributions would amount to C^j, at $w+2$ his accumulated contributions would equal $C^j(1+i) + C^j$, and at any age z the accumulated contributions would equal $C^j s_{\overline{z-w}|}$. The present value of future refunds at age w may be computed using

$$PVFRW^j = \sum_{z=w}^{y-1} \frac{C_z}{D_w} C^j s_{\overline{z+1-w}|}, \tag{3.3.2}$$

where we are assuming that refunds are made at the end of each year (exercise 3.2.7 should have proved to you the wisdom of this assumption).

Equation (3.3.2) can be rewritten as

$$PVFRW^j = \sum_{z=w}^{y-1} vC^j \frac{C_z}{D_w} \ddot{s}_{\overline{z+1-w}|} = vC^j \sum \frac{d_z}{l_w} \frac{v^{z+1}}{v^w} \frac{(1+i)^{z+1-w}-1}{d}$$

$$= vC^j \sum \frac{1}{d} \left(\frac{d_z}{l_w} - \frac{C_z}{D_w} \right) = vC^j \frac{1}{d} \left[\frac{l_w - l_y}{l_w} - \frac{M_w - M_y}{D_w} \right].$$

Applying equation (3.3.20), we can rewrite this as

$$PVFRW^j = vC^j \frac{N_w - N_y}{D_w} - C^j s_{\overline{y-w}|} \frac{D_y}{D_w}. \tag{3.3.3}$$

Substituting equation (3.3.3) into equation (3.3.1) we arrive at our expression for the normal cost:

$$NC^j = (B^j \ddot{a}_y^{(12)} - C^j s_{\overline{y-w}|}) \frac{D_y}{N_w - N_y}. \tag{3.3.4}$$

Now compare equation (3.3.4) to equation (2.3.1). Note that under a non-contributory plan the normal cost under the entry-age-normal method is designed to produce $B^j \ddot{a}_y^{(12)}$ for each employee j when he retires at age y. Under a contributory plan, as shown by equation (3.3.4), the normal cost need produce only this amount *less* accumulated employee contributions.

Turning our attention to the situation at age x (the actual attained age of employee j at time t), we see that his actual employee contributions accumulated at rate i are not necessarily equal to $C^j s_{\overline{x-w}|}$, even though all the assumptions work out, because the plan may have changed since he entered the plan or it may not even have existed when he was aged w. (Under the entry-age-normal cost method it is preferable always to compute the normal cost as though the plan was always in effect, so that when an employee terminates and is replaced by another employee with the same entry age there is no net increase in the normal cost on that account.)

Therefore, with all this in mind, let us again use the symbol AC_t^j to represent the actual accumulated employee contributions at age x. The accrued liability at age x for employee j is not just the present value of his future benefits (including his refund of contributions) minus present value of future normal costs, but is equal to the present value of future benefits less present value of future normal costs less the present value of future employee contributions, because the employee is helping to pay for his benefit.*

---

*Some actuaries would say that the accrued liability is equal to the present value of future benefits minus the present value of "total normal costs", but we have rejected that terminology and use the term "normal cost" to refer only to the employer portion.

The present value of future refunds consists in this case of two pieces: the present value of refunds of past contributions (those included in AC_t^j) plus the refund of contributions not yet made. The first of these two amounts we get from equation (3.2.2) and the second from equation (3.3.3):

$$PVFR_t^j = AC_t^j \frac{l_x - l_y}{l_x} + vC^j \frac{N_x - N_y}{D_x} - C^j s_{\overline{y-x}|} \frac{D_y}{D_x} . \tag{3.3.5}$$

Then the accrued liability for j at age x becomes

$$AL_t^j = B^j \ddot{a}_y^{(12)} \frac{D_y}{D_x} + AC_t^j \frac{l_x - l_y}{l_x} + vC^j \frac{N_x - N_y}{D_x}$$
$$- C^j s_{\overline{y-x}|} \frac{D_y}{D_x} - NC^j \frac{N_x - N_y}{D_x} - vC^j \frac{N_x - N_y}{D_x} ; \tag{3.3.6}$$

or

$$AL_t^j - AC_t^j = \left\{B_t^j \ddot{a}_y^{(12)} - \left[AC_t^j (1+i)^{y-x} + C^j s_{\overline{y-x}|}\right]\right\} \frac{D_y}{D_x}$$
$$- NC_t^j \frac{N_x - N_y}{D_x} . \tag{3.3.7}$$

The left side of equation (3.3.7) is the accrued liability minus the accumulated employee contributions and is sometimes called the *employer accrued liability*. Likewise, the terms in braces comprise the *employer* portion of the present value of future benefits — i.e., the amount that the employer must contribute over and above employee contributions. The term in brackets is the projected accumulated employee contributions at age y. Therefore, equation (3.3.7) can be interpreted as saying that the *employer* accrued liability equals the *employer* present value of future benefits minus the present value of future *employer* normal costs — as though the employer and the employee were operating separate pension funds each with its own contributions and benefits. Under this view of the situation we could imagine the employee contributing to a separate defined-contribution plan and the employer funding a so-called "floor plan".* Actually, there is no reason why a contributory plan could not be run this way — with actual interest on the fund being credited to employee contributions or even with two separate funds — but for reasons unknown to the author it almost never is.

*To an architect the term "floor plan" means a diagram of the rooms in a building, but to a pension actuary the term means a defined-benefit plan which provides pensions offset by those coming from a companion defined-contribution plan.

We now must analyze the behavior of the accrued liability from year to year in order to derive an expression for the actuarial gain. At time $t+1$ the employer accrued liability can be expressed as

$$AL^j_{t+1} - AC^j_{t+1} = \left[B^j_{t+1}\,\ddot{a}_y^{(12)} - AC^j_{t+1}(1+i)^{y-x-1} - C^j_{t+1}\,s_{\overline{y-x-1|}}\right]\frac{D_y}{D_{x+1}}$$

$$- NC^j_{t+1}\,\frac{N_{x+1}-N_y}{D_{x+1}}\;. \tag{3.3.8}$$

Also at time $t+1$, we compute a new normal cost for employee j equal to

$$NC^j_{t+1} = (B^j_{t+1}\,\ddot{a}_y^{(12)} - C^j_{t+1}\,s_{\overline{y-w|}})\,\frac{D_y}{N_w-N_y}\;, \tag{3.3.9}$$

because we have made new estimates of the projected benefit at retirement (B^j_{t+1}) and the annual rate of employee contributions (C^j_{t+1}). If we let $\Delta B^j = B^j_{t+1} - B^t_t$ and $\Delta C^j = C^j_{t+1} - C^j_t$ we can write

$$\Delta NC^j = (\Delta B^j\ddot{a}_y^{(12)} - \Delta C^j s_{\overline{y-w|}})\,\frac{D_y}{N_w-N_y}\;, \tag{3.3.10}$$

which shows us that the change in normal cost ΔNC^j depends only on ΔB^j and ΔC^j, the change in projected future benefits and contributions.

It will be convenient to call the expression within braces in equation (3.3.7) the *funding objective* and denote it by H_t. That is,

$$H^j_t = B^j_t\,\ddot{a}_y^{(12)} - AC^j_t(1+i)^{y-x} - C^j_t s_{\overline{y-x|}}.$$

Then remembering equation (3.2.4) we can write

$$H^j_{t+1} = H^j_t + \Delta B\,\ddot{a}_y^{(12)} - \Delta C^j s_{\overline{y-x-1|}},$$

or

$$\Delta H^j = \Delta B^j\ddot{a}_y^{(12)} - \Delta C^j s_{\overline{y-x-1|}}\,. \tag{3.3.11}$$

This shows that the change in funding objective is due solely to changes in projected benefit and projected employee contributions and not to any event which occurred during the year t to $t+1$. Note that there is a different "funding objective" for the normal cost in equation (3.3.9) and it is not necessarily the same as H^j_t. (Sometimes, for reasons stated earlier in this section, the projected benefit for purposes of computing the normal cost, as well as the projected employee contributions at retirement, is a ***hypothetical*** amount based on the supposition that the plan was always in effect since age w.)

We can now write

$$AL_{t+1}^j - AC_{t+1}^j = (H_t^j + \Delta H^j)\frac{D_y}{D_{x+1}} - (NC_t^j + \Delta NC^j)\frac{N_{x+1} - N_y}{D_{x+1}} .$$

(3.3.12)

Let the accrued liability at time $t+1$, assuming ΔB^j and ΔC^j are zero, be denoted by

$$\widetilde{AL}_{t+1}^j = AC_{t+1}^j + H_t^j\frac{D_y}{D_{x+1}} - NC_t^j\frac{N_{x+1} - N_y}{D_{x+1}} ,$$

(3.3.13)

so that

$$AL_{t+1}^j = AL_{t+1}^j + \Delta H^j\frac{D_y}{D_{x+1}} - \Delta NC^j\frac{N_{x+1} - N_y}{D_{x+1}}$$

and

$$AL_{t+1}^j - AC_{t+1}^j = \widetilde{AL}_{t+1}^j - AC_{t+1}^j + \Delta H^j\frac{D_y}{D_{x+1}} - \Delta NC^j\frac{N_{x+1} - N_y}{D_{x+1}} .$$

(3.3.14)

We can combine all of the above in the following algebraic development:

$$\begin{aligned}
\widetilde{AL}_{t+1}^j - AC_{t+1}^j &= H_t^j\frac{D_y}{D_{x+1}} - NC_t^j\frac{N_{x+1} - N_y}{D_{x+1}} \\[2mm]
&= \frac{D_x}{D_{x+1}}\left[H_t^j\frac{D_y}{D_x} - NC_t^j\frac{N_x - D_x - N_y}{D_x}\right] \\[2mm]
&= (1+i)\left[H_t^j\frac{D_y}{D_x} - NC_t^j\frac{N_x - N_y}{D_x} + NC_t^j\right] \\[2mm]
&\quad + q_x\left[\widetilde{AL}_{t+1}^j - AC_{t+1}^j\right] \\[2mm]
&= (AL_t^j - AC_t^j)(1+i) + NC_t^j(1+i) + q_x(\widetilde{AL}_{t+1}^j - AC_{t+1}^j) .
\end{aligned}$$

(3.3.15)

Finally, remembering equation (3.3.14) we can write

$$AL_{t+1}^j - AC_{t+1}^j = (AL_t^j - AC_t^j + NC_t^j)(1+i) + \Delta H^j\frac{D_y}{D_{x+1}} - \Delta NC^j\frac{N_{x+1} - N_y}{D_{x+1}}$$

$$+ q_x(\widetilde{AL}_{t+1}^j - AC_{t+1}^j) ,$$

or

$$AL_{t+1}^j = (AL_t^j + NC_t^j)(1+i) + C_t^j + \Delta H^j \frac{D_y}{D_{x+1}} - \Delta NC^j \frac{N_{x+1} - N_y}{D_{x+1}}$$
$$+ q_x(\widetilde{AL}_{t+1}^j - AC_{t+1}^j)\,.$$

(3.3.16)

Now harkening back to equation (2.2.2) we can sum equation (3.3.16) over the set $\mathbf{A}_{t+1}$ to get

$$AL_{t+1} = \sum_{\mathbf{A}_{t+1}} AL_{t+1}^j = \Big(\sum_{\mathbf{A}_t} AL_t^j + \sum_{\mathbf{A}_t} NC_t^j\Big)(1+i) + \sum_{\mathbf{A}_t} C_t^j$$
$$+ \sum_{\mathbf{A}_t \cap \mathbf{A}_{t+1}} \Big(\Delta H^j \frac{D_y}{D_{x+1}} - \Delta NC^j \frac{N_{x+1} - N_y}{D_{x+1}}\Big) + \sum_{\mathbf{A}_t} q_x(\widetilde{AL}_{t+1}^j - AC_{t+1}^j)$$
$$- \sum_{\mathbf{T}} \widetilde{AL}_{t+1}^j - \sum_{\mathbf{R}} \widetilde{AL}_{t+1}^j\,.$$

(3.3.17)

The fund balances are related by equation (3.2.9) so that the unfunded accrued liabilities for the two successive years are related by

$$UAL_{t+1} = (UAL_t + NC_t)(1+i) - C^{ER} - I_C$$
$$- \big[I - iF_t - I_C + I_P\big] - \Big[C^{EE} - \sum_{\mathbf{A}_t} C_t^j\Big]$$
$$- \Big[\sum_{\mathbf{T}} \widetilde{AL}_{t+1}^j - R - \sum_{\mathbf{A}_t} q_x(\widetilde{AL}_{t+1}^j - AC_{t+1}^j)\Big]$$
$$- \Big[\sum_{\mathbf{R}} \widetilde{AL}_{t+1}^j - P - I_P\Big] + \sum_{\mathbf{A}_t \cap \mathbf{A}_{t+1}} \Big(\Delta H^j \frac{D_y}{D_{x+1}} - \Delta NC^j \frac{N_{x+1} - N_y}{D_{x+1}}\Big)\,.$$

(3.3.18)

Thus, if all assumptions are realized, and if we correctly predict the employee contributions (and we have been assuming right along that we can do so) then all but the first three terms of equation (3.3.18) will be zero — which means that they constitute the actuarial gain, so we can write

$$Gain = (UAL_t + NC_t)(1+i) - C^{ER} - I_C - UAL_{t+1}\,.$$

(3.3.19)

The definition of actuarial gain is invincible!!

Exercises

3.3.1 Show that if $x < y$

$$\frac{1}{d}\left(\frac{l_x - l_y}{l_x} - \frac{M_x - M_y}{D_x}\right) = \frac{N_x - N_y}{D_x} - \ddot{s}_{\overline{y-x}|}\frac{D_y}{D_x}\,. \tag{3.3.20}$$

3.3.2 Prove equation (3.3.11), remembering that x is a function of t.

3.3.3 If the normal cost is a level amount between ages w and y, and the employee contributes a level amount C^j, why is not the normal cost equal to the non-contributory value (e.g., equation (2.3.1)) minus C^j, rather than equation (3.3.4)? Answer the question mathematically, and then in words you might use if your client (not an actuary) asked you the question.

3.3.4 Work out an alternative derivation of equation (3.3.18) by treating $PVFR_t$ as a separate accrued liability, as follows:

(a) What is the "normal cost" associated with $PVFR_t$? (Remember, there is an entry-age-normal accrued liability.) Establish the relationship between $PVFR_{t+1}$ and $PVFR_t$ putting the "normal cost" and other terms in the same relative positions as equation (3.3.17).

(b) Derive a similar equation expressing the present value of future employee contributions $PVFEC_{t+1}$ in terms of $PVFEC_t$.

(c) Finally, combine these equations with equation (2.2.5) to produce an alternative derivation of equation (3.3.18).

3.4 Individual Level Premium

You will recall from section 2.5 that under this cost method we start off when the plan is effective (or when an employee first joins the plan) by defining the normal cost for an individual the same as under the entry-age-normal method with $w = x$, as in equation (3.3.4):

$$NC_0^j = (B_0^j\,\ddot{a}_y^{(12)} - C_0^j s_{\overline{y-x}|})\frac{D_y}{N_x - N_y}\,. \tag{3.4.1}$$

This is the normal cost for employee j at time 0. At time 1, however, we do not follow the entry-age-normal method. Rather, we compute an incremental normal cost sufficient to fund the increase in projected benefit, as in section 2.5:

$$(\Delta NC)_1^j = \left[(\Delta B)_1^j \ddot{a}_y^{(12)} - (\Delta C)_1^j s_{\overline{y-x-1}|}\right] \frac{D_y}{N_{x+1} - N_y} \tag{3.4.2}$$

where $(\Delta C)_1^j$ is the change in j's contribution rate measured at time 1.

The present value of future benefits at time 1 includes refunds of employee contributions, so we can invoke equation (3.3.5) to write:

$$\begin{aligned} PVFB_1^j &= \left[B_0^j + (\Delta B)_1^j\right] \ddot{a}_y^{(12)} \frac{D_y}{D_{x+1}} + AC_1^j \frac{l_{x+1} - l_y}{l_{x+1}} \\ &\quad + v\left[C_0^j + (\Delta C)_1^j\right] \frac{N_{x+1} - N_y}{D_{x+1}} - \left[C_0^j + (\Delta C)_1^j\right] s_{\overline{y-x-1}|} \frac{D_y}{D_{x+1}} \\ &= \left[B_0^j + (\Delta B)_1^j\right] \ddot{a}_y^{(12)} \frac{D_y}{D_{x+1}} + C_0^j \frac{l_{x+1} - l_y}{l_{x+1}} + v C_0^j \frac{N_{x+1} - N_y}{D_{x+1}} \\ &\quad + v(\Delta C)_1^j \frac{N_{x+1} - N_y}{D_{x+1}} - \left[C_0^j + (\Delta C)_1^j\right] s_{\overline{y-x-1}|} \frac{D_y}{D_{x+1}} . \end{aligned} \tag{3.4.3}$$

The accrued liability at time 1 is equal to the present value of future benefits, less the present value of future normal costs, less the present value of future employee contributions; so

$$\begin{aligned} AL_1^j &= \left[B_0^j + (\Delta B)_1^j\right] \ddot{a}_y^{(12)} \frac{D_y}{D_{x+1}} + C_0^j \frac{l_{x+1} - l_y}{l_{x+1}} \\ &\quad + v\left[C_0^j + (\Delta C)_1^j\right] \frac{N_{x+1} - N_y}{D_{x+1}} - \left[C_0^j + (\Delta C)_1^j\right] s_{\overline{y-x-1}|} \frac{D_y}{D_{x+1}} \\ &\quad - \left[NC_0^j + (\Delta NC)_1^j\right] \frac{N_{x+1} - N_y}{D_{x+1}} - v\left[C_0^j + (\Delta C)_1^j\right] \frac{N_{x+1} - N_y}{D_{x+1}} \\ &= \left[B_0^j + (\Delta B)_1^j\right] \ddot{a}_y^{(12)} \frac{D_y}{D_{x+1}} + C_0^j \frac{l_{x+1} - l_y}{l_{x+1}} \\ &\quad - \left[C_0^j + (\Delta C)_1^j\right] s_{\overline{y-x-1}|} \frac{D_y}{D_{x+1}} - (B_0^j \ddot{a}_y^{(12)} - C_0^j s_{\overline{y-x}|}) \frac{D_y}{N_x - N_y} \frac{N_{x+1} - N_y}{D_{x+1}} \\ &\quad - \left[(\Delta B)_1^j \ddot{a}_y^{(12)} - (\Delta C)_1^j s_{\overline{y-x-1}|}\right] \frac{D_y}{N_{x+1} - N_y} \frac{N_{x+1} - N_y}{D_{x+1}} . \end{aligned} \tag{3.4.4}$$

Note that

$$\frac{N_{x+1} - N_y}{N_x - N_y} = 1 - \frac{D_x}{N_x - N_y} . \tag{3.4.5}$$

If we apply this to equation (3.4.4), the latter reduces to

$$AL_1^j - C_0^j = NC_0^j \frac{D_x}{D_{x+1}} . \tag{3.4.6}$$

This says that the ***employer*** accrued liability at time 1 (remember that the accumulated contributions at time 1 are just equal to one year's contribution without interest) equals last year's employer normal cost multiplied by D_x/D_{x+1}. Compare this with equation (2.5.6).

Now let us see how to update the accrued liability in the general case. At time t, the normal cost for j is equal to $NC_0^j + (\Delta NC)_1^j + \ldots + (\Delta NC)_t^j$ where $(\Delta NC)_t^j$ is the incremental normal cost necessary to fund the additional projected benefit $(\Delta B)_t^j$. At any time t the accrued liability equals present value of future benefits, minus present value of future normal costs, minus present value of future employee contributions. Therefore (letting x represent age at time t)

$$AL_t^j = B_t^j \ddot{a}_y^{(12)} \frac{D_y}{D_x} - NC_t^j \frac{N_x - N_y}{D_x} + AC_t^j \frac{l_x - l_y}{l_x} - C_t^j s_{\overline{y-x}|} \frac{D_y}{D_x} ,$$

or

$$AL_t^j - AC_t^j = \left(B_t^j \ddot{a}_y^{(12)} - AC_t^j (1+i)^{y-x} - C_t^j s_{\overline{y-x}|}\right) \frac{D_y}{D_x} - NC_t^j \frac{N_x - N_y}{D_x} . \tag{3.4.7}$$

At time $t+1$ we compute a new projected benefit $B_{t+1}^j = B_t^j + (\Delta B)_{t+1}^j$ and an incremental normal cost

$$(\Delta NC)_{t+1}^j = \left[(\Delta B)_{t+1}^j \ddot{a}_y^{(12)} - (\Delta C)_{t+1}^j s_{\overline{y-x-1}|}\right] \frac{D_y}{N_{x+1} - N_y} . \tag{3.4.8}$$

It follows that

$$\begin{aligned} AL_{t+1}^j - AC_{t+1}^j = &\left\{\left[B_t^j + (\Delta B)_{t+1}^j\right] \ddot{a}_y^{(12)} - AC_{t+1}^j (1+i)^{y-x-1} \right. \\ &\left. - \left[C_t^j + (\Delta C)_{t+1}^j\right] s_{\overline{y-x-1}|}\right\} \frac{D_y}{D_{x+1}} \\ &- \left[NC_t^j + (\Delta NC)_{t+1}^j\right] \frac{N_{x+1} - N_y}{D_{x+1}} . \end{aligned} \tag{3.4.9}$$

Note that

$$AC_{t+1}^j(1+i)^{y-x-1} + C_t^j s_{\overline{y-x-1}|} = AC_t^j(1+i)^{y-x} + C_t^j(1+i)^{y-x-1}$$

$$+ C_t^j\left[s_{\overline{y-x}|} - (1+i)^{y-x-1}\right]$$

$$= AC_t^j(1+i)^{y-x} + C_t^j s_{\overline{y-x}|},$$

(3.4.10)

so that

$$AL_{t+1}^j - AC_{t+1}^j = \left[B_t^j \ddot{a}_y^{(12)} - AC_t^j(1+i)^{y-x} - C_t^j s_{\overline{y-x}|}\right]\frac{D_y}{D_x}\cdot\frac{D_x}{D_{x+1}}$$

$$- NC_t^j\left(\frac{N_x - N_y}{D_x} - 1\right)\frac{D_x}{D_{x+1}} + (\Delta B)_{t+1}^j\,\ddot{a}_y^{(12)}\,\frac{D_y}{D_{x+1}}$$

$$- (\Delta C)_{t+1}^j s_{\overline{y-x-1}|}\frac{D_y}{D_{x+1}} - (\Delta NC)_{t+1}^j\,\frac{N_{x+1} - N_y}{D_{x+1}}\ .$$

(3.4.11)

The last three terms of equation (3.4.11) add to zero as a result of equation (3.4.8), so

$$AL_{t+1}^j - AC_{t+1}^j = (AL_t^j - AC_t^j + NC_t^j)\,\frac{D_x}{D_{x+1}}\ .$$

(3.4.12)

Equation (3.4.12) is thus the general rule for computing the *employer* accrued liability, of which equation (3.4.6) is just the particular case for the first year of participation. Since $\dfrac{D_x}{D_{x+1}} = \dfrac{1+i}{1-q_x}$ we can transform equation (3.4.12) into

$$AL_{t+1}^j - AC_{t+1}^j = (AL_t^j - AC_t^j + NC_t^j)(1+i) + q_x(AL_{t+1}^j - AC_{t+1}^j)$$

or

$$AL_{t+1}^j = (AL_t^j + NC_t^j)(1+i) + C_t^j + q_x(AL_{t+1}^j - AC_{t+1}^j)\ .$$

(3.4.13)

The fund balances are related by equation (3.2.9) so we can incorporate equation (2.2.2) to get

$$
\begin{aligned}
UAL_{t+1} = {} & (UAL_t + NC_t)(1+i) - C^{ER} - I_C \\
& - \left[I - iF_t - I_C + I_P\right] - \left[C^{EE} - \sum_{\mathbf{A}_t} C_t^j\right] \\
& - \left[\sum_{\mathbf{T}} AL_{t+1}^j - R - \sum_{\mathbf{A}_t} q_x(AL_{t+1}^j - AC_{t+1}^j)\right] \\
& - \left[\sum_{\mathbf{R}} AL_{t+1}^j - P - I_P\right] .
\end{aligned}
\tag{3.4.14}
$$

Compare this with equation (3.3.18). What is the difference between the two? Why is there a difference? (If you don't know, reread section 2.5 for a discussion.)

Obviously, the actuarial gain is the sum of the last four terms of equation (3.4.14), so once again we can define

$$
Gain = (UAL_t + NC_t)(1+i) - C^{ER} - I_C - UAL_{t+1} \tag{3.4.15}
$$

a result which by now has attained the stature of a fundamental law of the universe!

Exercises

3.4.1 Derive equation (3.4.14) from first principles.

3.4.2 What changes (if any) to equation (2.5.18) should be made before applying it to a contributory plan? Remember the basic relationship (3.3.1)!

3.5 *Entry Age Normal With Salary Scale*

When salary increases are assumed — i.e., when you employ a "salary scale" in the valuation — things get a bit more complex. Employee contributions are nearly always based on salary, but often are not a simple percentage of salary. They may be "integrated" with social security taxes: for example, the annual employee contribution might be computed as 1% of salary up to the taxable wage base plus 2% of the excess over the wage base. In the United States, furthermore, the taxable wage base is indexed to rise with national-average wages. All this means that it is difficult to derive simple expressions for present value of future refunds and present value of future employee contributions, except in special situations (which will be developed in the exercises).

Let $\gamma(S)$ be annual employee contributions expressed as a function of salary. Then the present value of future contributions at age w may be expressed as

$$PVFCW_t^j = \sum_{z=w}^{y-1} \gamma\left(S_t^j \frac{S_z}{S_x}\right) \frac{D_z}{D_w} \cdot v = \sum_{z=w}^{y-1} \gamma_z^j \frac{D_z}{D_w} v\,, \tag{3.5.1}$$

where we abbreviate $\gamma\left(S_t^j \frac{S_z}{S_x}\right)$, j's contribution at age z, by γ_z^j. Likewise, we can express the present value of future refunds at age w as

$$\begin{aligned} PVFRW_t^j &= \gamma_w^j \frac{C_w}{D_w} + \left[\gamma_w^j(1+i) + \gamma_{w+1}^j\right] \frac{C_{w+1}}{D_w} \\ &\quad + \ldots + \left[\gamma_w^j(1+i)^{y-w-1} + \gamma_{w+1}^j(1+i)^{y-w-2} + \ldots + \gamma_{y-1}^j\right] \frac{C_{y-1}}{D_w} \\ &= \sum_{z=w}^{y-1} AC_z^{j\prime} \frac{C_z}{D_w}\,, \end{aligned} \tag{3.5.2}$$

where $AC_z^{j\prime}$ denotes the accumulated contributions at age z (at the *end* of the year) given that the contributions in each future year are made on the basis of salary projected from S_t^j using the salary scale.

In order to accomplish these calculations we would generally have to use a "vector" approach, for example, the following:

(1) Compute a salary at each age from w to $y-1$ using for the salary at age z $S_t^j \frac{S_z}{S_x}$ where S_t^j is the actual annual rate of salary of employee j on the valuation date.

(2) Compute $\gamma_z^j = \gamma\left(S_t^j \frac{S_z}{S_x}\right)$ for each age.

(3) Compute $AC_z^{j\prime} = AC_{z-1}'(1+i) + \gamma_z$ at each age (where $AC_w' = \gamma_w^j$).

(4) Compute $\frac{D_z}{D_w} \cdot v$ at each age.

(5) Compute $\frac{C_z}{D_w}$ at each age.

(6) Now the present value of future contributions equals the inner or "dot" product of the vectors (2) and (4).

(7) And the present value of future refunds equals the inner product of vectors (3) and (5).

This method of computation is ideally suited for computers, but would be impossibly laborious with just a desk calculator. For this reason the entry-age-normal method with salary scale was almost never used for contributory plans in the pre-computer era.

The normal cost, which is now a percentage of salary (a separate percentage for each active employee) is then obtained by equating the present value of future normal costs and employee contributions to the present value of future pensions and refunds:

$$\sum_{z=w}^{y-1} U_t^j S_t^j \frac{s_z}{s_x} \frac{D_z}{D_w} + \sum_{z=w}^{y-1} \gamma_z^j \frac{D_z}{D_w} v = B_t^{j\prime} \ddot{a}_y^{(12)} \frac{D_y}{D_w} + \sum_{z=w}^{y-1} AC_z^{j\prime} \frac{C_z}{D_w} ,$$

or

$$NC_t^j = U_t^j S_t^j = \frac{B_t^{j\prime} \ddot{a}_y^{(12)} \dfrac{D_y}{D_w} + \sum_{z=w}^{y-1} \left(AC_z^{j\prime} \dfrac{C_z}{D_w} - v\gamma_z^j \dfrac{D_z}{D_w} \right)}{S_t^j \dfrac{s_w}{s_x} \dfrac{{}^sN_w - {}^sN_y}{{}^sD_w}} \cdot S_t^j$$

$$= \frac{PVFBW_t^j}{PVFSW_t^j} S_t^j . \qquad (3.5.3)$$

Stop for a moment and note that in equation (3.5.3) we have used $B_t^{j\prime}$ as the symbol for the projected benefit at retirement. This is because the normal cost is computed on the hypothesis that the person is just entering the plan at his own entry age. For example, suppose that a plan credits an annual pension at retirement of one-half percent of each year's pay up to the social security taxable wage base plus 1% of the excess over the wage base, and that contributions are 1% and 2%, respectively. We want the normal cost to reflect the cost at age w of providing that benefit, given that those contributions will be available to help pay the cost. In fact, the plan may be just getting under way and the employee might not have earned benefits (and made contributions) all the way from age w on this formula. But to compute the normal cost we assume this is the case! In the example of the preceding sentence, the projected benefit B_t^j based upon what we know the accrued benefit to be at age x (time t) is not going to be the same as $B_t^{j\prime}$, which assumes participation in the plan from age w. This separate definition of the projected benefit for purposes of computing the normal cost and the accrued liability is not limited to contributory plans but should be practiced generally with entry-age-normal: otherwise, if an employee with entry age w who has not always been in the plan should be replaced by another who is just beginning at the same age w, the normal cost would *increase* on that account alone even if all the assumptions were realized — producing the very instability the entry-age-normal cost method was designed to avoid.

We can now proceed to compute the accrued liability in roughly the same manner. We can leave "vectors" (1) and (2), above, in place; but we must use, instead of vector (3), a new array of projected accumulated contributions:

$$AC_x^j = (\textit{Actual accumulated contributions at time } t)(1+i)$$

$$AC_z^j = AC_{z-1}^j(1+i) + \gamma_z^j$$

$$\textit{for } z = x+1, \ldots, y$$

(3.5.4)

(The actual accumulated contributions is one of the items of information we must get from the employer in order to do the valuation.) Likewise, the projected benefit B_t^j at age y is estimated using the *actual* accrued benefit and estimated future accruals. Then we can compute the accrued liability at time t for employee j as

$$AL_t^j = B_t^j \ddot{a}_y^{(12)} \frac{D_y}{D_x} + \sum_{z=x}^{y-1} AC_z^j \frac{C_z}{D_x} - U_t^j S_t^j \frac{{}^sN_x - {}^sN_y}{{}^sD_x} - v \sum_{z=x}^{y-1} \gamma_z^j \frac{D_z}{D_x}.$$

(3.5.5)

Exercises

3.5.1 Assume that employee contributions are a flat percentage of salary each year and show how the formulas of this section may be simplified. What further simplifications can be made if $s_{x+1}/s_x = 1 + r$ (constant for all x)?

3.5.2 If it is impossible to simplify the equations of this section, and we must fall back on the generalized "vector" approach (which is actually used in computer programs to do valuations), does it help us to assume that $i = i'$? How did it help us before, in sections 3.1 through 3.3?

3.5.3 Using the rule, present value of future normal costs equals present value of future benefits *plus* present value of future refunds *minus* present value of future employee contributions, show how you would do a valuation of a salary-based plan using a salary scale under

(a) the aggregate entry-age-normal method (section 2.8);

(b) the frozen-initial-liability method; and

(c) the attained-age-normal method.

3.5.4 Why does the first term on the right of equation (3.5.1) have a factor of v?

3.5.5 Develop an expression for UAL_{t+1} in terms of UAL_t and other terms, and derive an expression for the actuarial gain. (Can you guess the answer in advance?)

3.5.6 Show how to apply the individual-level-premium cost method, with a salary scale, using the general method of this section. Don't guess the results, but actually derive them starting with the definition of normal cost, then seeing how the accrued liabilities progress from year to year. (Refer back to Chapter 2 if you have trouble.)

3.5.7 In sections 3.3 and 3.4 we showed that the normal cost and accrued liability for an individual could be expressed in terms of a "funding objective" equal to the present value of future pension less the employee contributions at age y. Rework the equations of this section so as to produce definitions of the normal cost and accrued liability in terms of a similar funding objective.

3.6 *The Modified-Cash-Refund Annuity*

This is a form of annuity peculiar to contributory pension plans. It provides a life annuity together with a lump-sum death benefit equal to the excess (if any) of employee contributions with interest to retirement (the commencement date of the pension) over the sum of the pension payments actually made before death — without interest. Thus, if the annuity is \$1 per year and the accumulated contributions at the commencement date of the pension are α, the death benefit is α at the moment of retirement; it then declines to $\alpha - \frac{1}{12}$ after the first monthly pension payment, and so forth. The death benefit reduces to zero when the sum of the payments equals α (that is, after α years).

The present value of this modified-cash-refund death benefit, at the commencement date of the pension, is

$$PVDB_x = \sum_{t=0}^{12\alpha-1} {}_{t/12}p_x \cdot {}_{1/12}q_{x+t/12} \cdot v^{(t+1)/12}\left(\alpha - \frac{t+1}{12}\right) \tag{3.6.1}$$

which can be used directly, if you have a computer, by interpolating the mortality table.

As a general rule, contributory plans do not express the amount of pension in terms of a straight life annuity — i.e., they do not have a life-annuity *normal form* — because if they did some employee might lose his contributions by premature death after retirement. Often the normal form is a life annuity with a period certain — five or ten years typically — which as we shall see is generally more valuable than the modified-cash-refund life annuity.

The traditional method of evaluating the MCR death benefit is to assume that it is payable at the end of the year of death. If the accumulated contributions at retirement are an integral multiple n of the *annual* pension B we have, from (3.6.1)

$$PVDB_x = \sum_{t=0}^{12n-1} {}_{t/12}p_x \cdot {}_{1/12}q_{x+t/12} \cdot v^{[t/12]+1}\left(n - \frac{t+1}{12}\right)$$

. . . where $\left[\frac{t}{12}\right]$ means largest integer in $\frac{t}{12}$. Then, assuming uniform distribution of deaths,

$$PVDB_x = \sum_{t=0}^{n-1}\sum_{m=0}^{11} \frac{1}{12}\frac{d_{x+t}}{l_x} v^{t+1}\left(n - t - \frac{m+1}{12}\right).$$

Now,

$$PVDB_x = \sum_{t=0}^{n-1} \frac{1}{12}\frac{C_{x+t}}{D_x}\sum_{m=0}^{11}\left(n - t - \frac{m+1}{12}\right)$$

$$= \sum_{t=0}^{n-1} \frac{1}{12}\frac{C_{x+t}}{D_x}\left[12(n-t) - \frac{13}{2}\right]$$

$$= \frac{1}{D_x}\Big[n(M_x - M_{x+n}) - (M_{x+1} - M_{x+n}) - \ldots$$

$$- (M_{x+n-1} - M_{x+n})\Big] - \frac{13}{24}\frac{M_x - M_{x+n}}{D_x}$$

$$= \frac{1}{D_x}\left[nM_x - R_{x+1} + R_{x+n+1} - \frac{13}{24}M_x + \frac{13}{24}M_{x+n}\right]$$

$$= \frac{1}{D_x}\left[nM_x - \left(R_x - \frac{11}{24}M_x\right) + \left(R_{x+n} - \frac{11}{24}M_{x+n}\right)\right]$$

$$= \frac{nM_x - R_x^{(12)} + R_{x+n}^{(12)}}{D_x}, \tag{3.6.2}$$

where $R_x^{(12)} \equiv R_x - \frac{11}{24}M_x$.

The value of the whole annuity with the death benefit then becomes

$$PVFB_x = \frac{N_x^{(12)} + nM_x - R_x^{(12)} + R_{x+n}^{(12)}}{D_x}, \tag{3.6.3}$$

where $N_x^{(12)} = N_x - \frac{11}{24}D_x$. Values of $PVFB_x$ for nonintegral n may be found by interpolation.

Note that for a given age x the value of a MCR annuity with "death-benefit ratio" n is a function of n — let's call it $M(n)$. $M(0)$ is just the present value of a straight life annuity. Suppose the annuity is payable continuously and the death benefit payable immediately after death; then

$$M(n) = \bar{a}_x + \int_0^n (n-t)\,{}_tp_x\,\mu_{x+t}\,v^t\,dt\,. \tag{3.6.4}$$

Taking the first derivative with respect to n, we get

$$\begin{aligned} M'(n) &= \lim_{h\to 0}\frac{1}{h}\Big[\int_0^{n+h}(n+h-t)\,{}_tp_x\,\mu_{x+t}\,v^t\,dt - \int_0^n (n-t)\,{}_tp_x\,\mu_{x+t}\,v^t\,dt\Big] \\ &= \lim_{h\to 0}\frac{1}{h}\Big[\int_h^{n+h}(n-t)\,{}_tp_x\,\mu_{x+t}\,v^t\,dt + h\int_0^{n+h}{}_tp_x\,\mu_{x+t}\,v^t\,dt\Big] \\ &= \bar{A}^{1}_{x:\overline{n|}}. \end{aligned} \tag{3.6.5}$$

Differentiating again:

$$M''(n) = {}_np_x\,\mu_{x+n}\,v^n\,. \tag{3.6.6}$$

From Taylor's theorem we know that

$$\begin{aligned} M(n) &= M(0) + nM'(0) + \frac{n^2}{2!}M''(0) + \frac{n^3}{3!}M'''(0) + \ldots \\ &= \bar{a}_x + n\cdot 0 + \frac{n^2}{2}\mu_x + \ldots \end{aligned} \tag{3.6.7}$$

so that

$$M(n) \approx \bar{a}_x + \frac{\mu_x}{2}n^2\,; \tag{3.6.8}$$

which shows that the MCR annuity is nearly equal to the life annuity plus a term proportional to n^2.

Equation (3.6.8) has a geometrical interpretation. From Figure 3.1 you can see that the amount of death benefit decreases uniformly from n at the commencement date to zero n years later. The present value of the death benefit is

$$\int_0^n (\textit{amount of death benefit at time } t)\,\mu_{x+t}\,{}_tp_x\,v^t\,dt\,.$$

Now μ_{x+t} increases exponentially with time and ${}_tp_x\,v^t$ decreases in the same way, so ${}_tp_x\,\mu_{x+t}\,v^t \approx \mu_x$, which can be brought outside the integral. What remains is just the area of the triangle in Figure 3.1, or $\frac{1}{2}n^2$. This leads directly to equation (3.6.8).

Figure 3.1
Modified-Cash-Refund Death Benefit

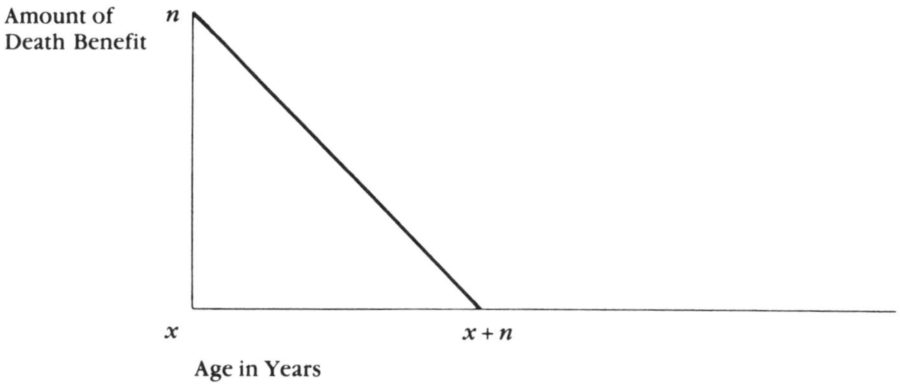

In actual practice n is seldom higher than 3 (virtually never as high as 5). At age 65 μ_x is roughly .02 on most mortality tables, so the maximum value of the death benefit is $.01(3)^2 = .09$. By comparison, the value of $\bar{a}_{65}$ is on the order of 9.0, so the death benefit adds at most $.09/9.00 = 1\%$ to the value of the straight life annuity. To put this in perspective, note that if your assumed interest rate is off by 1% (for example, if you are assuming 7% and you actually get 7.07%) the annuity value is also off by 1%. Obviously the value of the MCR death benefit can be ignored without significantly affecting the accuracy of a valuation.

If the death benefit under a contributory plan were ***installment refund*** instead of cash refund, then $M(n)$ would be a life annuity with n years certain (nCC). Some actuaries use nCC as an approximation to the value of the modified cash refund annuity with ratio n.

Exercises

3.6.1 A convenient way to obtain MCR values is to compute the exact value using equation (3.6.1) or (3.6.3) for, say, $n = 5$; then to use equation (3.6.8) to interpolate. Show that if $M(0) = \ddot{a}_x^{(12)}$ and $M(5)$ is known, then if we assume that $M(n)$ varies as n^2,

$$M(n) = M(0) + \frac{M(5) - M(0)}{25} n^2 .$$

3.6.2 Find the first three derivatives of $\bar{a}_{\overline{x:\overline{n|}}}$ (the nCC annuity paid continuously) with respect to n. How do these compare with those of $M(n)$?

3.6.3 Sometimes the MCR feature is carried over into optional forms such as joint-and-survivor. Derive an expression for a continuous 100% joint-and-survivor annuity of $1 per year with modified cash refund of n dollars — in terms of commutation functions.

3.6.4 Referring to exercise 3.6.3, can you derive an expression for a 50% contingent-annuitant pension with modified cash refund? ("Contingent-annuitant" means a joint-and-survivor form where the amount of annuity reduces only upon the death of the primary annuitant; "pure" joint-and-survivor annuities reduce on the death of either annuitant.)

3.6.5 Suppose there was a special form of MCR death benefit under which interest was credited on employee contributions even after the annuity commenced. Derive an expression for the present value of this form of annuity (assume that it is payable continuously, to make matters simple).

3.6.6 When $M(n) = n$ the annuity is called *full-cash-refund,* because the whole single premium is guaranteed to be paid. One way to compute the value of the full-cash-refund annuity is by taking a trial value n_0 then setting the next approximation $n_1 = M(n_0)$, etc. Will this process always produce a sequence $n_0, n_1, n_2, \ldots$ which approaches n? (Hint: draw a rough graph of $M(n)$; then show that for arbitrary n_0, $\left|\frac{n_2 - n_1}{n_1 - n_0}\right| < 1$ so that every repetition brings you closer to the point where $M(n) = n$.)

Chapter 4

Ancillary Benefits

4.1 *Ancillary to What?*

To pension actuaries any benefit provided by a pension plan, other than a life annuity commencing after the "normal retirement age", is called "ancillary" to the age-retirement pension. Thus, for example, disability pensions, survivor pensions and other death benefits, temporary early-retirement pensions, and severance benefits — including vesting provisions — are all deemed *ancillary* to the retirement pension.*

This viewpoint was implicit from the very beginning of our discussion in Chapter 2. We used a factor D_y/D_x to discount the value of the life annuity at age y back to age x, where the l_x's came from a "service table" which reflected all causes of leaving the group, including termination of employment, disability, and death. In making this discount we were implicitly assuming that no benefits were payable on account of any of these occurrences. In this chapter we shall discuss how to allow for the existence of such ancillary benefits when determining the cost of a plan.

*U.S. actuaries should remember, however, that the definition of "ancillary benefits" promulgated by the Internal Revenue Service is more restrictive than ours.

In Chapter 3 we examined extensively one kind of ancillary benefit; namely, the return of employee contributions upon termination of employment. But that benefit had one feature which made it easier to analyze than some others: it was payable regardless of the cause of leaving the active group — whether the termination was because of death, layoff, or voluntary resignation. When benefits are paid only upon termination of employment for certain specific reasons, the techniques for computing the value of these benefits are more difficult. Just to get our feet wet, let us first look at the most common ancillary benefit of all, vesting.

4.2 *Vesting — Unit-Credit Method*

Vesting is an ancillary benefit granted upon termination of employment for reasons other than death. The benefit itself is contingent upon surviving until the normal retirement age (or in some cases the early retirement age). This means that in order to place a value on the vesting "benefit" we shall need to divide q_x into two components, one representing the probability of leaving the group on account of death ($q_x^{(m)}$) and the other the probability of terminating employment for any other reason ($q_x^{(w)}$): $q_x = q_x^{(m)} + q_x^{(w)}$. In other words, we have a two-decrement service table.

In general, only a percentage of the accrued benefit is vested in each year of employment, so let VP_x^j be the vesting percentage at age x of employee j, expressed as a fraction between 0 and 1. The vesting percentage generally does not depend only upon the age but upon service as well; nevertheless, service and age advance in lock-step with the passage of time so we can use age as the independent variable for a given individual. If AB_t^j is j's accrued benefit at age x (time t), then $VP_x^j \cdot AB_t^j$ is the vested portion of the accrued benefit, the portion that cannot be lost solely because j terminates employment for reasons other than death (although it can be lost if j dies after terminating but before his pension begins). If we were simply to compute the accrued liability for j as $AB_t^j \dfrac{D_y}{D_x} \ddot{a}_y^{(12)}$, taking D_y/D_x from the service table, we would be implying that the accrued benefit is forfeited upon termination, because $q_x^{(w)}$ is a part of q_x in the service table. Clearly we must add back the present value of future vesting of the existing accrued benefit AB_t^j.

If j terminated employment in the year t to $t+1$, assuming that termination took place at the end of the year, he would derive a "benefit" with a value of $VP_{x+1}^j \cdot AB_t^j \cdot {}_{y-x-1|}\ddot{a}_{x+1}^{(12)}$ — where the deferred annuity is computed using interest and mortality only, because once the employee is vested no other decrements can affect the value of the benefit. This means that for the first year we have to add $C_x^{(w)}/D_x$ times the "benefit" where $C_x^{(w)} = q_x^{(w)} l_x v^{x+1}$ and where l_x is taken from the service table. For the next year, when j is aged $x+1$, we must add back $\frac{C_{x+1}^{(w)}}{D_x} \cdot VP_{x+2}^j \cdot AB_t^j \cdot {}_{y-x-2|}\ddot{a}_{x+2}^{(12)}$, and so forth. Note we are not adding the present value of any vesting of retirement benefits not yet accrued, because that would violate the logic of the unit-credit cost method, under which the accrued liability is the present value of accrued benefits. Continuing this process by induction you can see that in this case we should compute the accrued liability as

$$AL_t^j = AB_t^j \frac{D_y}{D_x} \ddot{a}_y^{(12)} + \sum_{z=x}^{y-1} \frac{C_z^{(w)}}{D_x} \cdot VP_{z+1} \cdot AB_t^j \cdot {}_{y-z-1|}\ddot{a}_{z+1}^{(12)}$$

$$= AB_t^j \left[\frac{D_y}{D_x} \ddot{a}_y^{(12)} + \sum_{z=x}^{y-1} \frac{C_z^{(w)}}{D_x} VP_{z+1}^j \cdot {}_{y-z-1|}\ddot{a}_{z+1}^{(12)} \right] . \tag{4.2.1}$$

Note that the bracketed factor in equation (4.2.1) depends on the sequence of vested percentages, VP_z^j, applicable to employee j.

In the special case where $VP_z^j = 1$ for all $z \geq x$ — i.e., where j is vested at time t — we have

$$AL_t^j = AB_t^j \left[\frac{D_y}{D_x} + \sum_{z=x}^{y-1} \frac{C_z^{(w)}}{D_x} \cdot \frac{D'_y}{D'_{z+1}} \right] \ddot{a}_y^{(12)} , \tag{4.2.2}$$

where the primed functions are computed using a mortality decrement only. If we assume that the mortality table comprises the same values of $q_x^{(m)}$ as used in the service table, we derive a particularly illuminating relationship, as follows.

Our service table comprised a sequence $\{l_x\}$ related by

$$l_{z+1} = l_z(1 - q_z^{(m)} - q_z^{(w)}), \tag{4.2.3}$$

and we have just introduced a new table $\{l'_x\}$ related by

$$l'_{z+1} = l'_z (1 - q_z^{(m)}) . \tag{4.2.4}$$

Since the radix of either table is immaterial to equation (4.2.2), let us assume that $l_x = l'_x$. Then

$$l'_{x+1} = l'_x (1 - q_x^{(m)}) = l_x - d_x^{(m)} = l_{x+1} + d_x^{(w)} , \tag{4.2.5}$$

and

$$l'_{x+2} = l'_{x+1}(1 - q^{(m)}_{x+1}) = (l_{x+1} + d^{(w)}_x)(1 - q_{x+1} + q^{(w)}_{x+1})$$
$$= l_{x+2} + d^{(w)}_x \frac{l'_{x+2}}{l'_{x+1}} + d^{(w)}_{x+1} , \tag{4.2.6}$$

and

$$l'_{x+3} = l_{x+3} + d^{(w)}_x \frac{l'_{x+3}}{l'_{x+1}} + d^{(w)}_{x+1} \frac{l'_{x+3}}{l'_{x+2}} + d^{(w)}_{x+2} , \tag{4.2.7}$$

and in general for any t,

$$l'_{x+t} = l_{x+t} + \sum_{k=0}^{t-1} d^{(w)}_{x+k} \frac{l'_{x+t}}{l'_{x+k+1}} . \tag{4.2.8}$$

Multiplying both sides of equation (4.2.8) by v^{x+t} we get

$$D'_{x+t} = D_{x+t} + \sum_{k=0}^{t-1} C^{(w)}_{x+k} \frac{D'_{x+t}}{D'_{x+k+1}} . \tag{4.2.9}$$

Then it follows that

$$\frac{D_y}{D_x} + \sum_{z=x}^{y-1} \frac{C^{(w)}_z}{D_x} \frac{D'_y}{D'_{z+1}} = \frac{D'_y}{D'_x} , \tag{4.2.10}$$

so that for a fully vested employee (equation (4.2.2)) we have

$$AL^j_t = AB^j_t \frac{D'_y}{D'_x} \ddot{a}^{(12)}_y ; \tag{4.2.11}$$

i.e., the accrued liability is computed on the mortality table only, with no other withdrawal assumed. This is the result we should have expected: For a fully vested employee we would suppose that the result of discounting for turnover and then adding back the accrued liability so discounted would achieve the same result as not discounting for withdrawal in the first place. Thus we see that equation (4.2.1) is completely general, even for employees who will not lose benefits on account of termination of employment for reasons other than death. This also means that we can use equation (4.2.11) in place of equation (4.2.1) for all employees who are fully vested on the valuation date — which saves a lot of work in some cases.

So much for the accrued liability; now let us see how the normal cost is affected. With the unit-credit method we get the normal cost by looking at two consecutive accrued liabilities, as we did in sections 2.2 and 3.2. Equation (4.2.1) becomes, one year later,

$$AL_{t+1}^{j} = AB_{t+1}^{j}\Big[\frac{D_y}{D_{x+1}}\,\ddot{a}_y^{(12)} + \sum_{z=x+1}^{y-1}\frac{C_z^{(w)}}{D_{x+1}}\cdot VP_{z+1}\cdot{}_{y-z-1|}\ddot{a}_{z+1}^{(12)}\Big]$$

$$= (AB_t^j + \Delta AB^j)\,\frac{D_x}{D_{x+1}}\Big[\frac{D_y}{D_x}\,\ddot{a}_y^{(12)} + \sum_{z=x}^{y-1}\frac{C_z^{(w)}}{D_x}\cdot VP_{z+1}\cdot{}_{y-z-1|}\ddot{a}_{z+1}^{(12)}$$

$$- \frac{C_x^{(w)}}{D_x}\,VP_{x+1}^{j}\cdot{}_{y-x-1|}\ddot{a}_{x+1}^{(12)}\Big]$$

$$= \frac{1+i}{1-q_x^{(m)}-q_x^{(w)}}\,\Big\{AL_t^j + \Delta AB\Big[\frac{D_y}{D_x}\,\ddot{a}_y^{(12)} + \sum_{z=x}^{y-1}\frac{C_z^{(w)}}{D_x}\cdot VP_{z+1}^{j}\cdot{}_{y-z-1|}\ddot{a}_{z+1}^{(12)}\Big]$$

$$- q_x^{(w)}\,v\,VP_{x+1}^{j}\,\widetilde{AB}_{t+1}^{j}\cdot{}_{y-x-1|}\ddot{a}_{x+1}^{(12)}\Big\}\,,$$

which implies

$$AL_{t+1}^{j} = (AL_t^j + NC_t^j)(1+i) - q_x^{(w)}\,VP_{x+1}^{j}\cdot\widetilde{AB}_{t+1}^{j}\cdot{}_{y-x-1|}\ddot{a}_{x+1}^{(12)} + q_x\,AL_{t+1}^{j}\,, \tag{4.2.12}$$

where the term containing $q_x^{(w)}$ represents the vesting benefits expected to be derived during the year and where $\widetilde{AB}_{t+1}^{j} = AB_t^j + \Delta AB^j$. We have denoted the normal cost for employee j as

$$NC_t^j = \Delta AB\Big[\frac{D_y}{D_x}\,\ddot{a}_y^{(12)} + \sum_{z=x}^{y-1}\frac{C_z^{(w)}}{D_x}\cdot VP_{z+1}^{j}\cdot{}_{y-z-1|}\ddot{a}_{z+1}^{(12)}\Big]\,. \tag{4.2.13}$$

The demonstration that this is a proper definition has been left as an exercise. Note that, as before, the unit-credit normal cost is just the additional accrued benefit multiplied by the same factor used to compute the accrued liability for employee j. This means again that we can apply equation (4.2.10) if the vesting percentage VP_x^j is equal to 1.

When a plan is contributory, the employee who terminates must often choose between a refund of his own contributions with consequent loss of some or all of his accrued benefit, and retention of a vested right to the full accrued benefit. Where the summation in equation (4.2.1) is being evaluated term-by-term (as usually it must be, because it can seldom be simplified) the relative advantage of these alternatives may be taken into account in each year separately: The alternative with the higher present value each year may be chosen as the "benefit" to be multiplied by $C_z^{(w)}/D_x$.

Exercises

4.2.1 Use the set relationship $\mathbf{A}_{t+1} = \mathbf{A}_t - \mathbf{T} - \mathbf{D}$ (where $\mathbf{D}$ is the set of employees active at time t who die before the end of the year) and the logical process of section 2.2 to show that equation (4.2.13) is really the "normal" cost. Do this by showing that all other terms are zero when the assumptions are exactly borne out. Show that this means that the gain is computed the same as before.

4.2.2 Some actuaries treat the vesting benefit under the unit-credit cost method in the following alternative way (called the "term-cost" approach):

(1) they compute the accrued liability using only the factor $\frac{D_y}{D_x}\ddot{a}_y^{(12)}$ from the brackets in equation (4.2.1), i.e., assuming no vesting; and

(2) they define the normal cost as

$$NC_t^j = \Delta AB^j \frac{D_y}{D_x}\ddot{a}_y^{(12)} + \frac{C_x^{(w)}}{D_x} VP_{x+1}^j \cdot \widetilde{AB}_{t+1}^j \cdot {}_{y-x-1|}\ddot{a}_{x+1}^{(12)} .$$

Show that the following statements about the term-cost approach are true:

(a) the accrued liability is understated;

(b) the normal cost is understated;

(c) the "term cost" is equal to one year's marginal actuarial loss due to (a) and (b) (see equations (4.2.12) and (4.2.13);

(d) the term-cost approach is not a correct application of the unit-credit cost method except in the trivial case where there is no assumed withdrawal for reasons other than death.

4.2.3 Suppose that the plan calls for "cliff" vesting, where the vested percentage is zero until completion of ten years of service and is equal to 1 thereafter. If the vesting "cliff" is reached at age $u \geq x$ it is possible to eliminate the summation sign in equation (4.2.1) by defining special functions M_x^a and R_x^a based on $C_x^a = C_x^{(w)} {}_{y-x-1|}\ddot{a}_{x+1}^{(12)}$. Show how equation (4.2.1) may be rewritten using these functions without a summation sign.

4.3 A Note About Multiple-Decrement Theory

The astute reader will have noted that in section 4.2 we apparently glossed over the distinction made in classical multiple-decrement theory between $q_x^{(m)\prime}$, the probability of mortality in an environment where that is the only decrement, and $q_x^{(m)}$, its counterpart when the withdrawal decrement is also present.

Actually, there was no logical flaw because the two decrements used were not independent: We chose $q_x^{(w)}$ to represent the probability of having left the covered group of employees *without having died before the end of the year.* We made no distinction between the employee who terminated employment and then died and the one who died before he had a chance to quit or be fired — in either case no vested pension resulted. Thus, our $q_x^{(w)}$ was dependent upon $q_x^{(m)}$, the probability of dying *in* or *out* of covered employment.

To say the same thing mathematically, remember that if we have n decrements $\mu_x^{(i)}$, then by definition

$$q_x^{(i)\prime} = 1 - exp\left(- \int_0^1 \mu_{x+t}^{(i)}\, dt\right) . \tag{4.3.1}$$

The probability of *not* being affected by at least one of the decrements during a year is then

$$p_x = 1 - q_x = exp\left(- \int_0^1 (\mu_{x+s}^{(1)} + \ldots + \mu_{x+s}^{(n)})\, ds\right) , \tag{4.3.2}$$

so that the probability of survival for a time $t \leq 1$ is

$$\begin{aligned} {}_tp_x &= exp\left(- \int_0^t (\sum_{i=1}^{n} \mu_{x+s}^{(i)})\, ds\right) \\ &= exp\left(- \sum_1^n (\int_0^t \mu_{x+s}^{(i)}\, ds)\right) \\ &= exp\left(- \int_0^t \mu_{x+s}^{(1)}\, ds - \ldots - \int_0^t \mu_{x+s}^{(n)}\, ds\right) . \end{aligned} \tag{4.3.3}$$

This means that

$$q_x = 1 - {}_1p_x = 1 - (1 - q_x^{(1)\prime}) \ldots (1 - q_x^{(n)\prime}) . \tag{4.3.4}$$

Now $q_x^{(i)}$ without a prime is the probability of being affected *first* by decrement i:

$$q_x^{(i)} = \int_0^1 {}_tp_x \, \mu_{x+t}^{(i)} \, dt \, . \tag{4.3.5}$$

In section 4.2 we did not make use of this probability because the nature of the vesting benefit did not require it (it did not matter whether death occurred before or after withdrawal for other reasons). Our $q_x^{(w)}$ of section 4.2, by comparison, was simply the quantity $q_x - q_x^{(m)}$, the probability of withdrawing but not dying.

There are, of course, occasions when you need a proper set of multiple-decrement q's, in which $q_x^{(i)}$ represents the probability of leaving the group on account of cause *i first,* before being affected by any of the other decrements. These must be obtained by approximation of equation (4.3.5) — one of which was that used in section 4.2, namely, that withdrawal occurs only at the end of each year. There are other such simplifying assumptions (e.g., that withdrawals occur at the beginning of the year, or in the middle of the year); the choice between them is one of taste.

Alternatively, considering that most of the assumptions made in pension funding work are fairly rough anyway, you may decide to choose $q_x \equiv \sum_{i=1}^{n} q_x^{(i)\prime}$ so that $q_x^{(i)} = q_x^{(i)\prime}$. The resultant "inaccuracy" is still within acceptable tolerances and this approach is widely used. For example, if you have two decrements the more accurate approach might be to approximate.

$$\begin{aligned} q_x^{(1)} &\approx q_x^{(1)\prime}(1 - \frac{1}{2} q_x^{(2)\prime}) \, ; \\ q_x^{(2)} &\approx q_x^{(2)\prime}(1 - \frac{1}{2} q_x^{(1)\prime}) \, . \end{aligned} \tag{4.3.6}$$

Note that $q_x^{(1)} + q_x^{(2)} = q_x = 1 - (1 - q_x^{(1)\prime})(1 - q_x^{(2)\prime})$.) If you used the gross approach, however, you might simply set $q_x = q_x^{(1)\prime} + q_x^{(2)\prime}$, in which case the error in q_x would be (from (4.3.6))

$$\begin{aligned} \delta q &= q_x^{(1)\prime} + q_x^{(2)\prime} - q_x^{(1)} - q_x^{(2)} \\ &\approx q_x^{(1)\prime} + q_x^{(2)\prime} - q_x^{(1)\prime} - q_x^{(2)\prime} + q_x^{(1)\prime} q_x^{(2)\prime} \\ &= q_x^{(1)\prime} q_x^{(2)\prime} \, . \end{aligned} \tag{4.3.7}$$

Thus, if $q_x^{(1)\prime} = .01$ and $q_x^{(2)\prime} = .05$ then $\delta q = .0005$ using the gross approach — an error small enough not to worry about.

The most important point to remember, though, is that whenever we undertake to divide q_x up into *independent* $q_x^{(i)}$ so that $q_x = q_x^{(1)} + \ldots + q_x^{(n)}$ we are necessarily introducing an approximation into our model of reality, because these $q_x^{(i)}$ are not, and cannot be, independent. To value ancillary benefits in terms of these $q_x^{(i)}$ we must deal *arbitrarily* with interaction between causes. In section 4.2 we dealt arbitrarily with the interaction between mortality and withdrawal by letting the withdrawals happen first and letting mortality operate only on the survivors. We could just as well have done the opposite — or made a more sophisticated approximation — the question is not one of accuracy but of consistency. Thus, while $q_x^{(i)}$ has only one theoretical definition (equation (4.3.5)), its definition in practice may vary.

Exercises

4.3.1 Given two independent decrements with forces $\mu_x^{(1)}$ and $\mu_x^{(2)}$, assume that $\mu_{x+t}^{(i)} = \mu_x^{(i)}$ for $0 \leq t < 1$ (i.e., μ_x is constant over the entire year). Show that

$$q_x^{(i)} = q_x \frac{\mu_x^{(i)}}{\mu_x^{(1)} + \mu_x^{(2)}} . \tag{4.3.8}$$

Can you extend this result to more than two decrements?

4.3.2 If, in constructing our service table, we had taken all withdrawals out of l_x at the *beginning* of each year, how would equation (4.2.1) have been affected? (Do you see why our definition of $q_x^{(w)}$ was tantamount to assuming that deaths occur at the beginning of each year?)

4.3.3 In our development of equation (4.2.11), which showed that proper allowance for vesting using a two-decrement service table for a fully vested employee produced the same result using no withdrawal decrement at all, we used a discrete model for the vesting liability. The same result can be determined more elegantly with a continuous approach as follows:

(a) Show that if we choose radices appropriately we can express our service table in the form $l_x = l_x^{(m)} \cdot l_x^{(w)}$, where $l_{x+1}^{(m)} = l_x^{(m)}(1 - q_x^{(m)\prime})$ and $l_{x+1}^{(w)} = l_x^{(w)}(1 - q_x^{(w)\prime})$.

(b) Show that the summation in equation (4.2.1) may be replaced by

$$\int_0^{y-x} \frac{l_{x+t}}{l_x} \mu_{x+t}^{(w)} v^t \left[\frac{l_x^{(m)}}{l_{x+t}^{(m)}} v^{y-x-t} \ddot{a}_y^{(12)} \right] dt .$$

(c) Show how this leads directly to equation (4.2.11).

4.4 Vesting — Entry-Age-Normal Method

As always, with entry age normal we begin by defining the normal cost — for which we need first to determine the present value of future benefits for each individual j at age w. The latter must now include the present value of future vesting as follows (using the same notation as in section 4.2):

$$PVFBW_t^j = B_t^{j\,\prime}\frac{D_y}{D_w}\ddot{a}_y^{(12)} + \sum_{z=w}^{y-1}\frac{C_z^{(w)}}{D_w}VP_{z+1}^j\widetilde{AB}_{t+z-x+1}^{j\,\prime}\frac{D_y'}{D_{z+1}'}\ddot{a}_y^{(12)}. \tag{4.4.1}$$

Note that this is the first time we have had occasion to refer to the *accrued* benefit under the entry-age-normal method. Now we need to generate a whole array of these accrued benefits from age $w+1$ to age y — a formidable task if we have no computer and we are using a salary scale, but not at all difficult otherwise: we just work up the arrays and multiply them term-by-term (i.e., take the inner product of the two "vectors"). Here again, the array of accrued benefits used to compute the normal cost is generally not the same as those used for the accrued liability, for reasons discussed at length in section 3.3.

The normal cost is then

$$NC_t^j = \frac{PVFBW_t^j}{PVFSW_t^j}S_t^j, \tag{4.4.2}$$

and the accrued liability is

$$AL_t^j = PVFB_t^j - NC_t^j\,\frac{{}^sN_x - {}^sN_y}{{}^sD_x}, \tag{4.4.3}$$

where

$$PVFB_t^j = \frac{D_y}{D_x}B_t^j\ddot{a}_y^{(12)} + \sum_{z=x}^{y-1}\frac{C_z^{(w)}}{D_x}VP_{z+1}\widetilde{AB}_{t+z-x+1}^j\frac{D_y'}{D_{z+1}'}\ddot{a}_y^{(12)}, \tag{4.4.4}$$

Note that $VP_{z+1}^j\widetilde{AB}_{t+z-x+1}^j \le B_t^j$. Therefore,

$$PVFB_t^j \le B_t^j\ddot{a}_y^{(12)}\left[\frac{D_y}{D_x} + \sum_{z=x}^{y-1}\frac{C_z^{(w)}}{D_x}\frac{D_y'}{D_{z+1}'}\right],$$

so that

$$PVFB_t^j \le B_t^j\ddot{a}_y^{(12)}\frac{D_y'}{D_x'}; \tag{4.4.5}$$

with equality being achieved only in the extreme case where $\widetilde{AB}_{t+z-x+1}^j = B_t^j$ and $VP_{z+1}^j = 1$. Therefore, unlike the situation with the unit-credit method, you do not get the same present value of benefits if you omit the withdrawal decrement for fully vested employees as when you use the decrement and add back the vesting liability. Even in a fully vested plan, if the entry-age-normal cost method is used with no withdrawal decrement there will be a gain on each termination. Refer back to your work on exercise 2.3.3 and note that this result (equation (4.4.5)) further strengthens the general proposition that entry-age-normal calls for faster funding than unit-credit.

The handling of vesting under other "projected-benefit" cost methods (e.g., individual-level-premium, frozen-initial-liability, attained-age-normal) is the same as under the entry-age-normal method because vesting affects only the present value of future benefits and not the present value of future salaries.

Sometimes the computation of the series $\{\widetilde{AB}^j_{t+z-x}, z = x+1, \ldots, y\}$ can be too time-consuming even for a computer (as with a social-security-offset formula, for example). Where a different projected benefit is used for the normal cost (for reasons discussed in section 3.5) the task for computing the sequence is even larger. In such cases the best approach is to interpolate geometrically between AB^j_t and $\widetilde{AB}^j_{t+y-x} = B^j_t(y)$ and between $\widetilde{AB}^{j\,\prime}_{t+w-x} \equiv 0$ and $\widetilde{AB}^{j\prime}_{t+y-x} = B^{j\prime}_t(y)$ (where the primed values are used to compute the normal cost).

Exercises

4.4.1 A plan provides a pension at retirement equal to the accumulation of units of pension earned in each year. The unit of pension each year is computed as 1% of that year's salary. (This is known in the trade as a "career-pay" plan.) Assume that the salary scale is uniform, i.e., that salaries increase at a constant rate r each year. Also assume that $B(y) \neq B'(y)$, because a special past service formula was in effect when the plan was established and the employee we are going to look at (employee j, of course!) had past service at the time the plan was established.

(a) What is the hypothetical accrued benefit of employee j at any age $z \geq w$?

(b) What is the accrued benefit for any age $z \geq x$?

(c) Write a complete equation for the normal cost for employee j at time t, using the hypothetical projected benefit from part (a) above.

(d) Write an expression for the accrued liability of employee j at time t.

(e) Have you simplified your answers as much as you possibly can, taking advantage of the geometrical salary-increase assumption?

4.4.2 Repeat the exercise above for employee j at time $t+1$, then work out an expression for the progression of accrued liability from time t to $t+1$ for employee j.

4.4.3 Assume that the plan covers only active lives, as we did in Chapter 2, and develop an expression for the gain, being careful to separate the components attributable to mortality from those attributable to withdrawal.

(a) From the equation thus generated, pick out the one which you would call the expected release of accrued liability on account of termination of employment.

(b) What is the actual accrued liability released? (Remember that when an employee actually does terminate with vesting you have to keep his new accrued liability on the books: do you know what this new accrued liability will be?)

4.4.4 Show how you would compute the cost of this same plan under the aggregate cost method. What effect does the existence of vesting in the plan have on the denominator of the expression for unit normal cost?

4.4.5 How would your answer to the previous exercise be modified if the plan were also contributory? Assume that employees must contribute one-half percent of salary for each year of plan participation. Before you begin work on this exercise, note that in most contributory plans the vesting percentage applies not to the entire accrued benefit but only to that portion of the accrued benefit which is attributable to employer contributions. In the United States, the accrued benefit attributable to employee contributions is computed as one-tenth of the accumulated contributions to date carried forward to age y with interest at 5%. You may make the exercise easier by assuming that i is also equal to 5%.

4.4.6 Prove that, under the entry-age-normal cost method, if the only decrements in the service table are mortality and withdrawal *and* if the vested benefit is equivalent to a cash refund of the accrued liability, then for a fully vested employee $AL_t' = AL_t$, where the primed accrued liability is computed on mortality decrement alone. (Assume that the actual and hypothetical accrued benefits are identical.) Note that this is the entry-age-normal counterpart to the result derived for unit-credit in section 4.2.

4.4.7 Can the EAN accrued liability for the vesting benefit *alone* be negative? When? Would such a negative accrued liability imply a flaw in logic?

4.5 Early Retirement

The typical retirement plan provides benefits at a stated "normal retirement age" which is commonly age 65. In valuing such plans the actuary often assumes that the retirement age y will be the normal retirement age. When the plan allows retirement at an age earlier than y, the retiring employee is usually given a choice between waiting until age y to begin receiving his full accrued benefit or taking a reduced amount of pension immediately.

If the plan is being funded on the unit-credit cost method, when an employee retires early with an immediate pension there will be a loss on this account unless the accrued liability at time $t+1$, assuming the employee retires during the year t to $t+1$, is the same as it would have been if the employee had not retired early. This means, if we assume the only decrement in effect for a person eligible for early retirement is mortality, that the early retirement benefit must be equal to the accrued benefit multiplied by the factor $N_y^{(12)}/N_x^{(12)}$ where x is the age at the time the pension commences (see exercise 4.5.1). This factor is called the "early-retirement reduction factor." Where the normal form is other than life annuity the factor is different.

In other words, if the unit-credit cost method is employed and the plan allows early retirement, then there will always be an actuarial loss occasioned by an early retirement, unless the early retirement benefit is equal to (or less than) the accrued benefit reduced by the application of an early retirement reduction factor based on the same interest and mortality assumptions as used in the valuation.

Under the entry-age-normal method the situation is a bit more complex. Suppose that the normal retirement benefit is \$1 per year for each year of service (we can always multiply our result by a factor if the plan is more liberal). Consider an employee j who is in the early retirement period, that is to say, has acquired at time $t-1$ the requisite age and service to be allowed to retire early under the plan. His accrued liability at time $t-1$ is then

$$AL_{t-1}^j = (y-w)\frac{D_y}{D_{x-1}}\ddot{a}_y^{(12)}\left(\frac{N_w - N_{x-1}}{N_w - N_y}\right). \tag{4.5.1}$$

If he retires early he will release at time t an amount of accrued liability equal to

$$\widetilde{AL}_t^j = (y-w)\frac{D_y}{D_x}\ddot{a}_y^{(12)}\left(\frac{N_w - N_x}{N_w - N_y}\right) \tag{4.5.2}$$

because he is no longer an active employee; but he will at the same time add an accrued liability equal to $AL_t^j = (x-w)\ddot{a}_x^{(12)}\cdot E$ because he is now a retired employee — where E is the early-retirement factor, yet to be determined.

In order to avoid an actuarial loss on account of retirement (see for example equation (2.3.10)), E must satisfy the relationship

$$E \cdot (x-w)\ddot{a}_x^{(12)} = (y-w)\frac{D_y}{D_x}\ddot{a}_y^{(12)}\left(\frac{N_w - N_x}{N_w - N_y}\right), \tag{4.5.3}$$

or

$$E = \frac{N_y^{(12)}}{N_x^{(12)}}\left[\frac{(y-w)}{(x-w)}\,\frac{N_w - N_x}{N_w - N_y}\right]; \tag{4.5.4}$$

which equals the unit-credit early-retirement factor multiplied by the term in brackets. The term in brackets is greater than or equal to 1 (exercise 4.5.2) so that, in this case at least, the required reduction for early retirement under entry-age-normal is *less* than that required for unit-credit. In other words, the plan could, if the cost were being determined by the entry-age-normal cost method, provide an early-retirement benefit greater than $N_y^{(12)}/N_x^{(12)}$ times the normal-retirement amount without incurring actuarial losses on account of early retirement. A corollary statement is that when early retirement benefits are reduced by applying a factor greater than $N_y^{(12)}/N_x^{(12)}$ and the cost is being determined under the unit-credit cost method, then to the extent that employees actually do retire early the cost of the plan is being understated. If the plan is funded under entry-age-normal the cost may or may not be understated depending on the actual reduction factors used by the plan.

In spite of the fact that in theory lower early-retirement reductions are possible under a plan which uses the entry-age-normal (or another "projected-benefit" cost method), any plan which provides early-retirement benefits which are greater than the factor $N_y^{(12)}/N_x^{(12)}$ multiplied by the accrued benefit is said to offer "subsidized" early-retirement benefits. Where subsidized early-retirement benefits are present in a plan — and especially where the unit-credit cost method is used — it is desirable to allow explicitly for the extra cost of early retirement by treating retirement itself as a decrement in the service table and thereby producing an increase in the unit-credit normal cost.

Where the entry-age-normal cost method is used and full actuarial reduction is applied to early-retirement benefits, the use of a separate decrement for retirement will often produce a lower normal cost, as may be seen from equation (4.5.4), because early-retirement benefits will be reduced more than is necessary to keep an actuarial loss from occurring.

Exercises

4.5.1 Show explicitly that there will be an actuarial loss (all other factors being equal) if an employee retires at age x with an early-retirement benefit greater than $AB_t^j \dfrac{N_y^{(12)}}{N_x^{(12)}}$, and if the cost method is unit-credit.

4.5.2 Show that if mortality is the only decrement $\left(\dfrac{N_w - N_x}{D_w}\right)/(x - w)$ is a monotonically decreasing function of x, and that consequently the term in brackets in equation (4.5.4) is generally greater than 1.

4.5.3 Derive an equation similar to equation (4.5.4) in the case where benefits are based on salary and a salary scale is used. Is this new hypothetical early-retirement factor also greater than the unit-credit factor? If not, under what conditions would it be less?

4.5.4 Show that the early-retirement factor $N_y^{(12)}/N_x^{(12)}$ is approximately an exponential function of x, as follows:

(a) Let the factor E be defined by $E(x) = \bar{N}_y / \bar{N}_x$ and write this as the quotient of two integrals.

(b) Assume μ_x is constant for all ages.

(c) Show that under these assumptions

$$E(x) = exp\left(-(\mu + \delta)(y - x)\right).$$

(d) What is the effect on $E(x)$ of an increase in the assumed interest rate? Does it raise or lower $E(x)$? What is the effect of a similar change in the assumed mortality rate? Does a proportional increase in the force of mortality have the same effect on $E(x)$ as the same proportional increase in the force of interest? How about an absolute increase in each?

4.5.5 Derive the counterpart of $N_y^{(12)}/N_x^{(12)}$ for plans whose normal form is other than life annuity:

(a) If the normal form is 10-years-certain-and-continuous (10CC);

(b) If the normal form is modified-cash-refund (note that in this case E depends on the death-benefit ratio as well as the age).

4.5.6 Suppose the plan of exercise 4.5.1 contained a provision which had the effect of paying out the entire accrued liability in case of death in the early-retirement period. What is the proper early-retirement factor in this case? (Answer: $(1+i)^{x-y}$.)

4.6 *Late Retirement*

Just as retirement before the normal retirement age y is called "early retirement", retirement after that age is called "late retirement". Suppose that employee j, expected to retire at age y, actually stays on until age $y+1$. Then: (1) the fund does not make the expected pension payments to him during the year; and (2) his benefit under the plan increases from B to $B+\Delta B$. The value of ΔB depends on the plan provisions pertaining to late retirement. The question which interests us is whether, if mortality and interest experience is exactly as assumed, there is an actuarial gain (or loss) attributable to the event of late retirement.

Suppose we have l_y persons aged y at time t, each eligible for a pension of \$1 per year. In our valuation we have assumed that everyone already aged y will retire immediately, so the accrued liability for this group of employees is $l_y \ddot{a}_y^{(12)}$. Now, at time $t+1$ we discover that the entire group has decided to retire late: d_y of them have died with no pension and l_{y+1} have survived and are still actively employed. The pensions of the survivors have increased from \$1 to \$$(1+\lambda)$. At the same time, the fund has not had to pay the pensions expected to be paid during the year and as a result has $l_{y+1} \dfrac{N_y^{(12)} - N_{y+1}^{(12)}}{D_{y+1}}$ more on hand than it would have if the employees had retired as expected. The marginal increase in the unfunded accrued liability attributable to this group of employees having retired late is then

$$\lambda l_{y+1} \ddot{a}_{y+1}^{(12)} - l_{y+1} \frac{N_y^{(12)} - N_{y+1}^{(12)}}{D_{y+1}} ,$$

because $l_{y+1} \ddot{a}_{y+1}^{(12)}$ would be a part of the accrued liability whether the group had retired or not. This marginal gain will be exactly zero if

$$l_{y+1} \frac{N_{y+1}^{(12)}}{D_{y+1}} \lambda = l_{y+1} \frac{N_y^{(12)} - N_{y+1}^{(12)}}{D_{y+1}} ,$$

or, in other words, if

$$\lambda = \frac{N_y^{(12)}}{N_{y+1}^{(12)}} - 1 . \qquad (4.6.2)$$

Thus, in general, if an actuarial gain on account of late retirement is to be avoided absolutely, the benefits of late retirees should be increased by the ratio $N_y^{(12)}/N_{y+n}^{(12)}$ where $y+n$ is the age at actual retirement. Plans which compute late-retirement benefits in this fashion are said to provide "actuarially increased" late-retirement benefits.

If the late-retirement benefit at age $y+1$ is less than $N_y^{(12)}/N_{y+1}^{(12)}$ in our example, then the marginal gain on account of late retirement is positive. So if the late-retirement benefit is less than the accrued benefit at age y multiplied by $N_y^{(12)}/N_{y+1}^{(12)}$ there will be a gain — to the extent that any employees actually do choose to retire after age y. Conversely, if late retirement benefits are more than the "actuarially equivalent" amount, there will be a loss if late retirements occur. (It should be obvious that if no late retirements do occur in fact, then the provisions of the plan with respect to late retirement are immaterial.)

Some plans provide no increase in pension at all if employees retire after the normal retirement age, and under such plans there is unquestionably an actuarial gain, marginally speaking, every time a late retirement occurs. Other plans, however, treat "late retirement" no differently from normal retirement, and benefit accruals continue in the same way after age y as before. Whether there is a marginal actuarial gain on account of late retirements under such a plan depends on the ratio of the additional accrued benefit ΔB earned after age y, to B, the benefit at age y. It is clear from equation (4.6.2) that there will be a marginal *gain* if $\dfrac{\Delta B}{B} < \dfrac{N_y^{(12)}}{N_{y+1}^{(12)}} - 1$, there will be *neither* a gain or a loss if $\dfrac{\Delta B}{B} = \dfrac{N_y^{(12)}}{N_{y+1}^{(12)}} - 1$, and there will be a *loss* if $\dfrac{\Delta B}{B} > \dfrac{N_y^{(12)}}{N_{y+1}^{(12)}} - 1$.

In the case of early retirement we saw that it might be dangerous to assume that all employees will retire at a single age y — rather than including a retirement decrement in the service table — if the unit-credit method is used and if early-retirement benefits are more than the actuarial equivalent of the accrued normal-retirement benefit. Likewise, with late retirement: Depending on the propensity of employees to retire after age y, and on the benefits prescribed by the plan in case they do so retire, the cost of the plan can be overstated (or, in extreme situations, understated) by the use of a single assumed retirement age rather than a table of retirement probabilities.

Exercises

4.6.1 Show that the late-retirement increase factor is of the form e^{ct} where retirement occurs at age $y+t$. (Hint: $N_y^{(12)}/N_{y+n}^{(12)}$ is the inverse of the early-retirement factor; refer to exercise 4.5.4.) What is the value of c?

4.6.2 A plan providing actuarially equivalent early- and late-retirement benefits calls for a reduction of 1% in his accrued benefit when an employee retires at age 64-11/12 (where the normal retirement age is 65). What is the approximate increase in accrued benefit if the employee retires at age 65-1/12? Why?

4.6.3 If $\mu_{65} = .035$ and $\delta = .065$, approximately by what percentage will an employee's benefit increase if he stays active until age 66, under a plan which grants actuarial increases after normal retirement age? (Answer: 10.5%; do you see why?)

4.6.4 If you plotted the early- and late-retirement factors on semilog graph paper, what would be the shape of the curve (i.e., how would it deviate from a straight line)? Check your surmise by actually computing and graphing a set of such factors using any mortality table that comes to hand and an interest rate of, say, 8%.

4.6.5 A plan provides a pension equal to $10 per month times years of service. The normal retirement age is 65, but benefits continue to accrue at the $10 rate in case of late retirement. What is the percentage increase between ages 65 and 66 in the accrued benefit of an employee hired at age 30? If the actuarial increase factor at age 66 is 1.1, would you expect to have a loss if such an employee had been hired at age 60?

4.6.6 Does the size of the gain on account of late retirement depend on the cost method employed? Explain your answer thoroughly, defining each of your terms carefully.

4.7 *Retirement as an "Ancillary Benefit"*

Throughout the book, until now, we have implied a service table based on the assumption that all employees would retire exactly at y, the normal retirement age. When we allowed for the cost of ancillary benefits we simply added a term to the present value of the accrued normal-retirement benefit.

But now, if we use retirement as a decrement in the service table, then the retirement benefit itself is treated as though it were an ancillary benefit. For example, in the unit-credit method instead of expressing the present value of the accrued benefit as $AB_t^j \dfrac{D_y}{D_x} \ddot{a}_y^{(12)}$, we must express it as

$$AL_t^j = AB_t^j \sum_{z=x}^{\infty} \frac{C_z^{(r)}}{D_x} \cdot E(z+1) \cdot \ddot{a}_{z+1}^{(12)} , \tag{4.7.1}$$

where $E(z)$ is the actuarial-equivalence factor used to adjust for early or late retirement (if the plan does not have such an adjustment then E is just 1 everywhere). Note that the summation in equation (4.7.1) has an indefinite end, because there is no cutoff point in the service table anymore, as there was when we assumed everyone would retire at age y. Of course, in practice there is always some age at which the service table ends, just as there is always some age at which a mortality table ends — but there is no theoretical limit to it. Where the variable age z is too low for retirement to occur under the terms of the plan, the commutation function $C_z^{(r)}$ is simply equal to zero (because $q_z^{(r)} = 0$).

Continuing to look at the unit-credit method, recall that the normal cost is defined (or, more properly, derived) by analyzing the behavior of successive accrued liabilities:

$$
\begin{aligned}
AL_{t+1}^j &= (AB_t^j + \Delta B^j) \sum_{z=x+1}^{\infty} \frac{C_z^{(r)}}{D_{x+1}} E(z+1)\, \ddot{a}_{z+1}^{(12)} \\
&= AB_t^j \sum_{x}^{\infty} \frac{C_z^{(r)}}{D_{x+1}} E(z+1)\, \ddot{a}_{z+1}^{(12)} - (AB_t^j + \Delta B^j) E(x+1) \frac{C_x^{(r)}}{D_{x+1}} \ddot{a}_{x+1}^{(12)} \\
&\quad + \Delta B \sum_{x}^{\infty} \frac{C_z^{(r)}}{D_{x+1}} E(z+1)\, \ddot{a}_{z+1}^{(12)} \\
&= \frac{D_x}{D_{x+1}} \left[AL_t^j - v q_x^{(r)} E(x+1) \widetilde{AB}_{t+1}^j\, \ddot{a}_{x+1}^{(12)} + \Delta B^j \sum_{x}^{\infty} \frac{C_z^{(r)}}{D_x} E(z+1)\, \ddot{a}_{z+1}^{(12)} \right] \\
&= AL_t^j (1+i) + \Delta B^j (1+i) \sum_{x}^{\infty} \frac{C_z^{(r)}}{D_x} E(z+1)\, \ddot{a}_{z+1}^{(12)} \\
&\quad - q_x^{(r)} \widetilde{AL}_{t+1}^j E(x+1) \ddot{a}_{x+1}^{(12)} + q_x \widetilde{AL}_{t+1}^j \,.
\end{aligned}
\tag{4.7.2}
$$

The second term in (4.7.2) is obviously the normal cost for employee j, with a year's interest, so:

$$
NC_t^j = \Delta B^j \sum_{x}^{\infty} \frac{C_z^{(r)}}{D_x} E(z+1)\, \ddot{a}_{z+1}^{(12)} \,. \tag{4.7.3}
$$

This is a more general form of the term inside the summation sign in equation (2.2.4), because if $d_z^{(r)} = 0$ for $z < y-1$, and $d_{y-1}^{(r)} = l_{y-1} - d_{y-1}^{(-r)}$ (where $d_z^{(-r)}$ represents the sum of all decrements *except* $d_z^{(r)}$), then

$$C_{y-1}^{(r)} = l_{y-1}\,v^y - d_{y-1}^{(-r)}\,v^y$$

$$= D_{y-1}\,v - C_{y-1}^{(-r)}\,,$$

(4.7.4)

so

$$NC_t^j = \Delta B^j \frac{C_{y-1}^{(r)}}{D_x}\ddot{a}_y^{(12)} = \Delta B^j \left(\frac{D_{y-1}\,v}{D_x} - \frac{C_{y-1}^{(-r)}}{D_x}\right)\ddot{a}_y^{(12)}\,.$$

(4.7.5)

This is the same as that derived in section 2.2 because in that section there was no retirement decrement at age $y-1$, so *all* the decrements in the service table were assumed to be for causes other than retirement:

$$\frac{D_y}{D_x} = \frac{l_y\,v^y}{D_x} = \frac{(l_{y-1} - d_{y-1}^{(-r)})\,v^y}{D_x} = \frac{D_{y-1}\,v - C_{y-1}^{(-r)}}{D_x}\,.$$

(4.7.6)

Note that we still have to add the normal cost due to vesting or other ancillary benefits to equation (4.7.3) above. Retirement has become just another among many possible ancillary benefits — benefits considered ancillary to the "null plan", which provides no pension benefits at all!

Exercises

4.7.1 Why is it "obvious" that the second term of equation (4.7.2) represents the normal cost? Review the development of equations (2.2.1) through (2.2.4).

4.7.2 Derive the counterparts to the equations of section 2.3 (for the entry-age-normal method without salary scale) when a retirement decrement is present in the service table.

4.7.3 Using section 2.9 as a guide, show how to express the normal cost under the aggregate method when retirement is a decrement in the service table. Can you see why the unit normal cost might decrease if you went from a single assumed retirement age to a table of retirement probabilities?

4.7.4 Show that under the unit-credit cost method with retirement treated as an "ancillary benefit" the accrued liability is the same as derived in section 2.2 if all benefits are adjusted by the "actuarial equivalence" factor $N_y^{(12)}/N_x^{(12)}$.

4.8 *Other Ancillary Benefits*

These may be handled in the same manner as those discussed in prior sections. For a "benefit" which is "payable" in case an employee leaves the group on account of cause k, we simply compute the benefit payable (or new liability incurred) at age $z+1$ and sum the products of each of those with the corresponding value of $C_z^{(k)}/D_x$. Where $q_z^{(k)}$ is a function of length of service as well as age, you will have, in effect, a different service table for each age at hire, but the formulas take the same form. Likewise, if the assumptions differ by employment classification or by sex: If you subdivide the group finely enough you will reach a point at which age becomes the only independent variable.

Our approach of assuming payment of ancillary benefits at the end of the year was deliberate. That assumption allowed us to use $q_x^{(k)}$ such that $q_x = q_x^{(1)} + \ldots + q_x^{(n)}$ and thereby to avoid questions of which event occurred first during the year. The alternative approach, namely to assume payment immediately upon separation from the group, will be explored in the exercises. Whichever approach you choose, you should be sure that you are being consistent. In particular, you should be able to show that if the benefit upon separation for cause k is a refund of the entire accrued liability, then the accrued liability will be the same as if you had ignored that decrement entirely. This test for consistency ensures that if the entire accrued liability is paid out on account of any kind of separation from the group, regardless of cause, then no decrements need be assumed in computing it. This is the logical generalization of the result proved in section 4.2 and in exercise 4.4.6.

While we shall defer until Chapter 6 a thorough discussion of how you go about choosing the probabilities $q_x^{(k)}$, and whether or not to go to the trouble of allowing specifically for the cost of the various ancillary benefits, it is important to be aware that such a specific allowance is, generally speaking, more important when you are using the unit-credit cost method than the entry-age-normal or similar methods. The reason is that many common ancillary benefits are equal in value to the present value of accrued benefits — which is to say the accrued liability under the unit-credit method, whereas under "projected-benefit" methods the accrued liability is generally greater than the present value of accrued benefits. There are situations, however, in which this generalization does not hold and you should be careful to look at every case on its merits.

While we looked at some post-retirement ancillary benefits in Chapter 3, we have not dealt with them in this chapter so far. Post-retirement ancillary benefits are simply various kinds of death benefits, the valuation of which will be apparent from your study of life contingencies. We shall nonetheless look at some of these as well as other kinds of pre-retirement ancillary benefits in the exercises.

Exercises

4.8.1 ***Bridge Benefit***

A "bridge benefit" is a supplemental early-retirement pension in the form of a temporary life annuity payable until social security (or other governmental pension) benefits begin — or until the death of the pensioner if that occurs first. Suppose that a plan provides a bridge benefit of \$300 per month to any employee who retires before age 62, payable until age 62. Assuming that the service table contains a retirement decrement, derive a formula for computing the present value of such a benefit (don't forget the regular early-retirement benefit, too!).

4.8.2 ***Social-Security-Adjustment Option***

Under this option an employee retiring before age 62 (or whenever the governmental pension is assumed to begin) gets a larger benefit to begin with and a smaller benefit later on. In particular, the social security benefit at age 62 is estimated as an annual amount SS; then an initial benefit amount B' is determined such that the combination of a temporary life annuity of B' per year until age 62 and an amount $B' - SS$ beginning at age 62 and continuing for life is actuarially equivalent to the early retirement pension otherwise available.

(a) If B is the early retirement benefit payable at age x (< 62) in the normal form of life annuity, write a formula for B' in terms of SS, B, and $N_{62}^{(12)}/N_x^{(12)}$.

(b) In your answer to (a) did you allow for the possibility that

$$B < SS\,\frac{N_x^{(12)} - N_{62}^{(12)}}{N_x^{(12)}}\ ?$$

(c) If the normal retirement age is 65 and you are given a table of early-retirement factors, can you compute the amount of the social security adjustment option without additional tables? (Answer is "yes", but show how to do it!)

4.8.3 ***"Joint-and-Survivor" Options***

(a) A plan provides that any retiring employee can elect to have his pension be paid in the form of a 100% joint-and-survivor ("last-survivor") annuity. If the present value of the optional form is to be the same as that of the life annuity commencing at age x, by what factor must the life-annuity amount be multiplied?

(b) Derive a formula for the actuarial-equivalence factor for the "contingent-annuitant" option under which the pensioner receives a constant life annuity regardless of the survival of the contingent annuitant, but if the pensioner dies and is survived by the contingent annuitant then a fraction p is continued for the life of the latter. Show that this option factor is always less than 1.

(c) If $f(1)$ is the factor derived in part (a) above, and $f(p)$ is the factor derived in part (b), show that

$$\frac{1}{f(p)} = (1-p)\frac{1}{f(0)} + p\frac{1}{f(1)} ; \tag{4.8.1}$$

in other words, you can get the value of the $p\%$ factor by "harmonic interpolation" between 0% and 100%.

(d) What is the option factor for converting from life annuity to the "pure" joint-and-survivor form, under which the annuity reduces to a fraction p of its original value upon the death of *either* the primary or the joint annuitant? If $p = ½$, under what conditions will this option factor be greater than 1? If you are given $f(1)$ from part (a) above, can you compute the option factor for the pure J&S form with $p < 1$?

(e) Express the 100% J&S factor for the case of continuous annuities in terms of integrals and then take the partial derivative of the factor with respect to $\delta = log(1+i)$. Is this derivative positive or negative? Can you tell the effect on the value of the factor of an increase in the assumed interest rate i?

4.8.4 ***Continuous Functions***

A certain plan has only two pre-retirement ancillary benefits: a flat death benefit of $1,000, and a severance benefit of $500. Your service table has only two decrements, death and severance.

(a) What is the present value at age $x < y$ of all pre-retirement ancillary benefits, assuming payment at the end of the year?

(b) Write an expression in the form of an integral for the present value of all ancillary benefits if payment is immediate. How would you approximate this integral using functions from your service table?

4.8.5 ***Automatic Spouse's Benefit***

This is a pre-retirement ancillary benefit wich provides that if the employee dies after reaching his earliest retirement age, but before actually retiring, he will be presumed to have retired just before dying and to have elected a contingent-annuitant option with p continued to the spouse.

(a) Assuming that the early retirement factor is $E(z)$, write a general expression for the present value of this ancillary benefit.

(b) If mortality is the only decrement and the accrued benefit is the same at all ages, and if the early retirement and joint-and-survivor benefits are actuarially equivalent on the same assumptions as used to fund the plan, can you simplify your answer to part (a) above?

4.8.6 ***Disability Retirement***

The retirement pension which we have been discussing so far in this book is sometimes called an "age-retirement" pension to distinguish it from disability retirement, which is particularly prevalent in the plans for governmental employees and for members of labor unions.

(a) Suppose a plan provides a disability pension payable for life equal to the unreduced accrued benefit, and that age retirement is assumed to occur only at age y. Write an expression for the present value of the disability benefit.

(b) Another plan provides a disability benefit equal to the regular early-retirement benefit (actuarially reduced). Write an expression for the present value of this disability benefit assuming that there is a retirement decrement in the service table. (Note the symmetry of the retirement and disability decrements. Does it make sense to assume age retirement at age y while using a special decrement for disability?)

(c) A third plan pays no disability pensions as such, but allows the age-retirement benefit to accrue as long as the employee is disabled (and receiving benefits under a separate disability program). What is the present value of this "benefit" at age x? Could we simply treat disabled employees as actives in determining the cost of such a plan?

4.8.7 ***Long-Term Disability (LTD)***

A self-insured LTD plan provides that if a participant in the plan becomes totally and permanently disabled he or she will receive a lifetime pension equal to one-half of current salary; there are no other benefits payable under the plan.

(a) How would you express the cost of such a plan under the unit-credit cost method? What is the "accrued benefit" under such a plan?

(b) How would you compute the cost of such a plan under the aggregate cost method?

4.8.8 ***Termination Indemnity***

In Mexico and many other countries, outside North America, employers are required by law to pay terminating employees a lump-sum cash severance benefit. Suppose the amount of the severance payment is computed as one month's pay for each year of service and that the employer wishes to set up a proper cost accrual for this benefit on his books.

(a) How would you determine the cost of this benefit using the unit-credit cost method?

(b) How would you determine it under the entry-age-normal cost method?

(c) Would there be any gain or loss due to interest?

4.8.9 ***More Joint-and-Survivor***

(a) Assume all annuities are paid continuously and write an expression for the 100% joint-and-survivor option factor analogous to that of exercise 4.8.3.

(b) Show that there exists some average value of μ_x — call it $\bar{\mu}$ — such that $\bar{a}_x = \dfrac{1}{\bar{\mu} + \delta}$. (Hint: express $\bar{a}_x$ and $\bar{A}_x$ as integrals and let $\bar{\mu}$ be the average value weighted by ${}_tp_x\, v^t$.)

(c) Assume that μ_x is constant for all ages and rewrite your answer to part (a) in terms of μ and δ. Call the factor $f(\mu, \delta)$.

(d) Evaluate $f(\mu, \delta)$ for $\mu = .025$ and $\delta = .065$. (Answer: 0.82.)

(e) Derive an expression for $\dfrac{\partial f}{\partial \mu}$. What is the effect on $f(\mu, \delta)$ of an increase in the assumed mortality rate?

Chapter 5

Assets

5.1 *What Are They?*

Since the very beginning (in Chapter 2) of our discussion of how to determine the cost of pension plans, we have implied the existence of a "fund" which has a value F_t at time t, which increases each year by the addition of "interest" and "contributions", and which is depleted by payments of benefits and other expenses (see equation (5.1.1), below). The benefits and expenses are certainly well defined quantities but we have so far not taken the trouble to define F_t and "contributions" precisely. We have not done so because it is not easy!

If the "fund" is an entity whose books are kept separate from those of the employer's own enterprise, then we can at least define the "contributions" unambiguously by simply counting the dollars that are received by the fund from the employer (and/or the employees). But if the "fund" is merely a reserve on the books of the employer, as it often is, then the net increase in the value of that reserve from year to year, after benefit payments are made, may be called either "interest" *or* "contributions", or any combination of the two, unless we arbitrarily define one or the other. Actuaries are likely to resolve the issue by saying that "interest" is computed using the rate which has been assumed for cost purposes, and that the remaining increase in the book reserve is the "contribution." But there is no unique way to differentiate between the two. This symmetry between interest and contributions in book-reserve plans, incidentally, is the reason many actuaries determine the cost of such plans assuming an interest rate of zero. Employers generally are not used to reserves which bear interest anyway, and do not care whether the actuary divides the cost into components, so this approach often works well — although it does not produce the same results as a positive interest rate.

Usually, however, there is a pension fund which is separate from the employer's business, so we do know precisely what the "benefits" and "contributions" are in a given year. This means that we can define interest in terms of two year-end fund values, or conversely we can define the fund value recursively with reference to the interest. The value of the fund, in turn, is a fundamental component of the determination of the cost of the plan: There is not a single cost method or type of plan so far discussed where the cost of the plan is independent of the value of the assets. In fact, a stronger statement can be made: The method of valuing assets is an integral part of the cost method. Change the definition of F_t and you necessarily change both the cost and the amounts by which the cost is adjusted in future years through amortization of gains and losses.

What are the restrictions on the definition of F_t? We know that when the plan is first established there are no assets, so $F_0 = 0$. And we know that from year to year the sequence of values $\{F_t\}$ should follow the recursion relation

$$F_{t+1} = F_t + I + C - B, \tag{5.1.1}$$

but are there any other restraints?

One school of thought says that the sole function of the pension fund is to generate investment income. Therefore, according to this point of view, the value of assets at any time is simply equal to the discounted value of future investment income (dividends, rents, interest on bonds, etc.) using the assumed interest rate i. This argument is bolstered by the notion that when plans are young contributions and investment income exceed benefit payments, and that eventually a plan reaches a state of maturity, or equilibrium, in which the contributions and the investment income exactly equal the benefit payments. Throughout the early stages of growth and into the period of maturity the plan is indifferent to the value that the actuary may place on the assets: Whether he places a small value on them and assumes a large interest rate or he puts a large value on the assets and assumes a small interest rate, it is of no concern to the plan. If the actuary says the fund is worth $20 million, but on the open market the assets could only be sold for $10 million, who cares? The assets do not have to be sold and the investment income continues.

The fallacy of that argument is that pension plans, like living things, are born, grow to maturity, and eventually die — either suddenly and unexpectedly (as through bankruptcy of the employer) or after a period of decrepitude and slow decline. In either case the death of the plan means the end of the period of equilibrium: Benefit payments must ultimately come, at least in part, out of the corpus of the fund itself. In other words, there will come a time when assets will have to be liquidated — turned to cash — in order to pay benefits. This follows logically from the fact that if all assumptions work out exactly, when the last pensioner draws his last check from the fund the fund will be exhausted: Sometime between now and then assets will have to be liquidated. Thus, we see that the market or cash value of the pension fund must enter into the determination of the cost of the plan, because in that last year the proper value of assets for purposes of determining cost must be the cash or market value, and not any arbitrary value. Furthermore, it is not sufficient to approach the last days of a pension plan determining the cost on the basis of an asset value which is wildly out of line with its market value, because this could necessitate large shifts in value toward the end, and a consequent distortion of the cost of the plan.

Therefore, we may state the following axiom of asset valuation for pension cost purposes: The sequence of asset values from year to year — a "time series" — should periodically intersect the time series of market values. The frequency of crossing of the two series is a matter of actuarial judgment — clearly the two should be in very close touch when a plan is in decline, for example — but there is no logical defense for an asset valuation method which totally ignores market value. Nevertheless, some sort of "book value" is often desirable so as to iron out purely random fluctuations in market value which would otherwise cause random fluctuations in cost.

In the case of bonds or other debt instruments held at amortized, or discounted, value, there is very little problem in assuring that the sequence of book values will coincide with the sequence of market values, because in the lifetime of every such investment there are at least two points where the book and market values coincide — at purchase and at maturity — so the sequence of book values can never get too far away from the sequence of market values. In other words, debt instruments are different in kind from other investments such as common stocks, real estate, and certain kinds of insurance contracts, in that *there is always a point at which you get your money back!*

The problem of asset valuation, then, arises primarily in situations where a pension fund has an *equity* interest in some enterprise — whether through common stock, real estate ownership, participation in mutual funds or other pooled trusts, or ownership of group annuity contracts with no definite maturity date — or direct ownership of real property.

Exercises

5.1.1 A hypothetical pension fund is invested in a mixture of high-quality stocks and bonds. The employer, a large and stable public utility, engages you as actuary and says the following: "Whereas

(a) similar portfolios of investments have demonstrably over long periods of time yielded rates of return of about 7% per year; and whereas

(b) there is no plausible circumstance under which our company could go out of business, so the future flow of contributions is assured; therefore,

(c) we propose to place a value on our pension fund equal to the previous year's value, adjusted for contributions and benefit payments, credited with interest at 7%" (which is also your assumed rate, let us say).

What do you think of this proposal? List on a piece of paper the arguments you would make for or against it.

5.1.2 Select a large industrial corporation with publicly traded shares and determine the current rate of dividend payments on each share. Next, choose a long-term interest rate (say, the current yield to maturity on long-term government bonds) and compute the lump-sum value of all future dividends, assuming a reasonable rate of growth in the amount of the dividends and that they continue into perpetuity. Finally, compare your value for each share with that currently quoted on a major stock exchange, and with values of those shares over the past few years. What is the value of each share if the growth rate assumed is close to your assumed interest rate? What assumptions must the traders of these shares be making as to future dividends and interest rates in order to arrive at the traded price of the shares?

5.1.3 Suppose a plan participates in a pooled trust fund which invests entirely in bonds. A daily "unit value" is computed by dividing the market value of the portfolio by the number of units, or shares, outstanding. All transactions in and out of the trust are recorded in numbers of units. Any of the plans participating in the trust may determine its market value at any time by multiplying the number of units it holds by the unit value. No investment income or maturity of principal is paid out directly to a plan, but rather is reinvested and affects only the unit value.

(a) Can a given plan value its holdings in this bond fund at discounted value? If so how would this be accomplished?

(b) Are holdings of this kind debt instruments? When does repayment of principal to a particular participating plan occur?

(c) May the pooled fund value *its* holdings at discounted value? If it chose to do so, would that change your answer to part (a) above?

(d) Learn from your correct answers to the foregoing that it is not the type of investment held by a pooled fund that determines the type of investment held by the plans which invest in the pooled fund: Each *plan* has only an *equity* interest in the pool, whether the pool's investments are debt or equity!

5.1.4 *Amortized Value of Bonds*

Consider a bond maturing at par n years after issue, with semi-annual coupons $c/2$ for each \$1 of face amount. Suppose a pension plan purchases such a bond at issue paying a price P per unit face amount, to yield $i^{(2)}$ (bond yield rates are always quoted in terms of $i^{(2)}$).

(a) Show that purchase price may be expressed as

$$P = c a_{\overline{n}|}^{(2)} + v^n = 1 + (c - i^{(2)}) a_{\overline{n}|}^{(2)} . \tag{5.1.2}$$

(b) Suppose the bond is to be valued for pension-cost purposes on the valuation date at time t, a fractional year s after purchase ($0 < s < ½$). Show that its discounted value is

$$\begin{aligned} V_t &= (1+i)^s \left[1 + (c - i^{(2)}) a_{\overline{n}|}^{(2)} \right] \\ &= P + \left[(1+i)^s - 1 \right] P \end{aligned} \tag{5.1.3}$$

(the second term is called "accrued interest" in financial statements).

(c) What is the value of the bond at time $t+1$? Show that the two values are related by

$$V_{t+1} = V_t(1+i) - c(1+i)^s s_{\overline{1}|}^{(2)} \tag{5.1.4}$$

(d) A certain government bond carries a coupon of 8-3/8% payable semi-annually on February 15 and August 15; and matures at par on August 15, 2000. A plan purchased \$100,000 face amount of the bond on February 23, 1984, paying to the seller \$93,313 plus \$184 accrued interest. What was the amortized value on February 23, 1984? (Answer: \$93,497.) What is the yield to maturity? (Answer: 9.169%.) An actuarial valuation was made on November 1, 1984; what was the amortized value of these bonds on that date? (Answer: \$95,195.)

5.2 Smoothed Market Value

In section 5.1 we demonstrated that the "actuarial value" of assets — i.e., the value used for purposes of determining the cost of the plan — must bear some relationship to the market value. In particular, if $\{M_t\}$ is the time-series of market values, the time series $\{F_t\}$ of actuarial values should be defined in such a way as periodically to intersect $\{M_t\}$ — as it does, for example, when we hold bonds to maturity and let F_t equal the amortized value. For non-debt investments we have no such obvious smoothing method because the only value known is the market value, so we have to address two central questions: (1) is it *ever* proper to value non-debt investments at other than fair market value?, and (2) if it is, what smoothing technique should be used? Let us take question (1) first.

No matter which actuarial cost method we are using, the cost assigned to a given year has a component which may be described as amortization of previous actuarial gains. With the "individual" methods (unit-credit, entry-age-normal, individual-level-premium) there is an explicit amortization component, while under "aggregate" methods (frozen-initial-liability, attained-age-normal, aggregate) a portion of the normal cost is attributable to amortization of gains (see, for example, equations (2.6.10) and (2.9.8)). The gains in turn have in each case a component attributable to "interest" which we may represent in the typical case as follows

$$G_t^I = I - (iF_t + I_C - I_B) . \tag{5.2.1}$$

We have seen interest gains of this type often before (equations (2.2.7), (2.3.10), (2.4.8), (2.5.12), (2.6.10), (2.8.3), (2.9.8), and (2.10.7), for example). Depending on the amortization period, some portion of G_t^I is subtracted from other components of the total cost. Note that if i' is the rate actually earned on the fund, that is to say,

$$M_{t+1} = M_t(1 + i') + (C + I'_C) - (B + I'_B) , \tag{5.2.2}$$

where primed values indicate interest computed at rate i' , and if we define $F_t = M_t$, we have from equations (5.1.1) and (5.2.2):

$$I = i' M_t + I'_C - I'_B , \tag{5.2.3}$$

so the interest gain may be written

$$G_t^I = (i' - i)M_t + (I'_C - I_C) - (I'_B - I_B) . \tag{5.2.4}$$

The normal amortization or spreading of this interest gain is thus equivalent to counting, for cost purposes only, a fraction of the difference between the investment return computed at the real rate of return i' and that which we would have had if we had actually earned rate i. Equation (5.2.4) shows, furthermore, that the interest gain is roughly proportional to the market value of the fund M_t. This means that, as the fund grows, so does G_t^I for a given fluctuation $(i' - i)$. For an immature plan the amortization of G_t^I may be just a small fraction of the total cost, but for a mature plan it may loom very large indeed.

For example, imagine a plan whose total cost is 5% of covered payroll and whose fund has a market value of 300% of covered payroll. If gains are being amortized over five years, a fluctuation in actual rate of return of ten percentage points would mean an interest gain of roughly 30% of covered pay, which would affect the cost by roughly 20% of 30%, or 6% of covered payroll — more than 100% of the previous year's cost! A fluctuation of only five points would still affect the cost by 60% and even a fluctuation of one point would cause a cost change of roughly 12%. In such a case, given even minor random fluctuations in stock and bond prices, valuation at market value would result in an annoying volatility in the cost of the plan.

In sum, there are situations where the normal damping of $(i' - i)$ through amortization of the gains is not enough: If we want year-to-year stability in pension cost we have to apply extra damping, which means we have to use an artificial asset value in place of the actual market value.

So much for question (1). With respect to question (2) — what smoothing method to use — there is no single correct answer. First of all, the nature of the market for the investment must be taken into account: Does $\{M_t\}$ fluctuate widely? Does it have a stationary mean? If not, what is the secular trend of the mean? And so forth. The truth is, you do not know the answer to these questions — if you did, you would be rich, because you would have mathematical tool for successfully "playing the market." There have been many attempts to fit a time-series model to the stock market, for example, but to the author's knowledge none has been successful over a long period of years.* A glance forward at Figure 6.5.3 will show why.

There is a strong bias in accounting theory toward holding assets at original cost, and this method often works well for actuarial purposes, too, especially since the accounting reports of bank-trustees (for example) usually are based on original cost. As long as the portfolio does not turn over too rapidly, original-cost will produce a smooth series of actuarial values from year to year. On the other hand, if the market value of assets is moving rapidly in one direction (e.g., a prolonged "bull" or "bear" market), the turnover of the portfolio may be too slow to catch up, and the actuarial value may deviate too much from fair market. How much is too much is a matter for debate, but in the U.S. the Internal Revenue Service has said (roughly) that "too much"

*If you wish to try it yourself, you will find a valuable reference in *Time Series Analysis* by Box and Jenkins; Holden-Day, 1970.

means outside a "corridor" of plus or minus 20% of market value. A weakness of the original-cost method, then, is that if we set no such "corridor" around market value, we have freed $\{F_t\}$ from $\{M_t\}$, which violates the tenet of section 5.1; but if we set a corridor with rigid walls, we may bump into a wall and cause a sudden write-down or write-up in actuarial value, with consequent loss of smoothness in cost.

Another approach is to ignore original cost altogether and use an actuarial value of assets equal to a moving average of several years' market values. The averaging period would depend on your preference for smoothness over fit: If you average over just one year you are in effect setting actuarial value equal to current market value; if you average over a long period you run the risk of wandering too far away from current market.

In any case, when we use average market value, we do so in an attempt to average out random fluctuations in stock prices (for example). We do not want to average out permanent changes in principal value — such as contributions or benefit payments, so we cannot simply average the value of the fund for the last n year-ends. What we do want to dampen out are purely random fluctuations in the effective per-share price of the entire fund. The effective per-share price is, of course, the market value at any time divided by the number of "shares" outstanding (which is arbitrary in the case of a plan which invests all its own assets). Let this unit-value or share-value be denoted by P_t.

We may imagine that P_t is composed of a true underlying price $\bar{P}_t$ plus a random fluctuation Q_t:

$$P_t = \bar{P}_t + Q_t . \tag{5.2.5}$$

The sum over n years is

$$\sum_{t=1}^{n} P_t = \sum_{t=1}^{n} \bar{P}_t + \sum_{t=1}^{n} Q_t . \tag{5.2.6}$$

Since Q_t is assumed to be a random variable with mean zero, the Law of Large Numbers assures us that for any small positive number

$$\lim_{n\to\infty} Pr\{|\sum_{1}^{n} \frac{Q_t}{n}| > \epsilon\} = 0 , \tag{5.2.7}$$

so we can get $\frac{1}{n}\sum_{1}^{n}\bar{P}_t$ to any desired degree of accuracy from

$$\frac{1}{n}\sum_{1}^{n}\bar{P}_t \approx \frac{1}{n}\sum_{1}^{n}P_t , \tag{5.2.8}$$

simply by taking the value of n large enough. The trouble is, we don't want to know $\frac{1}{n}\sum_{1}^{n}\bar{P}_t$: We want a single value of $\bar{P}_t$. If the mean, or "true", price $\bar{P}_t$ were constant we would have

$$\bar{P}_t = \frac{1}{n}\sum_{k=t-n+1}^{t}\bar{P}_k = \frac{1}{n}\sum_{t-n+1}^{t}P_k\,, \tag{5.2.9}$$

which would be very convenient because it would mean we could get a particular value of the "true" price by averaging the actual per-share prices over a sufficiently long period. In order to use a moving-average approach, then, we must *assume* that $\bar{P}_t$ is stationary.

Now let us assume that our pension fund has 100% efficient cash management, so that we always have just enough cash around to pay benefits and expenses, but all else is invested at the end of each year. By this means we can assume that all transactions take place only at intervals of one year. Let K_t be the investable cash at time t. Then the market value at time t is obviously the sum of all units or shares purchased over the years, multiplied by the current price:

$$M_t = P_t\sum_{m=0}^{t}\frac{K_m}{P_m}\,. \tag{5.2.10}$$

The actuarial value, however, is based on the mean share price:

$$F_t = \bar{P}_t\sum_{0}^{t}\frac{K_m}{P_m} = \frac{1}{n}\sum_{k=t-n+1}^{t}P_k\sum_{m=0}^{t}\frac{K_m}{P_m}\,, \tag{5.2.11}$$

where we have used the approximation of equation (5.2.9). That is to say, we are going to use an n-year average price as our definition of the real per-share value at time t. Equation (5.2.11) may be put into a more understandable form as follows, by incorporating equation (5.2.10):

$$F_t = \underbrace{\frac{1}{n}(M_{t-n+1} + \ldots + M_t)}_{\text{average market value}} + \underbrace{\frac{1}{n}\sum_{k=t-n+1}^{t-1}\sum_{m=k+1}^{t}K_m\frac{P_k}{P_m}}_{\text{adjustment for cash flow}}\,. \tag{5.2.12}$$

Equation (5.2.12) shows that a simple average of market values, without adjustment for contributions and benefits, is not generally correct.

We usually do not have the unit values P_t for all prior years unless the entire fund is invested in a single pooled fund of some type, and it is a nuisance to have to keep track of them — or to reconstruct them for all prior years when we want to switch to a moving-average asset-valuation method. We generally do, however, have the last n years' financial reports, each of which reconciles the current and prior market values in this fashion:

$$M_{t+1} = M_t + K_{t+1} + A_{t+1} , \tag{5.2.13}$$

where K_t represents the actual net cash flow at time t and A_t represents net appreciation (i.e., any increase in market value not attributable to contributions, benefits, expenses, or investment income). If we let N_t represent the number of units in the fund at time t then

$$N_{t+1} = N_t + \frac{K_{t+1}}{P_{t+1}} . \tag{5.2.14}$$

i.e., the net number of units added at $t+1$ must be those purchased by the net cash flow K_{t+1}. Thus, by definition, we have

$$\begin{aligned} M_{t+1} &= P_{t+1}N_{t+1} = P_{t+1}N_t + K_{t+1} \\ &= P_tN_t \cdot \frac{P_{t+1}}{P_t} + K_{t+1} = M_t \frac{P_{t+1}}{P_t} + K_{t+1} . \end{aligned} \tag{5.2.15}$$

Therefore, combining equation (5.2.13) with (5.2.15), we get

$$\frac{A_{t+1}}{M_t} = \frac{P_{t+1}}{P_t} - 1 , \tag{5.2.16}$$

which shows that P_t is just an index of the rate of appreciation of the fund from year to year.

Since only ratios of P_t are significant, we can set $P_{t-n+1} = 1$ arbitrarily and run up the rest of the n values by the recursion relationship

$$\frac{P_{t+1}}{P_t} = 1 + \frac{A_{t+1}}{M_t} , \tag{5.2.17}$$

using values of A_t and M_t as given in the financial reports of the fund.

Finally, from equation (5.2.10) we get

$$\frac{M_t}{P_t} \equiv N_t = \sum_{m=0}^{t} \frac{K_m}{P_m} , \tag{5.2.18}$$

which, when combined with equation (5.2.11), yields

$$F_t = \bar{P}_t \sum_{m=0}^{t} \frac{K_m}{P_m} = \bar{P}_t N_t = \left(\frac{1}{n} \sum_{k=0}^{n-1} P_{t-k} \right) \frac{M_t}{P_t} . \tag{5.2.19}$$

This means we can achieve the result of equation (5.2.12) by the following simple process:

(1) Set $P_{t-n+1} = 1$;

(2) Compute $P_{t-n+2}, \ldots, P_t$ using (5.2.17);

(3) Plug these into (5.2.19) to get F_t.

Let us now see how this method would work using an actual numerical example. Suppose t is January 1, 1989, and we want to compute F_t on a four-year average basis. The financial statements of the fund are summarized in Table 5.2.1. Our first step is to compute a table of hypothetical unit values, setting the value on 1/1/86 arbitrarily equal to 1 and computing the rest by recursion, as in Table 5.2.2.

Table 5.2.1
Summary of Three Years' Financial Statements

		1986		*1987*		*1988*
Market value 1/1		$150,000		$196,500		$238,000
Transactions						
Contributions	$ 65,000		$ 62,000		$ 66,000	
Benefit payments	(22,000)		(24,000)		(25,000)	
Expenses	(6,500)		(7,000)		(7,500)	
Interest and Dividends	8,000		7,500		7,000	
		44,500		38,500		40,500
Appreciation						
Realized gains (losses)	(2,000)		6,000		(8,000)	
Increase (decrease) in unrealized appreciation	4,000		(3,000)		(42,500)	
		2,000		3,000		(50,500)
Market value 12/31		$196,500		$238,000		$228,000

Table 5.2.2
Computation of Unit Values

Time k	A_k	M_k	$P_k = P_{k-1}(1 + A_k/M_{k-1})$
1/1/86		$150,000	1.000000
1/1/87	$ 2,000	196,500	1.013333
1/1/88	3,000	238,000	1.028804
1/1/89	− 50,500	228,000	.810507
Average			.963161

Then $N_t = M_t/P_t = 228{,}000/.810507 = 281{,}305$; and $F_t = .963161(281{,}305) = 270{,}942$.

Remember that the method we have just outlined is valid only if the "real" or mean value of each yearly share price is constant for all years: If it increases steadily, decreases steadily, or fluctuates in any predictable way, then the method is invalid, because in such cases a linear average of P_t is not an unbiased estimate of the mean of the *random variable* P_t.

There are countless smoothing methods in use other than original-cost and moving-average-market. Some combine the two approaches by taking into account both original cost and current market value. Others write up original cost by an assumed rate of appreciation. The diversity of opinion on the matter is well displayed in Jackson and Hamilton's paper "The Valuation of Pension Fund Assets" (TSA XX, 1969), which discusses some thirty or forty different methods.

Exercises

5.2.1 Verify equation (5.2.12).

5.2.2 Using the example of Table 5.2.1, compute the average market value without adjustment for cash flow. (Answer: $203,125.) Do you see why the cash-flow adjustment is necessary?

5.2.3 Is our assumption that assets will yield a total rate of return *i* consistent with the assumption that $\bar{P}_t$ is stationary? If not, what adjustment would be called for in our moving-average technique?

5.3 The New-Money Method

This is one name for the method used by most insurance companies to allocate investment earnings among group-annuity contractholders (others are the "investment-generation method" and the "investment-year method"). So, before we can go on to discuss how to place a value on various types of insurance contracts for purposes of computing pension cost, we have to gain a thorough understanding of the workings of the new-money method.

Unlike savings accounts, which generally credit interest at an aggregate rate to all the depositors' accounts, group annuity contracts credit interest at rates which depend on the pattern of deposits over time, so each contract has its own rate of interest — called the *case rate* — different from other contracts of the same type. The new-money method was originally introduced in the early 1960's because insurance companies wanted to be able to credit the higher rates of interest available for new investments at that time, rather than to continue to credit a lower aggregate rate to all contractholders. The new-money method is far superior to the aggregate from the standpoint of the insurance company because it helps avoid the distortions which crop up when interest rates move either up or down: When an aggregate rate is used there is a tendency for contractholders to want to deposit more money when new-money rates are lower than the aggregate rate, and conversely, to withdraw money when new-money rates are higher than the aggregate rate.

There is no single, uniform, new-money method used by all insurance companies, each company having its own approach and peculiarities, but they all rest on the same logical foundation. We shall look at an idealized and simplified version of the new-money method, but every actuary should take pains to inform himself as the the actual workings of the method in any particular case because those details will affect either (a) the actuary's assumed investment return, or (b) the value he places on the contracts themselves. At the heart of the new-money method is the fact that the general assets of insurance companies are invested primarily in debt instruments — bonds and mortgages — ***which are held at amortized book value*** and which the insurer wants to *allocate* equitably to each contract.

If these debt instruments were valued at market, as are the bond "separate accounts" often attached to group-annuity contracts or in the pooled bond funds offered by large corporate trustees (and described in exercise 5.1.3), then transactions in and out of the fund would be based on the unit market value in effect at the time of the transaction. In other words, every time there was a deposit or a withdrawal from a pooled bond fund, the entire fund would be converted to cash, in effect, and then reinvested after the transaction; so there would be no inequity between participants in the fund who invested or withdrew more in one year than another.

The reasons for insurance companies holding their investments at amortized book, rather than market, value are rooted in history and law rather than business necessity, but one incentive is that when you value bonds at market the year-to-year return is volatile and often negative, whereas using amortized value you achieve a smooth series of positive rates of return.

Suppose we have a fund of money whose book value at any time t is F_t, and that this fund is to be allocated among n plans which participate in its maintenance. For the moment, assume also that none of the n plans is allowed to withdraw totally from participation so that we have exactly n segments for the entire period under discussion.

Assume furthermore that all the investments are in annual-coupon bonds which mature at par and are not callable. If the coupon rate is denoted by c and the yield to maturity is y, and if the bonds mature k years in the future, the price of the bond may be computed by

$$P(y,c,k) \;=\; c a_{\overline{k|}y} + (1+y)^{-k} \;=\; 1 + (c-y) a_{\overline{k|}}. \tag{5.3.1}$$

If we invest \$1 in such bonds at time 0, we purchase $1/P(y,c,k)$ of face amount which produces an annual coupon-interest payment of $c/P(y,c,k)$ — cash which we can reinvest the following year or use to pay benefits and expenses. At time k, the bond matures and produces $1/P(y,c,k)$ in cash, which can also be used for benefits, expenses, or reinvestment. Suppose for the moment that maturity is several years away so we can see what happens in the meantime.

The book value of this investment at time 0 is the same as the market value: \$1. At time 1 the book value becomes

$$\frac{P(y,c,k-1)}{P(y,c,k)} \;=\; 1 + y - c/P(y,c,k)\,. \tag{5.3.2}$$

Also at time 1 we have cash in hand of $c/P(y,c,k)$ so that the total value at time 1 of our \$1 investment is $1+y$ — just as we intended when we demanded the yield rate y in the first place! Thus a \$1 investment at time 0 produces (a) a cash coupon of $c/P(y,c,k)$, which may be spent or reinvested, and (b) a capital gain or asset writeup of $y - c/P(y,c,k)$. Only the *cash,* of course, is available for reinvestment — you cannot invest paper assets.

At time 2, the same \$1 originally invested at time 0 would generate cash income of $c/P(y,c,k)$, the same as the first year, and a writeup of

$$\frac{P(y,c,k-2) - P(y,c,k-1)}{P(y,c,k)}\,.$$

The process would continue in this fashion until time k, when (1) the final coupon $c/P(y,c,k)$ would be received, (2) the final writeup of $\dfrac{1 - P(y,c,1)}{P(y,c,k)}$ would be made, *and* (3) the bond would mature and pay back the face amount of $1/P(y,c,k)$.

Now, if the original investment had been $\$K_0$ instead of $1 and if each of the n plans had contributed K_0^j in cash, where $K_0 = \sum_{j=1}^{n} K_0^j$, then the book value of the entire fund at time 1 — which we shall denote by F_1 — would be the sum of

(a) the original investment $\sum_{j=1}^{n} K_0^j = F_0$;

(b) the first-year capital gain $\sum_1^n K_0^j \left[y - c/P(y,c,k) \right]$;

and

(c) the investment income $\sum_1^n K_0^j \, c/P(y,c,k)$;

or, $F_1 = \sum_1^n F_0^j (1+y)$, where $F_0^j = K_0^j$ . . . quite simple.

But at time 1, complication sets in. Each plan j makes a contribution C_1^j and pays out benefits B_1^j. Also, we get income of $I_1 = F_0 c/P(y,c,k)$, so the net cash available for reinvestment (assuming that none of the bonds has yet matured) is $K_1 = C_1 - B_1 + I_1$ — that is, it is available for reinvestment if it is positive! If it is negative, not only can we not invest it, but we must sell some of the bonds to raise cash.

Can we make the assumption that $C_1 - B_1 + I_1$ is non-negative? Probably so, because we have already assumed that there are no wholesale withdrawals of entire plans, and we are dealing with a supposedly sophisticated insurance company managing the pool: We can safely assume that the insurance company is able to anticipate its cash requirements without having to liquidate assets, because it has only routine benefit payments to make and these are pretty easily planned for, especially if there is a large group of plans participating. Also, it does not make sense to value bonds at book unless one intends to hold them until maturity, which is possible only if the portfolio generates enough cash without premature sales. Let us therefore assume that the net cash flow of the entire fund is always positive. By the way, this does not necessarily mean that we are assuming the value of the entire fund is always *increasing:* If there were no new contributions the insurance company should still see to it that maturing investments and interest income provide enough cash to handle benefit payments and expenses, even though the value of the entire fund in this situation would be decreasing.

We now reinvest K_1 in new bonds whose parameters y, c, and k are not necessarily those of the bonds purchased at time 0. Their price is $P(y_1,c_1,k_1)$ and we purchase $K_1/P(y_1,c_1,k_1)$ of face amount, so that at time 2 we have new coupon income of $c_1 K_1/P(y_1,c_1,k_1)$ and new capital gains of $y_1 K_1 - c_1 K_1/P(y_1,c_1,k_1)$ — in addition to those generated by the initial investment of K_0. The portion of K_1 attributable to plan j may be taken as

$$K_1^j = C_1^j - B_1^j + K_0^j c_0 / P(y_0, c_0, k_0) \; . \tag{5.3.3}$$

To help us keep track of all this, let us separate the portfolio by time of investment: Let F_{mt} be the portion of F_t generated by the net cash flow at time m, which we have called K_m, and let F^j_{mt} be the portion of F_{mt} allocated to plan j. Picture F_{mt} as a triangular matrix with a separate column for each year of investment, like this:

		Time of investment, m						
		0	1	2	3	4	.	.
Time of valuation, t	0	F_{00}						
	1	F_{01}	F_{11}					
	2	F_{02}	F_{12}	F_{22}				
	3	F_{03}	F_{13}	F_{23}	F_{33}			
	4	F_{04}	F_{14}	F_{24}	F_{34}	F_{44}		
	.	...	...	...	...	...	...	
	.	...	...	...	...	...	...	...

Now $K_0 \equiv F_{00}$ identically, and we know what the initial deposit of each plan was, namely K^j_0, so the portfolio at time 0 could have been allocated in only one way:

$$F^j_{00} = K^j_0 \,. \tag{5.3.4}$$

This gives us the top entry in the triangular matrix F^j_{mt}. In order to define the allocation method completely we need two more rules: one for computing the diagonal entries $F^j_{mm} = K^j_m$, and another for carrying F^j_{mt} forward to $F^j_{m,t+1}$. Let us tackle the second rule first.

The cash K^j_m invested at time m is carried on the books at time $t \le m + k_m$ at amortized book value F^j_{mt}, so that at time $t+1$ it has grown to

$$F^j_{m,t+1} = F^j_{mt}(1+y_m) - c_m F^j_{mm}/P(y_m,c_m,k_m) \,. \tag{5.3.5}$$

Meanwhile, it has generated investment income of $c_m F^j_{mm}/P(y_m,c_m,k_m)$, which adds to the new investable cash, $K_{t+1} \equiv F_{t+1,t+1}$. If $t+1 = m + k_m$ the bonds *mature* to provide $F^j_{mm}/P(y_m,c_m,k_m)$ additional cash, and the portion of assets assigned to time m becomes 0 for all future time. In a real portfolio these maturities would be staggered in time, rather than occurring all at once at time $t+k$, as in our simple model. Therefore, to make it easier to extend our model to more complex situations, let us define a *maturity* or *rollover rate*

$$r_{mt} = \begin{cases} 0 & t \ne m + k_m - 1 \\ 1 & t = m + k_m - 1 \,. \end{cases} \tag{5.3.6}$$

Our rollover rate is just an on-off switch because we purchase only one type of bond each year; in real life the rate would be a fraction between 0 and 1 because the portfolio would acquire bonds of varying durations. Let us also define an *investment-income rate* g_{mt} relative to current book value:

$$g_{mt} = c_m \frac{F^j_{mm}}{F^j_{mt}P(y_m, c_m, k_m)} = \frac{c_m}{P(y_m, c_m, k_m - t + m)} . \tag{5.3.7}$$

Then for all values of $t \geq m$ we can write

$$F^j_{m,t+1} = (1 - r_{mt})F^j_{mt}(1 + y_m - g_{mt})$$
$$\textit{for } m = 0, \ldots, t . \tag{5.3.8}$$

Note that $y_m - g_{mt}$ may be thought of as a writeup, or capital-gain, rate; so (5.3.7) says that $F^j_{m,t+1}$ is that portion of F^j_{mt} which does not roll over, written up to yield y_m.

Now let us turn our attention to the diagonal entries F^j_{mm}. The total coupon income received at time $t+1$ is $\sum_{m=0}^{t} g_{mt}F^j_{mt}$, and, as you can see from (5.3.7), maturing (rolled-over) investments provide $\sum_{m=0}^{t} r_{mt}(1 + y_m - g_{mt})F^j_{mt}$. So the total cash available for investment at time $t+1$ is

$$F^j_{t+1,t+1} = \sum_{m=0}^{t} F^j_{mt}(g_{mt} + r_{mt} + r_{mt}y_m - r_{mt}g_{mt}) + C^j_{t+1} - B^j_{t+1}$$
$$= \sum_{m=0}^{t} F^j_{mt}\left[g_{mt}(1 - r_{mt}) + r_{mt}(1 + y_m)\right] + C^j_{t+1} - B^j_{t+1} . \tag{5.3.9}$$

Note in (5.3.9) that the factors in brackets are characteristic of the entire portfolio: The term $g_{mt}(1 - r_{mt})$ reflects the cash investment income on bonds which have not matured, and the term $r_{mt}(1 + y_m)$ reflects the book value at time $m+1$ of the reinvested maturity proceeds.

Equations (5.3.4), (5.3.6), (5.3.7), (5.3.8), and (5.3.9) fully define the allocation of the fund for all years — i.e., completely describe the new-money method, at least in our simplified setting.

The effective rate of interest credited to the fund share of plan j at time $t+1$, as we said earlier, is called the *case rate,* which we shall denote by $\bar{y}^j_t$. The case rate can be found by dividing the fund balance at $t+1$ (adjusted for contributions and benefits paid at time $t+1$) by the balance at time t:

$$1 + \bar{y}_t^j = \frac{F_{t+1}^j - C_{t+1}^j + B_{t+1}^j}{F_t^j}$$

$$= \frac{\sum_{m=0}^{t} F_{m,t+1}^j + F_{t+1,t+1}^j - C_{t+1}^j + B_{t+1}^j}{\sum_{m=0}^{t} F_{mt}^j}$$

$$= \frac{\sum_{m=0}^{t} F_{mt}^j \left[(1 - r_{mt})(1 + y_m - g_{mt}) + g_{mt}(1 - r_{mt}) + r_{mt}(1 + y_m)\right]}{\sum_{m=0}^{t} F_{mt}^j}$$

$$= \frac{\sum_m F_{mt}^j (1 + y_m)}{\sum_m F_{mt}^j} . \qquad (5.3.10)$$

In other words, the case rate may be defined by

$$\bar{y}_t^j = \frac{\sum_m F_{mt}^j y_m}{\sum_m F_{mt}^j} ; \qquad (5.3.11)$$

i.e., the weighted average yield to maturity. Note that two different plans may have the same allocated share of the fund at time t (e.g., plans A and B may have $\sum_m F_{mt}^A = \sum_m F_{mt}^B$) but their rates of return — their case rates — will be *different* unless $F_{mt}^A = F_{mt}^B$ for all m (except in the trivial case where all the yield rates y_m are the same).

Why do we not simply use equation (5.3.10) to get $F_{m,t+1}^j$, instead of (5.3.3) through (5.3.9)? Because eventually the bonds purchased with K_m^j mature, and the cash received is reinvested in the new year; F_{mt}^j in that year declines to zero; i.e., in our simple model $F_{m,m+k_m} = 0$. But even in a portfolio of staggered maturities there comes a time when all of the assets in a particular investment-year "column" have rolled over into another column.

Now would be a good time to stop and work exercises 5.3.1 through 5.3.3. Note that for Plan B, equation (5.3.3) indicates a *negative* cash flow. In effect, Plan B is required to *sell* bonds back to the pool under the same terms as the pool as a whole is acquiring them. When interest rates are rising, as in parts (a) and (c) of the exercise, the net depositor obtains better overall rates of return (case rates) than the net borrower — and conversely when interest rates fall. This arrangement was agreeable to insurance companies during the 'sixties and 'seventies, because interest rates generally rose during the entire period (see Figure 6.5.2), so new customers — those most likely to be net depositors — got a better deal than older plans in the net-payment stage. With the proliferation of short-term deposit-only contracts ("guaranteed investment contracts", or GICs) with their heavy negative cash flow after the short (three- or five-year) deposit period, more attention is being paid to the proper "segmentation" of contracts according to their liquidity requirements. Another solution to the problem illustrated by exercise 5.3.3 might be to reconsider the wisdom of reinvesting all cash before using it for payments — i.e., reconsider strict allocation of new money according to equation (5.3.9) in favor of allocating only the overall excess of C_{t+1} over B_{t+1} (i.e., using all cash first for benefit payments, then for reinvestment).

Exercises

5.3.1 Prove equation (5.3.2).

5.3.2 Prove the rightmost portion of equation (5.3.7) and thus that g_{mt} is the same for all plans in the fund, i.e., is independent of j.

5.3.3 Assume that the fund is always invested in five-year bonds with 7% annual coupons. Let the new-money rates for the first four years of operation be

Time of Purchase	*Yield to Maturity*
0	5%
1	6%
2	7%
3	8%

(a) Plan A makes net contributions (after benefit payments) of $1,000 at times 0, 1, 2, and 3. What is the fund balance at time 3? (Answer: $4,360.51.) What are the case rates $\bar{y}_0^A$, $\bar{y}_1^A$, *and* $\bar{y}_2^A$? (Answer: 5.00%, 5.52%, and 6.24%.)

(b) Plan B makes a contribution of $5,000 at time 0 but then makes net *withdrawals* of $1,000 at times 1, 2, and 3. What are the case rates $\bar{y}_0^B$, $\bar{y}_1^B$, *and* $\bar{y}_2^B$? (Answer: 5.00%, 4.74%, and 4.25%.)

(c) Now, reverse the sequence of yield rates to make the sequence 8% at time 0, 7% at time 1, and so forth. What would the case rates for the two plans be? (Answer: Plan A — 8.00%, 7.48%, and 6.96%. Plan B — 8.00%, 8.14%, and 8.52%.)

5.3.4 *Market Value*

(a) If F^j_{mt} is the book value at time t of plan j's assets invested at time m, show that the market value at time t of those same assets is

$$F^j_{mm}\frac{P(y_t, c_m, m+k_m-t)}{P(y_m, c_m, k_m)}, \tag{5.3.12}$$

and that the ratio of market value to book value is

$$\varrho_{mt} = \frac{P(y_t, c_m, m+k_m-t)}{P(y_m, c_m, m+k_m-t)} \tag{5.3.13}$$

. . . i.e., is the same for all plans.

(b) Suppose a portion of the bonds purchased at time m were sold at time t and the cash reinvested. How would g_{mt} be affected? If we wanted to let r_{mt} reflect *sales* of bonds as well as maturities, how would its definition (equation (5.3.5)) have to be extended?

(c) Suppose a particular plan j wished to withdraw completely from the pool and receive a distribution of all its assets in *cash*. Show that the proper amount of the distribution would be $\sum_{m=0}^{t} \varrho_{mt} F^j_{mt}$. If every plan wanted to withdraw at time t, would there be sufficient funds if each plan recieved a distribution on this basis?

(d) Compute the market values of the fund balances at time 3 for plans A and B of exercise 5.3.3. Do the results surprise you?

(e) Some insurance companies compute market values by applying a single average value of ϱ to all plans. Is this practice equitable?

5.3.5 The new-money method outlined in this section is sometimes called the *declining-index* approach because F^j_{mt} eventually declines to zero as t increases and the bonds mature or are sold. An alternative (and equivalent) approach is to let maturities and realized gains stay in their original investment-year columns, but to define a matrix of interest rates y_{mt} such that F'_{mt} (the new definition of F_{mt}) increases indefinitely, and such that $\sum_{m=0}^{t} y_{mt} F'_{mt} = \sum_{m=0}^{t} y_m F_{mt}$. This is called the *fixed-index* approach because if all bonds were purchased at par, F'_{mt} would remain constant for all t. Show how to develop the matrix y_{mt}. Is there any advantage to one approach over the other?

5.4 *Group Annuity Contracts*

We shall now look at the problem of assigning a value, for the purpose of determining the cost of a pension plan, to a group annuity contract held as a plan asset. We shall not need to say anything about nonparticipating group annuity contracts (such as ones now known as "guaranteed investment contracts") because these are really a species of bond. It is the participating aspects of group annuity contracts which make them difficult to value.

Group annuity contracts come in many shapes and sizes but may be loosely categorized into three types, namely, deferred-annuity contracts, deposit-administration (DA) contracts, and immediate-participation-guarantee (IPG) contracts.

Under all types of group annuity contracts annuities are purchased (otherwise they wouldn't be group annuity contracts!). In the case of a deferred-annuity contract an actual deferred annuity is purchased for each unit of pension earned in each year (the unit-credit cost method is an outgrowth of this type of contract). Under a DA contract only immediate annuities are purchased, the remainder of plan assets being held in a deposit account or "active-life fund". Under an IPG contract no annuities are purchased at all as long as the contract remains in force, although annuities may be purchased when the contract terminates.

Behind every group annuity contract there is an experience account which records for the entire contract — i.e., for annuities actually purchased as well as unallocated funds — the actual interest earned (via the new-money method discussed in section 5.3), the actual expenses charged to the account, the actual benefits paid, and the contribution of the contract to the surplus of the insurance company (i.e., the company's "profit"). When this experience fund exceeds a certain limit set by the insurance company, a portion of the excess is paid to the contractholder as a dividend. Under a deferred-annuity contract the experience fund must exceed deferred-annuity reserves established by the insurer (which it may change unilaterally).

A deposit-administration contract is ostensibly separated into active- and retired-life portions. The insurance company issues a statement showing interest credited to and expenses charged to the active-life fund as a separate entity; but these credits and charges are not related to those actually recorded in the experience account. A dividend is payable when the experience fund equals 105% (or some similar ratio) of the active life fund plus the retired life reserves, which again are established unilaterally by the insurance company. The active-life fund thus is irrelevant except in the case where the interest and expense guarantees in the contract actually come into play — in which case there is never any dividend payable. Note that until annuities have actually been purchased under a DA contract there is never any dividend, or hardly ever, because the experience fund has recorded the actual heavy initial expenses of acquiring and establishing the contract.

The IPG contract does away with most of the guarantees in the other two types and shows actual interest credited and actual expenses directly in its accounting to the contractholder — i.e., it lays bare the experience fund and thus provides a guarantee of "immediate participation".

It is tempting to look at the balance in the experience fund as being the *value* of a group-annuity contract, but in general it is not. The reason is that the balance in the experience fund is not available for withdrawal in cash, as if it were a bank account. In fact, when a plan tries to convert a group annuity contract into cash it encounters a host of complex withdrawal and discontinuance provisions whose effect is usually to reduce the apparent assets in the experience fund.

What may be said about the experience fund is doubly true with respect to contract reserves — i.e., annuity reserves or active-life-fund balances. These amounts are determined on the *insurance company's* assumptions as to mortality, interest, and expenses; they have no real market value. Their value to a particular plan may be established only with reference to the *plan's* own assumptions.

Remember that we rejected in section 5.1 — on solid logical ground — the valuation of assets by discounting the future cash flow from the asset using the plan's interest assumption. We rejected it because this method lacks objectivity, because it mixes up the plan's actuarial assumptions with asset values and allows the cost of the plan to be determined with only distant contact with reality. We saw that the discounted-cash-flow method works only when the plan can be assumed to be immortal — an assumption which is always fallacious.

Just as the value of a common stock can properly be determined only by assuming that it is sold on a particular day and converted into cash, so it is with a group annuity contract. But when we go to convert such a contract into cash, we find, generally speaking, the following kinds of contractual provisions:

(1) Unallocated reserves are used to purchase the full accrued benefits of all plan participants on the termination date. Special rates generally apply to such a purchase (different from those which apply to an active contract); these may be nonparticipating.

(2) Unamortized acquisition costs (salesmen's commissions) are deducted.

(3) A contribution to surplus (profit margin) is subtracted, usually by multiplying the remaining balance by a factor such as 95%.

(4) The amount remaining in the experience fund after deducting the above items is subjected to a "market-value" adjustment. The latter is not usually handled with as much sophistication as the crediting of interest in the first place (exercise 5.3.4 shows how). The typical market-value adjustment is determined by computing the price of a \$1 bond with a coupon rate equal to the case rate, yield rate equal to the estimated new-money rate for the year (the actual new-money rate is, of course, never known until the insurance company has closed its books for a calendar year), and some arbitrary term to maturity. This unit price is then

multiplied by the refundable balance to get its "market value"; the "market-value adjustment" is simply the dollar difference between market and book values. Since interest rates have risen fairly steadily for the last several decades market-value adjustments have been nearly always negative, although in theory a positive market-value adjustment is possible.

Sometimes as an alternative to a "market-value" cashout a contract will allow a remaining balance in the experience to be paid out in installments over a period of several years, usually at a low aggregate interest rate specified in the contract.

Sometimes if the plan itself is not terminating, but only the insurance contract, the contract will forego the purchase of deferred annuities, and will thus make more reserves available for refunding through the cashout provisions. Sometimes also special terms can be negotiated with the insurance company, despite the contractual language. And there are often special provisions for "discontinuance" of future contributions, although usually that event is tantamount to termination of the contract.

The actual determination of market value is not an easy task. For example, you cannot generally completely cash out a deferred annuity contract — there are always reserves held back for annuities. Even when the excess balance in the experience fund is refundable, the exact amount of various penalties and market-value adjustments can only be determined by the insurance company, and insurers generally refuse to do this on a routine basis. This means that you, as actuary, will have to estimate the market value of such a contract as best you can. You cannot avoid this responsibility entirely, because you cannot be sure a value you place on the contract is reasonably close to market value unless you know, at least approximately, what the market value is! In order to determine the market value, in turn, you must first be thoroughly familiar with the contract, especially its discontinuance provisions. You must then place a value on any annuities purchased (which may mean estimating future dividends) and determine what experience reserves if any are refundable to the plan. Then you must estimate any penalties or market value adjustments and make allowance for any extended-payout provisions, to reduce the whole thing to a cash value. This value will necessarily be partly dependent on the interest assumption you are using to determine the cost of the plan, but that is unavoidable.

Be particularly careful of so-called "separate accounts". These are assets held by the insurance company outside their general account, and it makes a great deal of difference whether the separate accounts are accessible directly by the plan, or whether they must first pass back through the general account and, by so doing, subject themselves to withdrawal penalties. Also, some IPG contracts are successors to older DA or deferred-annuity contracts under which annuities were purchased: The annuity reserves may be shown as part of the IPG fund balance but they will revert to their prior status upon termination of the contract. In theory this is no hardship if the annuities are participating, but as we saw in section 5.3 the new-money method operates particularly harshly on plans with negative cash flows so the level of future dividends on repurchased annuities is problematical.

While you must know what the market value is, at least every few years or so, it is highly impractical to try to use market value every year to determine the cost of a plan. If the market value turns out to be very close to the value of the experience fund, or can be presumed to oscillate around it, there is a decided practical advantage to using the experience fund or a percentage of it as the assets represented by the contract.

Under a DA contract which is not likely ever to pay a dividend (some of these have had actual expenses far in excess of those guaranteed in the contract) it is proper to disregard retired lives entirely, and take the active life fund as the assets of the plan. On the other hand, if dividends are likely to be paid, this approach may substantially understate the value of the contract and thus overstate the cost of the plan. The reason this method is acceptable when there is *no* dividend payable is that you may then look upon the contract as an investment instrument which "matures" at retirement age for an amount equal to the value which you place on the annuity to be purchased.

With respect to deferred-annuity contracts, it has been traditional to avoid any actuarial valuation entirely and to simply let the cost of the plan be equal to the premiums less dividends and termination credits (under this type of contract the rates are determined without reference to any turnover rate, so there is a refund of most of the deferred-annuity reserve whenever a covered employee terminates). Note that if you decide that the cost of the plan is to be determined in this way you have implicitly decided to use the unit-credit cost method. You have also implicitly assumed that the turnover in the covered group is very small, that the interest on the experience fund is the same as the interest rate used to determine the purchase rates for the deferred annuities and that gains should be amortized in one year.

As you can see, valuation of group annuity contracts as pension fund asset is a very challenging task indeed. There are no hard and fast rules that can be applied to it but a few general principles should be observed:

(1) Always read the contract, and understand thoroughly what will happen if it terminates.

(2) Avoid the *fallacy of perpetuity:* Nothing lasts forever, especially a pension plan.

(3) Note what the "case rate" being credited to the experience fund is, and what course it is likely to take in future years.

(4) Know precisely what formula is used to make market-value adjustments, where these are applicable. Often the formula is not spelled out in the contract.

(5) Periodically, and no less frequently than every five years, determine as best you can the ratio of the market value of the contract to the value you are placing on it. Note any trends in this ratio and if necessary adjust your valuation method.

(6) Remember that an insurance contract is, in our terms, an "equity investment" because there is no definite maturity *date* nor any definite maturity *value.* This means that, as a general rule, insurance contracts cannot be held at face value.

Exercises

5.4.1 Why is there a market-value adjustment on separate-account assets which must come through the general account?

5.4.2 What rationale can you see for making market-value adjustments at contract termination, but not for routine benefit payments? (Hint: Review the assumptions underlying the new-money method.)

5.4.3 A pension plan holds as one of its assets an old DA contract with no active lives but several purchased annuities. Dividends flow from the contract back to the fund. Describe how you would place a value on this contract.

5.5 *Individual Life-Insurance Policies*

Many pension plans use individual life-insurance policies to fund all or part of the benefits provided by the plan. Often there is a trust which holds the policies and which invests plan assets other than the policies themselves. A plan whose assets consist entirely of individual policies is said to be *fully insured;* one whose assets comprise policies and other assets is called *split-funded.* In a split-funded plan the assets other than the policies themselves are referred to as the *side fund.* Valuation of the side fund itself has already been covered because it is usually invested in stocks, bonds, and other marketable securities. We shall in this section try to reason out what value to place on the policies.

At first glance the question looks trival, because the policies have at all times a cash surrender value so we know exactly what the market value is, right down to the penny. Furthermore, these cash values form a smooth sequence from year to year and are not subject to random price fluctuations, so from that standpoint they are ideal for pension-cost purposes. We are tempted then to leap to the conclusion that assets in the form of individual policies should always be valued at straight market value.

But when an individual-policy plan is newly established and when the policy premiums represent a significant portion of the total cost of the plan, the fact that the cash surrender values are zero for the first year or two can cause severe distortions in the cost. This means that the cash value should not be used as the asset value for cost purposes, at least in the first few years of operation.

Under most individual-policy plans when a participant retires he receives a distribution of the policy itself along with other plan benefits. So it is quite proper to view the policy as maturing at normal retirement age y, whether or not it is of a type (retirement-income or endowment) which naturally matures at a certain time. This means that it is proper to value an individual policy at discounted value, just as we might treat bonds which are being held to maturity.

The discounted present value of the future cash flow to the plan from an individual policy may be expressed as

$$V_t^j = CSV_y \frac{D_y}{D_x} + \sum_{z=x}^{y-1} \left[\frac{C_z^{(m)}}{D_x} DB_{z+1}^j + \frac{C_z^{(w)}}{D_x} CSV_{z+1}^j - \frac{D_z}{D_x} NP_z^j \right] \tag{5.5.1}$$

where CSV_z equals the cash surrender value at age z, DB_z represents the death benefit at age z, NP_z is the net premium (policy premium less dividend) at age z, and $q_x^{(w)}$ is the probability of withdrawing from the plan for reasons other than death or retirement during the year. If we let the value of the side-fund assets be A_t (which may or may not be allocated to individual participants) we can express the fund balance for cost purposes as

$$F_t = A_t + \sum_{\mathbf{A}_t} V_t^j \tag{5.5.2}$$

where we have assumed that the policies on the lives of employees who have retired or terminated with vested rights have been cashed in.

The unit-credit cost method is almost never used in an individual policy plan, because the policies themselves carry level premiums and the admixture of the two might result in negative costs. Therefore, the unfunded accrued liability under whatever cost method is used may be taken as the present value of future benefits, less assets, less the present value of future normal costs. The present value of future benefits may be written

$$PVFB_t = \sum_{\mathbf{A}_t} \left[B\ddot{a}_y^{(12)} \frac{D_y}{D_x} + \sum_{z=x}^{y-1} \frac{C_z^{(m)}}{D_x} DB_{z+1} + \sum_{z=x}^{y-1} \frac{C_z^{(w)}}{D_x} SB_{z+1} \right]. \tag{5.5.3}$$

where we have assumed the same death benefit from the plan as from the policies themselves and where SB_z represents the severance benefit from the plan, whether that is the present value of a deferred pension, a cash refund, or some other benefit. The present value of future normal costs may be written

$$PVFNC_t = \sum_{\mathbf{A}_t} \sum_{z=x}^{y-1} NC_z \frac{D_z}{D_x}, \tag{5.5.4}$$

so that if we combine the foregoing equations we can write the unfunded accrued liability as

$$UAL_t = \sum_{\mathbf{A}_t} \left[(B\ddot{a}_y^{(12)} - CSV_y) \frac{D_y}{D_x} + \sum_{x}^{y-1} \frac{C_z^{(w)}}{D_x} (SB_{z+1} - CSV_{z+1}) - \sum_{x}^{y-1} (NC_z - NP_z) \frac{D_z}{D_x} \right] - A_t. \tag{5.5.5}$$

If there is no assumed withdrawal from the plan for reasons other than death (which is often the case with these plans because they are so small), or if the severance benefit is actually equal to the surrender value at each age, then equation (5.5.5) boils down to

$$UAL_t = \sum_{\mathbf{A}_t} (B\ddot{a}_y^{(12)} - CSV_y) \frac{D_y}{D_x} - A_t - \sum_{\mathbf{A}_t} \sum_{x}^{y-1} (NC_z - NP_z) \frac{D_z}{D_x} . \tag{5.5.6}$$

Equation (5.5.6) suggests that we view such a plan as comprised of two side-by-side plans: one a completely insured plan with the normal cost equal to the net premium, and the other, a plan providing a pension supplementing those provided by the policies. When we look at the plan in this way we are assuming that the proper cost to be assigned to the insured portion is the net premium. This assumption is convenient but is not necessarily correct — the net premium can be large in early years and may reduce to zero in later policy years. Nevertheless, this is the approach commonly taken because it is so convenient.

If we treat the side fund separately we then produce an unfunded accrued liability and a normal cost which are independent of the policy except to the extent that the policies mature to provide a portion of the projected benefit at retirement (and of course to the extent that dividends from the policies are deposited back into the fund and represent a gain).

Note, however, that if you treat the insured portion and the side fund separately and apply a certain cost method to the side fund, that is not the same as applying that cost method to the plan as a whole.

In cases where individual policies are being held by a plan which is not an individual-policy plan — i.e., one which does not call for the regular purchase of insurance policies for participants — it is probably best to value the policies at their surrender values, because then the cost method is being applied, properly, to the entire plan. The use of discounted value is appropriate where the policy is funding a particular plan benefit, in which case the totally insured portion may be isolated in the manner described above.

5.6 *The Big Picture*

It is time once again to step back out of the trees and see if we can get a good view of the forest. We need to put the question of asset valuation in perspective with all the rest of the concepts and techniques we have been examining so far in the book.

By now it should be clear that regardless of the actuarial cost method we are using we can define an unfunded accrued liability by

$$UAL = PVFB - PVFNC - F \, , \tag{5.6.1}$$

where *PVFB* is the present value of future benefit payments as of the valuation date, *PVFNC* is the present value of future normal costs (including employee contributions), and *F* is the value of the pension fund (or book reserve) which we had determined according to the principles set forth in this chapter.

Now note that the *cost method* proper tells how *PVFNC* is computed, while the asset-valuation method determines how *F* is computed. *PVFB* is independent of the other terms. The cost of the plan — which is the sole object of our quest — depends not only on the normal cost (which is determined by the cost method) but also on the *gain:* Where we use that term in the largest sense as *any unexpected decrease in UAL,* as defined by equation (5.6.1). The gain in turn depends on both *PVFNC* and *F*, and thus on both the cost method and the asset valuation method. Therefore, just as much care should be lavished on *F* as on *PVFB* or *PVFNC*, because they are all interlocked.

Now the term *F* in equation (5.6.1) is what pins our cost determination to reality. If we use a value for *F* which is arbitrary and not related to any actual ability to convert the pension fund to cash, then we destroy that vital link to the real world. That is why we cannot blithely abandon cash or market value just to eliminate annoying gains. We can, of course, smooth out random fluctuations in asset values (making sure of course that what we are smoothing our are truly random fluctuations) and we can allow ourselves the luxury of evaluating certain kinds of investments by discounted cash flow — but only those which have a definite maturity value (and which are likely to be held to maturity). We must always avoid the temptation to insulate the plan cost from reality by putting a value on assets which cannot be realized in cash within a finite time period.

Note that our asset value and our assumed interest rate are linked: In equation (5.1.1), for example, there is never any question about the transactions (contributions and benefit payments) but the interest term *I* is a balancing item which links the two year-end fund balances, and *I* is assumed to be generated by the assumed rate *i* acting on the value of the fund F_t.

Equation (5.6.1) tells us that the assets must be coordinated with *PVFB*: We cannot count in *F* monies which are included in *PVFB*. For example, if an employee is owed a benefit payment for the month preceding the valuation date, but *PVFB* includes only future benefit payments, then *F* should be reduced. Likewise with employer contributions. Thus, payables and receivables must be accounted for in the valuation of assets. Ideally, they should be adjusted for the assumed interest rate, i.e., by discounting any payables or receivables back to the valuation date; otherwise, they become in effect non-interest-bearing assets, contrary to our assumption that assets earn interest at rate *i*. Also, in this connection, remember from section 2.9 that under the aggregate cost method assets must always include amounts charged as pension cost in previous years.

Some actuaries like to think of equation (5.6.1) in terms of an "actuarial balance sheet":

"Assets"	"Liabilities"
• Assets on hand • Unfunded accrued liability • Present value of future employer contributions • Present value of future normal costs	• Various components of the present value of future benefits
Total "Assets"	Total "Liabilities"

Clearly, both columns must add to the same total, so the balance sheet balances. Note that the unfunded accrued liability falls in the "assets" column, because it is a part of the present value of future contributions. But listing anything called a "liability" under the heading of "assets" invariably raises questions (see section 2.2) from those familiar with financial accounting. Also, the balancing item (present value of future normal costs) falls in the left-hand column rather than the right-hand one (where "net worth" is usually shown in a conventional balance sheet).

Exercises

5.6.1 Show in detail how equation (5.6.1) applies to each of the cost methods discussed in Chapter 2. For those cost methods where we did not explicitly define an actuarial gain, what happens to the "gain" as that term is used in this section (i.e., any unexpected decrease in *UAL*)?

Chapter 6

Assumptions

6.1 *Actuarial Science vs. Actuarial Art*

You have by now accumulated a fairly complete kit of actuarial tools for determining the cost of a pension plan. You know something about how and why cost methods work, how to put a value on plan assets, and how to deal with employee contributions and ancillary benefits. But none of these tools can be used without a set of actuarial assumptions: a service table, a post-retirement mortality table, an assumed interest rate, etc. If we had taken up the subject of pension cost in operational order, we would have discussed how to choose these assumptions before discussing how to use them. But that would have been confusing, because you would not have had any motivation for choosing assumptions at all! Now that you have been through five chapters (you didn't cheat and skip ahead did you?) you must at least once have asked the question "But how do I decide what assumptions to use?"

Unfortunately, we shall not be able to answer that question with the same degree of mathematical rigor that we were able to bring to bear on the subject of cost methods and related matters. While most actuaries would find little in the preceding chapters to disagree with, no two actuaries ever seem to agree on the proper choice of actuarial assumptions for a particular plan at a particular time. When we come to choosing assumptions we are entering the subjective realm of actuarial art and leaving the precise and mathematical world of actuarial science. This means that we cannot prescribe exactly how to choose actuarial assumptions for a particular situation, but we can discuss some general principles. There is a surprising amount of logic that can be brought to bear, despite the subjective nature of the task.

There is a natural order to choosing assumptions, and we shall follow it in this chapter. First, we shall discuss the components of the service table, which govern *when* we expect a particular benefit to be paid. Second, we shall take up secondary decrements, such as post-retirement mortality, mortality of disabled lives, etc. — which govern *how long* we expect the benefit to be paid. Finally, we shall take up the salary-increase and interest assumptions, which govern *how much* will be paid and the discounted value of the payments.

But before we attack the question of what we can do in the way of choosing assumptions rationally, we have to stop for a while and remind ourselves of what we can *not* do, because, surprising as it may seem, when we strain for a precision that is unattainable, we actually lose accuracy.

6.2 *An Actuarial Paradox*

In life insurance work, the emphasis of actuarial theory is on determining the proper magnitude of reserves (analogous to our accrued liabilities) and premiums (analogous to our normal costs). Gains or losses are considered only a minor nuisance, one which can be minimized by proper selection of mortality rates, lapse rates, etc. The law of large numbers makes life-company experience much more predictable than that of the typical pension plan, so the actuary's attention is on the precision of his assumptions. In life insurance work, the precision of the outcome can actually be improved by putting more effort into choice of assumptions. In pension work, by contrast, the focus of the actuary's attention must be on the precision of the outcome, or in other words, on the size of gains and losses. The pension actuary must face squarely the fact that he is always going to be wrong, often by a wide margin.

Of course, an actuary dealing with a very large pension plan — one with as many participants, say, as there are policyholders in a life insurance company — does not have to approach his work differently from the life-insurance actuary. But most pension plans are not large — most, in fact, have fewer than 100 participants — so there are usually insurmountable limitations on the precision with which we can determine the cost of the plan. These limitations arise from two facts: (1) we are attempting to model the behavior of a probabilistic, or stochastic, process, and (2) we are dealing with discrete events: An individual either leaves the group or stays.

We saw in Chapter 2 that in general the pension cost which we assign to a particular year has three components, namely, the normal cost, the amortization of the inital unfunded accrued liability, and the amortization of the accumulated gains and losses. When the cost is redetermined the following year, the change in cost is entirely predictable, except for that additional component which will arise because of the actuarial gain in the coming year. Thus, in general, the pension cost assigned to a particular year is the sum of a deterministic component and a probabilistic component. For example, look back at equation (2.4.8). One component of the gain was a term $\sum_{\mathbf{T}} \widetilde{AL}^j_{t+1} - \sum_{\mathbf{A}_t} q_x \widetilde{AL}^j_{t+1}$. We did not emphasize the point at the time, but the actual release of accrued liability on account of termination is a *random variable,* whose mean or expected value is $\sum_{\mathbf{A}_t} q_x \widetilde{AL}^j_{t+1}$ assuming, of course, that q_x is truly the probability of terminating employment). The quantity $\sum_{\mathbf{T}} \widetilde{AL}^j_{t+1}$ is just one possible value of the random variable; if we could turn back the clock and rerun the year we would generally get a different value.

In the general case, as we saw in Chapter 4, the service table comprises a number of probabilities $q_x^{(k)}$ such that $q_x = q_x^{(1)} + \ldots + q_x^{(m)}$ $(m \geq 1)$, and the component of the actuarial gain attributable to any one of these decrements is of the form

$$\sum_{\mathbf{T}^{(k)}} \widetilde{AL}^j_{t+1} - \sum_{\mathbf{A}_t} q_x^{(k)} \widetilde{AL}^j_{t+1}$$

where $\mathbf{T}^{(k)}$ is the subset of $\mathbf{A}_t$ which actually succumbs to decrement k. The pension cost for the subsequent year will contain a fraction (depending upon the amortization period for gains) of that gain and consequently the same fraction of the portion of the gain attributable to decrement k. Now the surprising fact is that if either (1) $q_x^{(k)}$ or (2) the number of persons in set $\mathbf{A}_t$ is *small,* the accuracy of our pension cost may actually be improved by ignoring $q_x^{(k)}$ altogether! To see how this can be, let us conduct the following "thought experiment".

Suppose the accrued liability of every member of set $\mathbf{A}_t$ is 1 and that the probability of "dying" is $q = .005$. Assume that we have 100 persons in the set, so the expected release of accrued liability is $1/2$. Since the probability of dying acts independently on each member of the set we have

$$Pr\{\textit{exactly n deaths}\} = \binom{100}{n} q^n (1-q)^{100-n}$$

$$\approx \frac{(.5)^n}{n!} e^{-.5} \tag{6.2.1}$$

where $0 \leq n \leq 100$ and $q = .005$, and we approximate the binomial by the Poisson distribution. Then we can set up the following table:

Table 6.2.1

Actual Number of Deaths N	$Pr(X = N)$	*Cumulative Probability* $Pr(X \leq N)$
0	.60653	.60653
1	.30327	.90980
2	.07582	.98562
3	.01264	.99826
4	.00158	.99984
5	.00016	1.00000

Now we can run a Monte Carlo experiment by generating random numbers between 0 and 1 and assigning the number of deaths as follows: If the random number is less than .60653 we say that no one died during the year; if it is between .60653 and .90980 we say that one death occurred; and so forth. Let us also imagine that we have two observers of this experiment, A and B, whose task is to predict the number of deaths that will occur in a given year. Observer A reasons that since the mean number of deaths is 1/2, that is his best estimate, so he predicts that the number of deaths will be 1/2 — notwithstanding the fact that he knows he cannot have half a death. Observer B, on the other hand, even though he knows that the probability of death is .005, guesses that there will be no deaths. This means that Observer A is always going to be in error by an amount $|\sum_{\mathbf{D}} 1 - \sum_{\mathbf{A}_t} q| = |X - \frac{1}{2}|$, where X is the actual number of deaths occuring during the year — the number of persons in set **D**. Likewise, Observer B will always be in error by $|X| = \sum_{\mathbf{D}} 1$, because he does not "expect" any deaths. Now we choose 30 random numbers to represent 30 repeats of the experiment and we get the results shown in Table 6.2.2.

To our surprise, we find that Observer B's strategy is the better one, because the expected value of his absolute error is smaller than that of Observer A. Of course, neither observer did a particularly good job in any given year, but given the size of the group and the small probability there was no way to do a good job in absolute terms. By the way, the outcome shown in Table 6.2.2 was no accident, as you will see when you get to exercise 6.2.1.

The result of the experiment is a consequence of the fact that in a Poisson process such as this (or more properly, in a process such as this which can be approximated by the Poisson distribution) if the probability of no deaths at all, namely, $\frac{(qn)^0}{0!} e^{-qn} = e^{-qn}$ is greater than 1/2, then $E(|X - qn|) > E(|X|) = qn$,

Table 6.2.2

Trial #	*Random #*	*No. of Deaths*	*Absolute Error*	
			Obs. A	*Obs. B*
1	.69179	1	.5	1
2	.27982	0	.5	0
3	.15179	0	.5	0
4	.39440	0	.5	0
5	.60468	0	.5	0
6	.18602	0	.5	0
7	.71194	1	.5	1
8	.94595	2	1.5	2
9	.57740	0	.5	0
10	.38867	0	.5	0
11	.56865	0	.5	0
12	.18663	0	.5	0
13	.36320	0	.5	0
14	.67689	1	.5	1
15	.47564	0	.5	0
16	.60756	1	.5	1
17	.55322	0	.5	0
18	.18594	0	.5	0
19	.83149	1	.5	1
20	.76988	1	.5	1
21	.90229	1	.5	1
22	.76468	1	.5	1
23	.94342	2	1.5	2
24	.45834	0	.5	0
25	.60952	1	.5	1
26	.00770	0	.5	0
27	.41583	0	.5	0
28	.65793	1	.5	1
29	.69721	1	.5	1
30	.98539	2	1.5	2
Total		17	18.0	17

where X is the random variable representing the actual number of deaths. To prove this theorem, let $\lambda = qn$; then

$$E(|X-\lambda|) = \sum_{k=0}^{[\lambda]} (\lambda - k)f(k) + \sum_{[\lambda]+1}^{\infty} (k-\lambda)f(k)$$

where $$f(k) = \frac{\lambda^k}{k!}e^{-\lambda}\,. \tag{6.2.2}$$

By our hypothesis

$$e^{-\lambda} > \frac{1}{2} \Leftrightarrow 2 > e^{\lambda} \Leftrightarrow \lambda < \log 2 = .693$$
$$\Rightarrow [\lambda] = 0.$$

(6.2.3)

Therefore,

$$\begin{aligned} E(|X-\lambda|) &= \lambda e^{-\lambda} + \sum_{k=1}^{\infty}(k-\lambda)f(k) \\ &= \lambda e^{-\lambda} + \sum_{1}^{\infty} kf(k) - \lambda\sum_{1}^{\infty} f(k) \\ &= \lambda e^{-\lambda} + \lambda - \lambda(1-e^{-\lambda}) = 2\lambda e^{-\lambda} \\ &= \lambda(2e^{-\lambda}) > \lambda(2e^{-\log 2}) = \lambda = E(|X|) \end{aligned}$$

(6.2.4)

which proves the theorem.

This theorem may be interpreted as follows. You might imagine that if you knew beforehand what the probability of a certain event was, the pension cost would be more accurate if you took that knowledge into account than if you ignored it. But the reality is that as the probability of no "deaths" increases — i.e., as q or n (or both) decrease — we reach certain fundamental *limits of certainty*. If thereafter we attempt to refine our model further, we simply introduce more uncertainty into the cost. This result sheds interesting light on the requirement of U.S. actuaries that their assumptions reflect their best estimate of future experience. If we interpret "best estimate" to mean that the expected value of the absolute deviation of the result from the estimate is to be minimized, then for a one-person plan, for example, the best estimate must be no terminations at all, except where the probability of survival for one year is less than 1/2; i.e., the only possible decrement that could be used in the service table for a one-person plan is that of retirement, under which the probability of leaving the plan, say at age 65, is greater than 1/2.

Another interesting corollary is that if we know the probability of death among active participants is roughly .005, and if their accrued liabilities are about equal, then we must have at least 138 persons to make it worthwhile to use that knowledge! With a smaller group we actually improve the accuracy of our cost calculation by ignoring mortality altogether. Other decrements, such as disablement, are even more unpredictable and require an even larger group if they are to be used explicitly.

Note, however, that in general accrued liabilities are not all equal, so q_x is not distributed binomially. Thus, the point at which q_x is so small as better to be ignored may vary considerably from the ideal case we have been examining. But *where* that point lies is less important than the fact that it exists.

Exercises

6.2.1 Using a published table of random numbers, or a random-number generator on your calculator or computer, or by another means of your own devising — prepare a table of 30 random numbers between 0 and 1 and run a new Monte Carlo experiment along the lines of that shown in Table 6.2. Are you surprised that your results are similar? If so, repeat the experiment several times.

6.2.2 Consider a pension plan covering only the following three employees:

Name	*Age*	*Accrued Liability*	q_x
Smith	25	10	.001
Brown	40	100	.002
Green	55	1,000	.009

(a) What is the expected release of accrued liability on account of mortality? (Answer: 9.21)

(b) There are exactly eight possible outcomes for the coming year with respect to mortality. List all eight showing in each case (i) the accrued liability released and (ii) the corresponding probability.

(c) Enter next to each outcome from (b), above, the actuarial gain as a result of that outcome.

(d) Compute the statistical expected value of the absolute value of the gain. (Answer: 18.2.)

(e) If, as a result of ignoring mortality, the accrued liabilities of the three persons are respectively, 13, 123, and 1152 — but the probabilities q_x are still valid — what is the expected value of the absolute gain? (Answer: 10.6.)

(f) In choosing assumptions for this plan should the actuary ignore mortality, even if he knows what the probabilities are? (Answer: yes.)

6.2.3 Consider a plan covering a single employee, whose acrued liability is A and whose probability of leaving employment within one year is q. Let X be a random variable representing the actual accrued liability released in the coming year.

(a) How many outcomes of the "experiment" of observing this plan for one year are possible?

(b) List all outcomes, showing in each case the actuarial gain on account of termination of employment (i.e., the actual accrued liability released less the expected release).

(c) Show that $E(|X|) = q \cdot A$.

(d) Show that $E(|Gain|) = E(|X - qA|) = 2q(1-q)A$.

(e) Show that $E(|X|) < E(|X - qA|)$ if and only if $(1-q) > 1/2$.

6.2.4 Consider a plan covering two employees whose accrued liabilities are, respectively, A_1 and A_2, and whose probabilities of terminating employment within one year are, respectively, q_1 and q_2. Assume

$$q_1A_1 + q_2A_2 < min\ \{A_1, A_2\}\ ;$$

That is, that the probabilities are small in relation to the accrued liabilities. Also, let X denote the accrued liability actually released during any particular year (i.e., in any hypothetical repetition of a given year).

(a) Show that $E(|X - E(x)|) = 2(1-q_1)(1-q_2)E(X)$.

(b) Show that if q_1 and q_2 are actually the probabilities of termination, but we ignore them anyway, and that as a result of ignoring them the amounts of the accrued liabilities are unaffected, then

$$E(|X|) < E(|X - E(X)|) \Leftrightarrow (1-q_1)(1-q_2) > 1/2\ .$$

(c) Note that the result of (b) above is independent of the magnitudes of A_1 and A_2, so that in this restricted situation we have again proved that if the probability of no one terminating during the year is greater than 1/2, then the best estimate of the number of terminations is 0 rather than $E(X)$.

(d) Can you extend this result to the case of three or more employees? Is the restriction that the mean release be less than the minimum accrued liability a realistic one?

6.2.5 (a) Given n Bernoulli trials with probability of success q, show that if we require that the probability of no successes whatever in n trials be less than 1/2, this is equivalent to requiring $q > \frac{\log 2}{n}$.

(b) If we interpret each trial as an employee and the probability q as the probability of terminating, how small may q be if there are 10 employees? 100 employees? 1,000 employees? 10,000 employees?

6.3 *The Service Table*

The service table, as we have said earlier, is the set of probabilities of leaving the group of employees covered by the plan within one year, whether by reason of death, disability, retirement, layoff, resignation, or any other event. Before you rush into constructing an elaborate service table, you should first pause and ask yourself (bearing in mind the discussion in the preceding section) whether there is any statistical justification for having a service table at all. Although we did not prove in section 6.2 any ***universal*** rule for making this decision, our discussion strongly implied the following general guideline: To justify any service table at all there must be a better-than-even chance of at least one termination of employment each year. This "even-money" rule applies to the service table as a whole as well as to its individual components, so your refinement of the service table should stop at the point where you are dealing with a decrement so small that you would not bet even money on at least one occurrence per year in the covered group. You may refine your service table beyond that point if you like, but only at the risk of introducing a greater variability in the pension cost.

The most common reason for leaving the group of active employees covered by the plan is usually one ***other*** than death, disability, or retirement. We shall henceforth refer to terminations of this kind as "terminations", and refer explicitly to terminations on account of death, disability, or retirement. Even for very large groups "termination" is the most common reason for leaving the covered group, as a rule, so it is well to begin constructing your service table by considering this phenomenon first.

The employee most likely to terminate is usually one in his first year of employment. This stands to reason because before an employee is hired he and his employer do not know each other as well as they will a few months later — and familiarity often breeds contempt, which may in turn lead to resignation or discharge. Also, when there is a business downturn an employer tends to lay off the most recently hired employees first.

As time goes on, however, if the employee does not terminate he becomes more attached to his job and his employer more attached to him, with the result that after a period of, say, ten or fifteen years it becomes very unlikely that an employee will terminate. Thus, in most employee groups with which the author has become acquainted, the probability of terminating depends primarily on the length of service, or seniority, of the employee in question: the probability being very high in the first year of employment and diminishing to a very low number after a decade or two of service.

The author has observed that the inclination to terminate decays exponentially as the employee remains in service, so you can construct a very satisfactory set of probabilities of termination by assuming that the "force of termination" is of the form

$$\mu_t^{(w)} = ae^{-bt}, \tag{6.3.1}$$

where t is the seniority measured in years and a and b are constants (which would be different, of course, for different employee groups). From equation (6.3.1) it follows that

$$q_t = 1 - exp\left(-\int_0^1 \mu_{t+s}^{(w)}\, ds\right)$$

$$\Rightarrow -\log(1-q_t) = \int_0^1 ae^{-b(t+s)}ds = -\frac{a}{b}e^{-bt}(e^{-b}-1)$$

$$\Rightarrow \log\frac{1}{1-q_t} = colog(1-q_t) = ce^{-bt}, \tag{6.3.2}$$

where $c = \frac{a}{b}(1-e^{-b})$.

If you have sufficient experience data when you first are called upon to compute the cost of a given plan, you can estimate the parameters b and c directly, but otherwise you can usually get surprisingly good results by asking the employer the right questions. For example, if you ask him, based on his experience, what proportion of a hypothetical group of 100 newly hired employees he would expect to be still on the job a year later, he might answer, "Sixty." Then you can write

$$p_0 = .6 = 1 - q_0. \tag{6.3.3}$$

If you follow this question with, "How many of that sixty who survive would you expect to be around at the end of the second year?" He might answer, "Forty." Then you can write

$$_2p_0 = .4 = (1-q_0)(1-q_1). \tag{6.3.4}$$

From equation (6.3.2) you get

$$\log\frac{1}{.6} = ce^{-b\cdot 0} = c = .5108, \tag{6.3.5}$$

and from equation (6.3.4):

$$- \log {}_2p_0 = - \log .4 = - \log(1 - q_0) - \log(1 - q_1)$$

$$= ce^0 + ce^{-b} = c(1 + e^{-b})$$

$$\Rightarrow .9163 = .5108(1 + e^{-b})$$

$$\Rightarrow \frac{.4055}{.5108} = e^{-b} = .7938 . \tag{6.3.6}$$

With this information you can quickly run up Table 6.3.1 (computing the first column first).

Table 6.3.1

t	$x \equiv - \log(1 - q_t) = .5108(.7938)^t$	$q_t = 1 - e^{-x}$
0	.5108	.4000
1	.4055	.3333
2	.3219	.2752
3	.2555	.2255
4	.2028	.1836
5	.1610	.1487
6	.1278	.1200
7	.1014	.0964
8	.0805	.0773
9	.0639	.0619
10	.0507	.0494
11	.0403	.0395
12	.0319	.0314
13	.0254	.0251
14	.0201	.0199
15	.0160	.0160

You can chop off this table at the point where the probability becomes too small to be statistically useful, remembering the discussion of section 6.2. In this way you can construct a very good table of termination probabilities in just a few minutes by asking only two questions of the employer — which he is usually able to answer quite accurately, in the author's experience.

For very large groups there is a measurable residual force of termination left even after very long periods of service (in some industries there is a high level of employment instability which has nothing to do with length of service). For these situations you can improve on the foregoing estimate considerably by using a force of termination of the form

$$\mu_t^{(w)} = a + be^{-ct} . \tag{6.3.7}$$

The parameters are somewhat more difficult to estimate in this case but the improved fit with actual experience may justify the extra effort. Some actuaries use age as well as service, and some use a model based on age alone — which, in the case where all employees are hired at the same age, is the same as a service-related table. In precomputer days it was simply not feasible to construct multiple tables of commutation functions corresponding to different attained ages and different ages at hire. Also, in the era before our modern hand-held calculators, exponentiation was not as simple as pressing a button, so it was not common to think much about $\mu_t^{(w)}$ before computing the tables of $q_t^{(w)}$.

Just remember that the correct model for the termination decrement is the one that actually *works* — that can be verified by collecting data after the assumption is set. In pension work you seldom have the luxury of having complete experience data when you first arrive on the scene, so you most often have to make the best *educated guess* you can with very limited exposure to the situation. This means that you should not only be imaginative when you initially set the assumptions but be ready to change when actual evidence proves that you were wrong. A corollary to this admonition is that you should not construct a model with so many parameters that you have no hope of ever gathering enough data to estimate them reliably; in particular, this means that unless you have a plan covering tens of thousands of employees, you cannot measure the probability of termination separately for each year of seniority and/or each age and then graduate the results — because this amounts to having a separate parameter for each cell. Therein lies the advantage of a model such as equation (6.3.1) or (6.3.7): The parameters are few and the model produces a nice smooth table.

The actual probabilities of termination will vary greatly from employer to employer, owing to differing employment conditions, customs of different industries and so on, so you must usually construct the termination decrement separately for each pension plan, either using one of the techniques outlined above or one of your own devising. If the group is small, the retirement decrement may be the only one left to consider, because the chances of someone dying or becoming disabled may be too small to be useful. However, where a mortality assumption is justified, it is usually reasonable to use one of the many published mortality tables, both because you will probably never accumulate enough mortality experience in the usual pension plan to estimate parameters accurately, and because there is no sense in duplicating effort. A compromise approach might be to assume Gompertz' law

$$\mu_x = ae^{bx} , \tag{6.3.8}$$

or Makeham's

$$\mu_x = a + be^{cx} , \tag{6.3.9}$$

and estimate the parameters a, b, and c from a combination of the published table and actual experience. Two advantages accrue from this hybrid approach: (1) your service table is nice and smooth, and (2) you can use equation (4.3.5) directly, by numerical integration, to get $q_x^{(m)}$ and $q_x^{(w)}$, because you know $\mu_x^{(k)}$ for every real value of x. Furthermore, it is usually easier for a computer to recompute a table of q's using two or three parameters than to store the entire table or read it from tape or disk.

Disability is a hazard which appears to have the same kind of "force" as mortality: i.e., it appears to increase exponentially with increasing age. This is not too surprising because mortality may be thought of as the extreme form of disability. Unless you have a very large employee group, however (perhaps 1,000 or more), the probabilities are simply too small to use. The parameters of $\mu_z^{(i)}$ are highly dependent on the definition of disability contained in the plan (if there is no disability benefit in the plan it is usually easier to treat mortality and disability as a single decrement), the waiting period for benefits, the nature of the job, etc., so care should be used in adopting tables of disablement probabilities from other employee groups. The *Reports* issues of the *Transactions of the Society of Actuaries* are a good source of raw data for a first estimate, but careful monitoring of actual experience with the plan in question is indispensable. Some law-enforcement groups, for example, show disability as the cause of a large majority of retirements under their pension plans, because of special additional benefits for disability; on the other hand, in certain white-collar situations termination of employment on account of disability is a very rare event.

Once you have decided what the values of $q_x^{(k)\prime}$ are for each decrement you can use the results of exercise 4.3.1 to get tables of $q_x^{(k)}$; or you can develop formulas for $\mu_x^{(k)}$ and use a more sophisticated numerical integration technique; or, as we said in section 4.3, you can simply use the "gross" approach of adding together the values of $q_x^{(k)\prime}$. In any case, the set of values of $q_x^{(k)}$ is the desired result: Your choice of techniques is not terribly important. Make sure, however, that $\sum_k q_x^{(k)} \le 1$ for every possible x. Note that we have generally used x as a shorthand for all the parameters upon which q may depend: age, length of service, sex, job classification, or whatever factors you deem relevant.

Which brings us at last to the retirement decrement. We have left it for last because it is fundamentally different from most of the others. The forces of termination, mortality, and even disability may be viewed as largely independent of the provisions of the plan (except in extreme cases), whereas the inclination to retire is definitely not.

To gain perspective on the probability of retirement, imagine for a moment a group of employees — ordinary wage-earners rather than highly paid executives or professionals — who have no retirement plan whatsoever, either private or governmental. Such employees would retire — could retire — only when their own savings were sufficient or when they were forced to leave work owing to the decrepitude of old age. In this situation the "force of retirement" would probably look something like Figure 6.3.1.

Figure 6.3.1
Force of Retirement *in Vacuo*

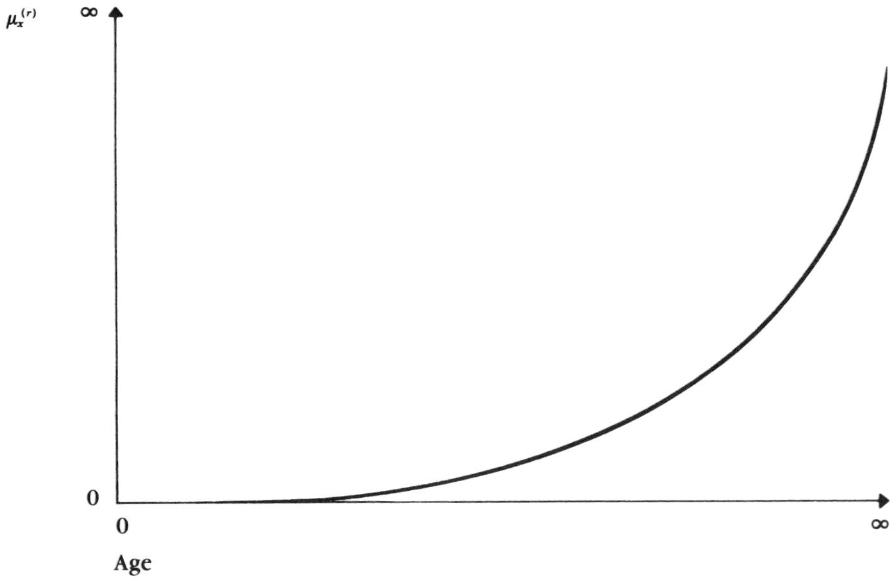

There is some age at which it simply becomes impossible to continue working no matter what financial resources are lacking; at that age the pressure to retire — the force of retirement — becomes infinite. Also at that age, of course, the distinction between retirement and disability becomes blurred. This line of reasoning could lead us into an almost metaphysical discussion of what "retirement" is, but we have more pressing things to consider and will leave this philosophical question as an unwritten exercise.

Referring still to Figure 6.3.1: At younger ages the shape of the curve is governed more by the employees' financial ability to retire than by physical inability to continue working. For example, if an employee had accumulated five or ten years' pay in savings his propensity to retire would be much higher than if he had accumulated one year's pay or less. The nature of the job would also influence "retirement", which for some occupations (e.g., military service) is just another word for change of occupation. Nevertheless, for any particular employee group we can imagine a function $\mu_x^{(r)}$ in the pristine setting where there are no external retirement benefits.

If we now introduce a retirement pension, such as social security old-age benefits, we in effect inject into an employee's life instant financial resources at whatever age the pension becomes payable. Suppose, for example, that a governmental old-age pension is payable to everyone in our group at age 65. Then $\mu_x^{(r)}$ would change and look something more like the curve in Figure 6.3.2.

Figure 6.3.2
Force of Retirement with Simple Plan

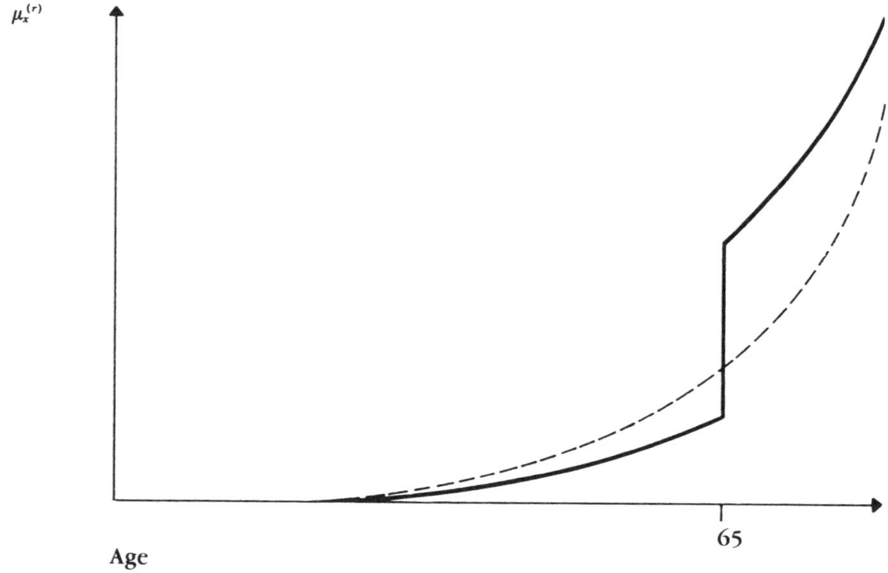

Close to age 65 the force of retirement is depressed below its "natural" value because employees tend to delay retirement until the government pension starts. Then at age 65 a sudden jump to a higher level takes place, and the force of retirement stays higher because the governmental pension is always available. Another way of looking at it is to imagine a whole family of natural $\mu_x^{(r)}$ curves similar to that of Figure 6.3.1 — one for each level of financial resources: A group of relatively well-off employees would presumably fall on a higher curve than a group of poor workers. The hypothetical government pension simply shifts a particular group of employees into a higher resource category — like a quantum jump to a new energy level in atomic physics. The size of the vertical jump at age 65 would depend on the relative financial impact of the government pension: If it were low in relation to the worker's pay the jump would be smaller than if the pension were more generous.

When we now superimpose a private pension plan on the natural inclination to retire, as modified by the presence of the government system, we may introduce a number of such discontinuous jumps in the $\mu_x^{(r)}$ curve, corresponding to the various ages at which pensions become payable — for example, age 55 for early retirement under the private plan, age 62 for reduced social security, age 65 for full pension and full social security, and so forth. Also, the slope of the curve is modified in between each of these discontinuities because of the tendency to wait for the next eligibility age and because the pensions add to the employee's wealth more rapidly toward the end.

A third variable affecting $\mu_x^{(r)}$, besides age and wealth, is direct pressure, either from the employer's mandatory retirement rules or a general peer pressure due to social custom (if your friends are all retiring at age 65 you tend to want to do so, too). Thus, in the real world the shape of $\mu_x^{(r)}$ tends to look more like Figure 6.3.3.

Figure 6.3.3
Force of Retirement with Complex Plan

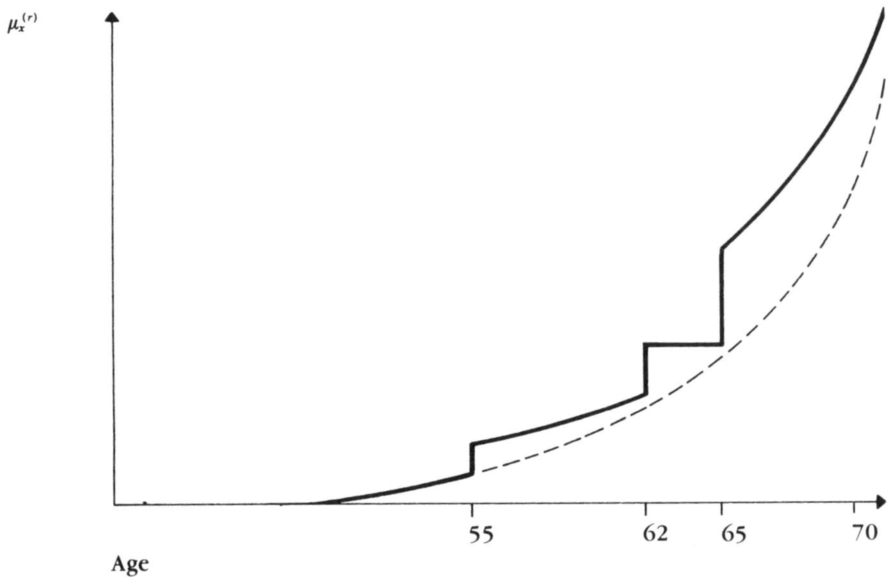

It is not necessary that $\mu_x^{(r)}$ be increasing between each of the discontinuities — it may get such strong "shocks" from benefit eligibility and the delaying effect that it actually decreases between, say, ages 62 and 65.

If we were to continue this line of reasoning we would have to decide how much additional pressure to retire is added when each higher level of retirement benefits becomes available, and thereby be able to estimate the height of each jump in the curve. But such an approach would be of academic interest only, because the resulting probabilities would likely be no more accurate than some kind of "seat-of-the-pants" estimate, by the actuary or the employer, of the probabilities of retirement themselves. Obviously, these probabilities vary with age and service and also do not form a monotonically increasing sequence. They are also difficult to verify by actual experience, because peoples' inclination to retire has something to do with their faith in the future, and thus rests in part on the general condition of the economy.

In many situations it is difficult to imagine that by using a table of probabilities of retirement you will be gaining anything in accuracy over simply assuming a single retirement age — particularly where you are not using the unit-credit method (i.e., you are using a projected-benefit cost method) and where the plan exerts strong pressure to retire at a single age, usually age 65, by making actuarial reductions for early retirement (see section 4.5). Furthermore, the computations are usually simplified if a single retirement age is assumed.

Assuming a single retirement age is tantamount to assuming a force of mortality like that illustrated in Figure 6.3.4.

Figure 6.3.4
Force of Retirement when Single Retirement Age Assumed

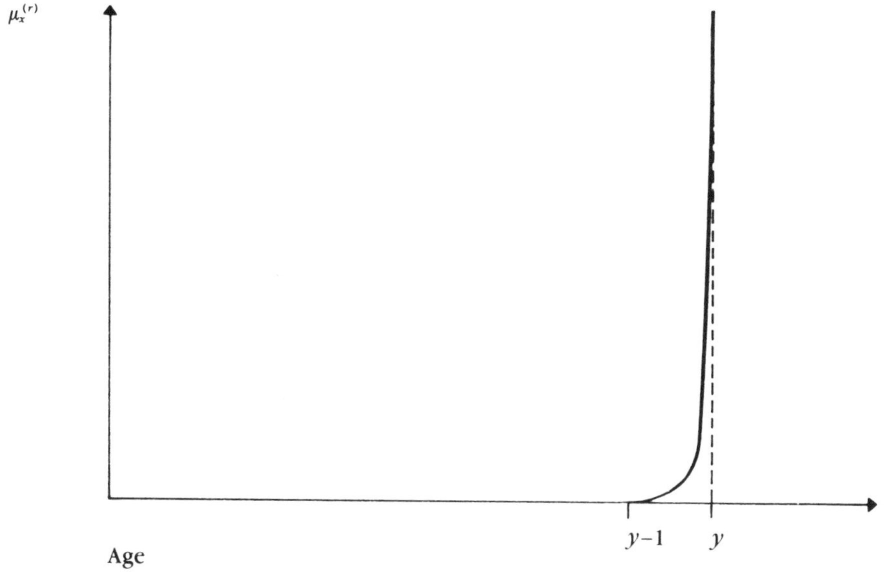

Note that under this assumption $\mu_x^{(r)}$ is zero everywhere except just before the assumed retirement age y, where it approaches infinity, thus insuring that $q_{y-1}^{(r)} = 1$. In situations where you cannot justify assuming a single retirement age, e.g., where early retirement benefits are "subsidized" and/or the unit-credit cost method is being used you have no choice but to assume retirement probabilities based on age, service, benefit level, and whatever other parameters may be important. Rarely can the choice be made scientifically — you will simply have to use your best judgment (and it is precisely the ability to make this kind of judgment that distinguishes the actuary from the technician). You may, to simplify calculations, find that single retirement age which produces the same pension cost as a table of probabilities, remembering to re-examine your assumption if the plan changes.

Whichever way you approach the probability of retirement — through a single age or a table of probabilities — the retirement decrement will close out the service table, in the sense that if you decide to compute values of l_x, these will approach zero as the force of retirement approaches infinity.

There may be other events resulting in termination which are important for certain employee groups — for example, there may be different benefits for service-related disability than for other kinds, or the plan may be contributory, in which case employees are usually allowed to withdraw from the plan voluntarily while remaining in employment. For each of these situations you must analyze the forces behind each event and develop a set of probabilities accordingly. It is usually best to begin by thinking about μ rather than q, because the former is independent of the other decrements. Even if all you can manage is a rough sketch such as Figure 6.3.3, you will have a good start on analyzing the situation. Then you can ask whether the shape of the curve is linear, geometrical, or otherwise, and devise a way to estimate the parameters using whatever data are available. One luxury you are not allowed is that of postponing the decision, because it is your duty to compute the cost of the plan and to do so you must assume something!

Exercises

6.3.1 The employer tells you that out of 100 newly hired employees he would expect only 50% to remain employed for a whole year. Out of the remaining 50 only 35 would still be employed at the end of this second year. Assuming that the force of termination is described by equation (6.3.1), compute $q_t^{(w)\prime}$ for $t = 0, 1, \ldots 15$. (Answer: .50000, .30000, .16768, .09012, .04744, ...)

6.3.2 Given the information of exercise 6.3.1 and the additional information that $\mu_t^{(w)}$ never falls below 5% no matter how large t gets, use equation (6.3.7) to develop values of $q_t^{(w)\prime}$ for $t = 0, 1, \ldots 15$.

6.3.3 Explain why Figure 6.3.4 shows the proper form of $\mu_x^{(r)}$ when retirement is always assumed to occur at age y. What difference does the shape of $\mu_x^{(r)}$ over the age interval $(y-1,\ y)$ make, as long as $\sum_k q_{y-1}^{(k)} = 1$?

6.3.4 Show that if Gompertz' law holds over a two-year interval centered on age x, i.e.,

$$\mu_{x+t} = ae^{b(x+t)}, \quad -1 \le t < 1, \tag{6.3.10}$$

then $e^b = \dfrac{colog\, p_x}{colog\, p_{x-1}}$, which in turn implies

$$\mu_x = \frac{\Delta log\, f_{x-1}}{\Delta f_{x-1}} \tag{6.3.11}$$

where $f_x = 1/colog\, p_x = 1/log(1/p_x)$ and Δ is the forward-difference operator. If $q_{64} = .020517$ and $q_{65} = .022562$, what is μ_{65}? (Answer: .021742.)

6.3.5 (a) Assume μ_x is constant for each age, that is, it is a step function, and that it follows Gompertz' law for integral ages. You observe a set of employees $\mathbf{A_0}$ and observe that a subset $\mathbf{D}$ die (no-one terminates for any other reason). Let L be the probability of this event occurring and show that

$$colog\, L = \sum_{\mathbf{A_0-D}} colog\, p_x + \sum_{\mathbf{D}} colog\, q_x, \tag{6.3.12}$$

where $colog\, p_x = ae^{-bx}$. Describe a method for computing the parameters a and b from equation (6.3.12). (This is the "maximum-likelihood" approach.)

(b) Suppose you decide arbitrarily to take $b = .095$. How would you solve for a? Which of the two parameters would you expect to vary most from group to group (i.e., if you had to pick one arbitrarily which one would be easier to estimate from other experience data)?

6.4 *Secondary Decrements*

In general actuarial parlance, these are probabilities which are conditional or contingent upon the occurrence of a primary decrement. In the case of pension plans, of course, the primary decrement is leaving employment, as reflected in the service table, and the most important secondary decrement is mortality after retirement. In many situations you will have other secondary decrements as well, such as the probability of remaining disabled after having become disabled, or the probability of retiring after having terminated with a deferred vested pension — but we shall concentrate primarily on post-retirement mortality because the principles for choosing it are universally applicable, and because virtually all plans which pay pensions from their own resources (i.e., which are not insured) must make use of this important decrement.

At first glance there is not much new to say about the choice of the post-retirement mortality table. Obviously, it should represent your best estimate of the mortality rates of the group you are working with. Often when the service table makes use of a published mortality table, the same table is used for post-retirement as well as pre-retirement mortality (even though there is evidence that, all things being equal, retired people are more likely to die than working people). The post-retirement table might even be select-and-ultimate if you suspect ill health as a prime motivation for retirement; and it is possible to refine the post-retirement mortality assumption further by having separate tables for males and females, hourly and salaried employees, or for any other subdivisions of the entire group that you think are pertinent. These are all considerations that you have undoubtedly encountered earlier in your actuarial career.

But our inquiry cannot stop there. We want to know how to choose the *best* assumption, or at least how best to go about choosing an acceptable one. And we need to know how precise we should be, and in what circumstances more or less precision is called for.

Before we go any further we should remark that from the point of view of that portion of the group of plan participants which is already retired, the post-retirement mortality table constitutes the *primary* decrement — analogous to the service table for active employees — so if you have only retired employees in your plan the choice of mortality tables is governed by the principles already discussed in sections 6.2 and 6.3. We shall concern ourselves here only with post-retirement mortality as a secondary decrement.

For active employees (and others not yet on pension) the post-retirement mortality table governs the fundamental units by which the normal cost and accrued liability are measured, because it determines $\ddot{a}_y^{(12)}$, the factor which converts periodic payments to lump sums. Note that year-to-year gains and losses do not reflect deviations from this assumption until employees retire, at which time the post-retirement mortality table becomes the primary decrement. So, if the post-retirement mortality table is "wrong", it will affect pension costs for years to come before they begin to be corrected by gains or losses. Therefore, we want to be sure that our choice of this assumption is as good as it can be.

But how good is that? And what is "good"? A perfect post-retirement mortality table would be one which, given that the interest assumption were exactly realized, yielded a precise value of $\ddot{a}_y^{(12)}$, on average, for the group in question. We know, of course, that it cannot be precise for each participant individually because that would require each to live exactly t years where $\ddot{a}_{\overline{t}|}^{(12)} = \ddot{a}_x^{(12)}$ — whereas we know that the retired lifetimes of participants will in reality be spread out over a wide range. Rather, we hope that the *average* value of $\ddot{a}_{\overline{t}|}^{(12)}$ will be $\ddot{a}_x^{(12)}$ as computed on our mortality table.

One way we can realize that hope is to choose the "right" mortality table; but even if we do that, since we are dealing with probabilities, we may find the actual result falling far from the mark due to the fact that only a certain finite number of pensioners will ever retire under a given plan, whereas to be sure of having the sample mean coincide with the theoretical mean we need an almost infinite number of trials. To put it a little differently, there are two ways for an actuary to turn out wrong in his determination of pension cost:

(1) He may choose the wrong assumption; i.e., in this case the wrong mean value $\ddot{a}_y^{(12)}$; and/or

(2) The actual results realized when events play themselves out deviate from the true mean because of chance fluctuation.

Now laymen (i.e., persons who have no understanding of stochastic processes) usually assume that these two sources of error are independent; they assume that, even though there is a scattering of results on either side of the mean, you stand the best chance of predicting the result if you ascertain the mean with as much accuracy as you can. We shall see that the opposite is true; namely, that the two sources of error are in practice indistinguishable, so that there is a *cloud of uncertainty* surrounding the true pension cost. The situation is analogous to that of a telescope, which can resolve objects on the moon (for example) only down to a certain minimum size. Any further fine-tuning of the focusing knob cannot improve the image so as to allow the viewer to perceive objects smaller than that minimum size. Just so, actuaries or any other human beings can predict pension costs only to a point — and beyond that point further striving for accuracy is fruitless.

To address first one side of the argument, let us suppose for a moment that we actually ***know*** the probabilities of dying which apply to a given group of employees after retirement, and see what kind of statistical noise is inherent in our calculations of annuity values. To make the analysis simpler, suppose also that pensions are paid continuously, so that our cost calculations are based on $\bar{a}_y$ rather than $\ddot{a}_y^{(12)}$. Now consider a continuous life annuity of $1 per year commencing at age y for a particular individual. Its present value is

$\bar{a}_{\overline{T}|}$ where T is the person's remaining life-span after age y (remember we are still supposing that our assumed interest rate is exactly realized). Now T — the post-retirement life-span — is a number which eventually will be known but which when the employee has just retired is only a *random variable.* Because we are assuming that our mortality table is correct, we know that

$$Pr\{t \leq T < t + \Delta t\} = {}_tp_x \, \mu_{x+t} \Delta t \tag{6.4.1}$$

for arbitrarily small time intervals Δt; so

$$f(t) = {}_tp_x \, \mu_{x+t} \tag{6.4.2}$$

is the probability-density (or distribution) function for the random variable T. We can see that it integrates to 1 just as a proper distribution function should —

$$\int_0^\infty f(t)\,dt = \int_0^\infty {}_tp_x \mu_{x+t}\,dt = -\int_0^\infty d({}_tp_x) = 1, \tag{6.4.3}$$

and we can compute the mean of the distribution as

$$E(T) = \int_0^\infty t f(t)\,dt = \int_0^\infty t(-d\,{}_tp_x) = \underbrace{-t\,{}_tp_x \Big|_0^\infty}_{0} + \int_0^\infty {}_tp_x\,dt$$
$$= \int_0^\infty {}_tp_x\,dt \equiv \mathring{e}_x\,. \tag{6.4.4}$$

That is to say, the expected future life-span at age x is equal to the "life expectancy" at that age (which is good because otherwise we should be using the term "life expectancy" in some non-statistical sense). Unfortunately, we sometimes call $\bar{a}_x$ the "present value" of a life annuity, whereas in fact it is only the *expected* present value:

$$E(\bar{a}_{\overline{T}|}) \equiv \int_0^\infty \bar{a}_{\overline{t}|} f(t)\,dt = \int_0^\infty \frac{1}{\delta}(1 - e^{-\delta t})\,{}_tp_x \mu_{x+t}\,dt$$
$$= \frac{1}{\delta} - \frac{1}{\delta}\bar{A}_x = \bar{a}_x\,. \tag{6.4.5}$$

As we said earlier, T is a random variable when the pension commences so we cannot compute the true present value of the life annuity, $\bar{a}_{\overline{T}|}$, at retirement but can only estimate it. If we estimate it as $\bar{a}_x$ (assuming retirement at age x), then when the pensioner dies we shall find that we were wrong in our estimate by an amount $|\bar{a}_{\overline{T}|} - \bar{a}_x|$. The statistical expected value of the square of this error is, of course, the *variance* of $\bar{a}_{\overline{T}|}$:

$$Var(\bar{a}_{\overline{T|}}) \equiv \int_0^\infty (\bar{a}_{\overline{t|}} - \bar{a}_x)^2 f(t)\,dt$$

$$= \sigma^2 = \int_0^\infty \bar{a}^2_{\overline{t|}} f(t)\,dt - \bar{a}_x^2 .$$

(6.4.6)

This variance is a decreasing function of the interest rate δ (as you will see in exercise 6.4.1) so the variance takes its largest value when $\delta = 0$:

$$\sigma^2 \equiv Var(T) = \int_0^\infty (t - \mathring{e}_x)^2 f(t)\,dt$$

$$= 2\int_0^\infty t\,{}_tp_x\,dt - \mathring{e}_x^2 .$$

(6.4.7)

Now what we should like to do is get some idea of the size of this variance, but to do so we shall have to know a little bit more about the distribution function $f(t)$ than we do already. This function is not completely arbitrary because it is implicit in our chosen mortality table, and it is a well established fact that μ_x — especially at older ages — follows Gompertz' law quite closely,* i.e., it increases geometrically; so

$$\mu_{x+t} = \mu_x e^{ct}$$

(6.4.8)

for some constant c. This, in turn, means that

$$- \log {}_tp_x \equiv \int_0^t \mu_{x+s}\,ds = \int_0^t \mu_x e^{ct}\,dt = \frac{\mu_x}{c}(e^{ct} - 1),$$

(6.4.9)

so we can write

$$f(t) = {}_tp_x\,\mu_{x+t} = \mu_x exp\left(ct - \frac{\mu_x}{c}(e^{ct} - 1)\right)$$

(6.4.10)

— which is the general expression of what we shall henceforth refer to as the *"Gompertz distribution"*. Figure 6.4.1 shows the curve of a typical Gompertz distribution for $\mu_x = .0204$ and $c = .097$ (roughly equivalent to

---

*See Tennenbein and Vanderhoof, "New Mathematical Laws of Select and Ultimate Mortality", TSA XXXII, page 119 for an excellent discussion of this assertion

Figure 6.4.1
Typical Gompertz Distribution

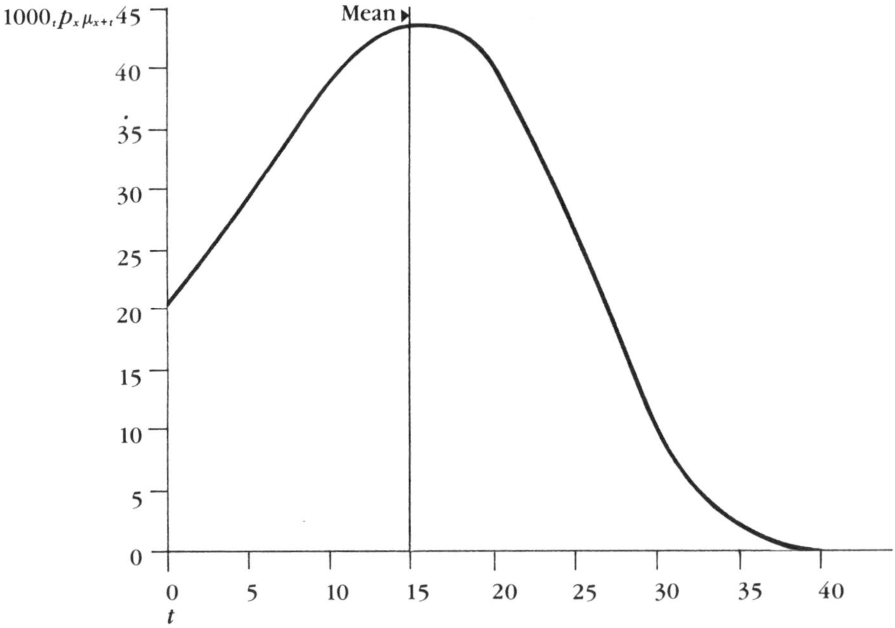

the 1971 GAM male table at age 65).* Note furthermore that the cumulative distribution function is

$$F(t) \equiv \int_0^t f(s)ds = {}_tq_x = 1 - {}_tp_x \,. \tag{6.4.11}$$

(Further interesting properties of the Gompertz distribution are explored in the exercises.)

It would be nice if we could compute the variance of the Gompertz distribution directly from equation (6.4.7), but unfortunately the form of ${}_tp_x$ (equation (6.4.9)) is such that it does not permit direct integration. Figure 6.4.2 shows the graph of ${}_tp_x$ for the Gompertz distribution depicted in Figure 6.4.1. We can get a rough approximation to the integral of ${}_tp_x$ by approximating the curve of Figure 6.4.2 by a straight line. This is illustrated in Figure 6.4.3, in which the dashed line is the true curve of ${}_tp_x$, while the deviation of that curve from the straight-line approximation is represented by the error

*Thanks to W. H. Wettersrand, who gives a useful table of Gompertz parameters for common mortality tables in his interesting paper, "Parametric Models for Life Insurance Mortality Data: Gompertz's Law over Time", TSA XXXIII.

Figure 6.4.2
${}_tp_x$ under Gompertz Distribution

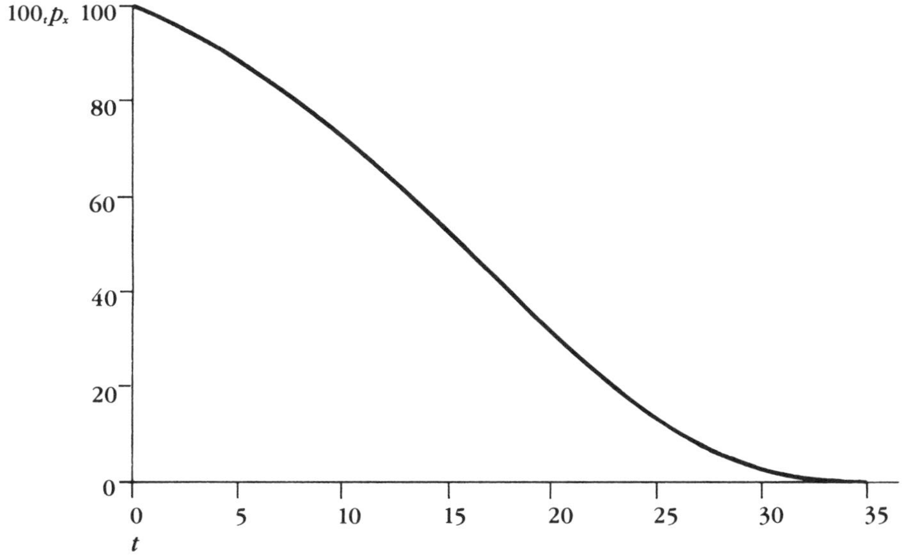

Figure 6.4.3
Linear Approximation to ${}_tp_x$

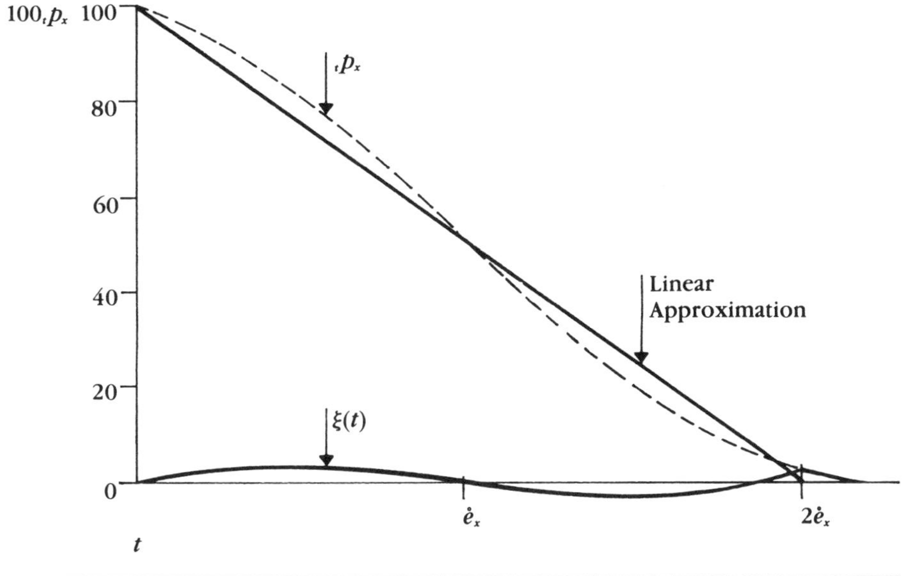

function along the abscissa. We have drawn a straight line through the points on the curve at $t = 0$, $t = \mathring{e}_x$ and $t = 2\mathring{e}_x$. The error function may be defined mathematically as

$$\xi(t) = \begin{cases} {}_tp_x - 1 + \dfrac{t}{2\mathring{e}_x} & 0 \le t \le 2\mathring{e}_x \\ {}_tp_x & t > 2\mathring{e}_x \,. \end{cases} \tag{6.4.12}$$

Note that because of our clever positioning of the straight line, the integral of the error function is 0 (exercise 6.4.4).

Using this straight-line approximation we can write the integral in equation (6.4.7) by substituting equation (6.4.12):

$$\begin{aligned} \sigma^2 + \mathring{e}_x^2 &= 2\int_0^\infty t\,{}_tp_x\,dt = 2\int_0^{2\mathring{e}_x} t\left(1 - \frac{t}{2\mathring{e}_x}\right)dt + 2\int_0^\infty t\,\xi(t)\,dt \\ &= \frac{4}{3}\mathring{e}_x^2 + 2\int_0^\infty t\,\xi(t)\,dt \,. \end{aligned} \tag{6.4.13}$$

You will see (exercise 6.4.4) that the integral at the end of equation (6.4.13) is negative but relatively small (refer to Figure 6.4.3); if we just neglect it we get

$$\begin{aligned} \sigma^2 + \mathring{e}_x^2 = \frac{4}{3}\mathring{e}_x^2 &\Leftrightarrow \frac{\sigma^2}{\mathring{e}_x^2} = \frac{1}{3} \\ \Rightarrow \frac{\sigma}{\mathring{e}_x} &= \frac{1}{\sqrt{3}} = .577 \,. \end{aligned} \tag{6.4.14}$$

Since the neglected error term was negative we can round this down to the approximation

$$\frac{\sigma}{\mathring{e}_x} \approx \frac{1}{2} \,. \tag{6.4.15}$$

Actually, for the sample Gompertz distribution of Figure 6.4.1 the true value of σ is 0.526 (exercise 6.4.3) but the approximate equation (6.4.15) is good enough for our purposes. Note that the property of the standard deviation being a nearly linear function of the mean distinguishes the Gompertz distribution from others, such as the Poisson (whose standard deviation is the square root of the mean) and the Normal (whose standard deviation is independent of the mean).

Now if instead of just one person in our group we had n persons all aged x, we might estimate the present value of the n pensions as $n\bar{a}_x$; but when history was written we should find the true value to have been $\sum_{j=1}^{n} \bar{a}_{\overline{T_j}|}$, where T_j is the future life-span of person j. In other words, the actual average present value of the life annuity would be $\frac{1}{n}\sum \bar{a}_{\overline{T_j}|}$. We are interested in the mean squared deviation of this "sample mean" from its mean, $\bar{a}_x$ — i.e., in the variance of the sample mean. Since we want to look at the worst case, the one with the largest variance, we shall examine the sample mean future life span $\frac{1}{n}\sum_{j=1}^{n} T_j$ against its mean, $\mathring{e}_x$. You will remember from statistics that the sample mean is approximately normally distributed about the underlying mean (in this case $\mathring{e}_x$), with standard deviation equal to $\sigma/\sqrt{n}$ where σ is the underlying standard deviation (this is the Central Limit Theorem). Thus, with about 95% confidence we should expect the average future life-span (i.e., the sample mean) to fall within two standard deviations on either side of its mean:

$$\mathring{e}_x - 2\frac{\sigma}{\sqrt{n}} < \frac{1}{n}\sum T_j < \mathring{e}_x + 2\frac{\sigma}{\sqrt{n}}. \tag{6.4.16}$$

Now in our case we have a direct relationship (equation (6.4.15)) between the standard deviation and the mean, so (6.4.16) reduces to

$$\mathring{e}_x\left(1 - \frac{1}{\sqrt{n}}\right) < \frac{1}{n}\sum T_j < \mathring{e}_x\left(1 + \frac{1}{\sqrt{n}}\right). \tag{6.4.17}$$

The above relationship tells us that, even if we knew the correct mortality table in advance, in order to have 95% confidence in the outcome we should have to allow an error of $\pm\, \mathring{e}_x/\sqrt{n}$. Thus, the accuracy of our estimate is limited by the number of persons observed, as shown in the following table:

Table 6.4.1
95% Confidence Limits for $\mathring{e}_x$

n	*Percentage Range*
1	±100%
10	32
50	14
100	10
500	4
1,000	3
5,000	1
10,000	1

Since the variance of $\bar{a}_{\overline{T}|}$ is slightly smaller than σ, being smallest for largest δ, these ranges represent outside limits. Nevertheless, you can see that even with exact foreknowledge of the mortality function we would have to have a very large number of persons in the group to be able to come very close to *predicting* their average future life-span, or average life annuity.

On the other hand, in real life we do not have exact foreknowledge about μ_{x+t}; we can only estimate its parameters. How do we go about making the best estimate? If there is a "best" estimate then it must be the one which most closely predicts the post-retirement life expectancies of the persons *actually covered by the plan.* In other words, the goodness of the estimate would have to be judged by the *real* results — not what we think they ought to have been. Because each pension plan stands on its own financially (except when it purchases non-participating retirement annuities from an insurance company, in which case there is no choice of post-retirement mortality table to be made) there can be no measure of performance other than the actual experience of the plan.

Now suppose our hypothetical plan covers a group of persons of whom n eventually retire at age y. Observers A and B (our friends from section 6.2) each set out to pick the "best" mortality assumption. That is, each one tries as best he can to predict $\bar{T} = \dfrac{1}{n}\sum_{j=1}^{n} T_j$. They choose their assumptions and we act as judges to see who has done the better job. Since we can measure their performance only against the experience of *this plan,* we decide to wait until all n persons have died and compute the actual value of $\bar{T}$. Observer A's mortality table has predicted the value to be $\mathring{e}_x^A$ while B's table predicts $\mathring{e}_x^B$, and let us say the actual value turns out to be $\bar{T} = L$. Which observer has made the bet-better assumption? (The notion that there is a *best* assumption implies a way to measure the goodness of assumptions.)

One of the two observers must come closer to predicting L — say it is Observer A. At first we might be tempted to say that A was the winner, but upon reflection we should realize that it is quite possible that B chose the right mortality table and that, given a large number of such trials as we have just completed, he might have been proven the winner; i.e., it may be that our single sample produced a value $\bar{T} = L$ which is quite far from the true mean $\mathring{e}_x$. Thus we have to entertain the possibility that B is right, notwithstanding that his estimate was not closer to the actual result than A's. (We might have a clear-cut winner in this case, however, if A's estimate was quite close to L and B's was further than two standard deviations away from it — standard deviations compute on B's distribution of course. But although there is always the possibility that B was just unlucky, when the result falls far enough from B's estimated mean we can conclude that his mean was in error.)

In the likely event that the answer fell within two standard deviations of A's mean *and* within two standard deviations of B's mean we should be forced — using this "hypothesis test" — to accept both the hypothesis that A had made the correct choice *and* the hypothesis that B had made the correct choice.

Likewise, if we had a third observer who was also participating in the contest, as long as his mean $\mathring{e}_x$ was such that

$$\mathring{e}_x(1 - \frac{1}{\sqrt{n}}) < L < \mathring{e}_x(1 + \frac{1}{\sqrt{n}}) \tag{6.4.18}$$

then he too could make a valid claim to having made the correct assumption. Now the relation (6.4.18) is algebraically equivalent to

$$\frac{L}{1 + \frac{1}{\sqrt{n}}} < \mathring{e}_x < \frac{L}{1 - \frac{1}{\sqrt{n}}}$$

$$\Rightarrow \left|\frac{L}{\mathring{e}_x} - 1\right| < \frac{1}{\sqrt{n}}, \tag{6.4.19}$$

so we see that *any* mortality assumption which produces an estimate of life expectancy in the indicated range must necessarily be judged acceptable. Furthermore, there is no statistically defensible way of *ranking* the various assumptions which are deemed acceptable — i.e., there is no best assumption *even in hindsight!* This tells us that not only do we not know in advance what the "best" mortality assumption is, but it may prove impossible for anyone at any time to discern which of several different assumptions about post-retirement mortality is "best".

The inequalities (6.4.19) may be interpreted as a *maximum resolving power:* If the relative error in the outcome $\overline{T}$ compared to the prediction $\mathring{e}_x$ is less (in absolute value) than $1/\sqrt{n}$, then we cannot tell whether and to what extent the error was due to a bad guess or to bad luck. Any attempt to make such a distinction is without logical basis. The resolving power of a telescope is limited by the phenomenon of diffraction: fuzziness around the edges due to the wave nature of light. Likewise the resolving power of the actuarial valuation of a pension plan is limited by the probabilistic nature of the event being observed.

But what does the maximum resolving power tell us? It says that any attempt to guess the average future life-span of 10,000 persons aged x to an accuracy greater than 1% is fruitless. Likewise, *any* mortality table will do an adequate job of predicting the life-span of a single person (which is why single-person plans do not, as a rule, pay pensions as they fall due, but rather pay a lump-sum distribution at retirement or buy an annuity). For a group of 100 pensioners your best efforts will allow only 10% accuracy; you need 400 persons to get 5% and so on (see Table 6.4.1). And in the end, when you measure actual experience against your assumption, you will not know whether your result was bad luck or bad guess, nor in what proportion.

The resolving power also applies to other secondary decrements, for example, disabled-life mortality. Since even large plans commonly never have more than 50 pensioners, you have considerable latitude in choosing such a table because your maximum resolving power is ±14%.

With small plans (under 25 participants, say) you may choose almost any mortality table and expect it to produce an estimate of life-span within a tolerance of ±20%. Male/female distinctions are impossible to prove or disprove in these cases, and if you have a large number of such plans you could use the same table for all and still make the claim that you chose the assumption for *each plan* as accurately as humanly possible! This is a fortunate phenomenon because the small plan generally cannot afford a lot of attention from expensive actuaries, and often needs to take advantage of the savings which may be realized by being batched with other plans of similar size for actuarial purposes.

In a very large case, on the other hand (perhaps 10,000 lives or more), you would rightly be expected to estimate the average life-span to within 1% of the actual result — or, failing that, to make an apology for having chosen the wrong mortality table to begin with. In such a case, a full-scale mortality study is in order.

Exercises

6.4.1 Prove that $Var(\bar{a}_{\overline{T|}})$ (equation (6.4.6)) declines as δ increases; and that therefore

$$\frac{Var(\bar{a}_{\overline{T|}})}{\bar{a}_x} < \frac{Var(T)}{\mathring{e}_x} \tag{6.4.20}$$

for $\delta > 0$. (Hint: First show that the derivative of the variance of a random variable is twice the covariance of the random variable and its derivative.)

6.4.2 Prove the rightmost equality of equation (6.4.7). (Hint: Integrate by parts.)

6.4.3 ***The Gompertz Distribution***

(a) Assume that $\mu_x = .0204$ and $c = .097$ in equations (6.4.9) and (6.4.10), and compute tables of $f(t)$ and ${}_tp_x = 1 - F(t)$ for $t = 0$, 5, 10. . . . Check your values against those plotted on Figures 6.4.1 and 6.4.2.

(b) Using the results of (a) above, compute the mean future life span using Simpson's rule or some other numerical integration technique. (Answer: $\mathring{e}_x = 15.034$.)

(c) Compute the *median* of $f(t)$. Is it identical to the mean? Prove it.

(d) What is the *mode* of $f(t)$. (Answer: 16.074.) For what values of the parameters μ_x and c is the mode zero?

(e) Compute the standard deviation of the future life-span using numerical integration. (Answer: 7.905.)

(f) Using $\delta = .07$, compute $\bar{a}_x$. Then compute it for $\delta = .12$. (Answers: 8.507 and 6.259.)

6.4.4 ***Linear Approximation to*** $_tp_x$

(a) Show that the area under the error curve $\xi(t)$(equation (6.4.12)) is exactly zero.

(b) Show that if $_tp_x$ is defined as

$$_tp_x = \begin{cases} 1 - \dfrac{t}{2\mathring{e}_x} & 0 \le t \le 2\mathring{e}_x \\ 0 & t > 2\mathring{e}_x . \end{cases} \tag{6.4.21}$$

then the mean life-span is $\mathring{e}_x$.

(c) Show that $\int_0^\infty t\xi(t)\,dt$ is negative. Before starting out, look at Figure 6.4.3 and give a verbal rationale.

(d) Make a very rough numerical estimate of the error term in equation (6.4.13). Does your result square with your result in exercise 6.4.3?

6.4.5 A closed group of n persons, all aged x, is retiring at the same time and on the same respective amounts of pension. Your best estimates of δ and $\bar{a}_x$ are .10 and 7.0, respectively. It has been proposed to value these pensions as perpetuities rather than as life annuities. What is the largest value of n that will make this approximation fall within the limit of resolution? (Answer: 5.)

6.4.6 An actuary estimates the average future life-span at age 65 of a group of 1,500 pensioners to be 16.0 years. After all have died, the average actually turns out to be 16.5 years. Was the actuary's assumption — in hindsight, acceptable? If the critical range were expanded to *three* standard deviations, would the assumption then be acceptable?

6.4.7 Two actuaries are called upon to choose a mortality assumption for a group of 200 pensioners. A's assumption implies an average future life span of 15.3 years. B's assumption implies 16.2 years. A accuses B of being too conservative, and B responds by accusing A of being too liberal. You are asked to mediate the dispute as a disinterested third party. To the surprise of everyone, without further ado or any additional data, you immediately announce your judgment. What is it, and why?

6.4.8 A plan covers just one person who will retire at age 65 with a pension of $10,000 per year payable continuously. The plan is invested in such a way as to earn interest at exactly $e^\delta - 1 = i$ per year, indefinitely. The plan would like to have on hand at age 65 the sum of:

(i) the present value of an annuity certain for the life expectancy of the participant; and

(ii) the single premium for a stop-loss insurance policy which would make any future pension payments due after the participant had reached his life expectancy.

Both the plan and the reinsurer use the mortality table of exercise 6.4.3 and the transaction is free of expenses on all sides. What is the premium for the stop-loss policy?

6.5 *Interest, Inflation, and Salary Increases*

We come at last to the choice of i, the assumed rate of investment return on the pension fund. Let us begin by noting that i is not an estimate of interest rates generally, but is the assumed rate of investment return on the particular fund we are concerned with. That is to say, it must reflect not only the type of investments made by the fund, but also how those investments are valued. As we saw in section 5.6, i and the asset valuation method are married to each other by the definition of interest gain (equation (5.2.1)): i is the rate which, acting on F_t and transactions during the year, produces I, the dollar investment return.

There are situations in which i is not an assumption at all, but a fact. A book-reserve plan is one such situation. Or, for another example, if you have a plan covering only pensioners and if investment income and maturing debt exactly match the projected pension payments — i.e., if the fund is "immunized" — then you can value the fund at amortized value and (except for mortality gains or security defaults) the rates of return in every future year can be determined precisely. So, the rate of return or, in the second example, the sequence of rates of return $\{i_t\}$, is not always an "assumption".

There are, on the other hand, situations where *i* is completely assumed. For example, a new plan having no pensioners and no assets cannot know in advance the rate of return it will actually realize on its investments. In this case, we have to assume the rate or rates of return on *future* investments. Furthermore, because our objective is to minimize interest gains, and because interest gains are proportional to the amount of the fund (see equation (5.2.4)), we are most concerned with those rates of return which will obtain many years into the future, when the fund reaches its maximum value. (Incidentally, every pension fund reaches a maximum value at some time, because, as we emphasized in Chapter 5, no pension plan is immortal.)

In general, therefore, the choice of *i* is part fact and part assumption — the proportion of each depending on the situation. Since the portion which is factual needs no discussion, we shall concentrate our attention on the assumed part: that is, we shall focus our attention on how to predict future rates of return on future investments.

First let us consider debt investments. When an investor buys a bond, for instance, he runs two kinds of risk: The first is that the debtor will default on payments of interest or principal; the second is that the value of the debt when repaid will not be the same as the value of the loan at the outset, owing to debasement of the currency. Unfortunately, there seems to be no such thing as a currency which does not consistently lose value — as illustrated by Figure 6.5.1, which shows the purchasing power of the U.S. dollar from 1920 through 1983. Although there have been periods where the value increased, it has declined in almost every year in the last half-century. (Note that if you wish to prepare a similar graph for another currency you should use a logarithmic vertical scale rather than a linear one, so that percentage declines appear equally spaced — otherwise the small value of the currency in the later years will make it appear that the debasement is proceeding at a slower rate than it is in fact.) The reasons for currency debasement have been the subject of heated debate — a sure indication that they are not known; the author has no new facts or theories to contribute to that debate. For purposes of *this* discussion we need only bear in mind the fact that there is at present no quantitative theory of economics powerful enough to predict future rates of inflation — even for short periods.

Now, of course, investors are not stupid. If they imagine that currency debasement will proceed at instantaneous rate β then they know that the real value of a unit principal repayment after t years will be $e^{-\beta t}$, so that, if they charge interest at rate δ, (i.e., at annual rate $i = e^{\delta} - 1$), the total proceeds of the loan — interest and principal — after t years will be $e^{\delta t} e^{-\beta t} = e^{(\delta - \beta) t}$, so that the "real" rate of return will be $\delta - \beta$. That investors do tend to set interest rates which are high enough to affort them a real rate of return is illustrated in Figure 6.5.2. The solid line shows the actual yields on short-term U.S. Government bonds, expressed as continuous rates. The dashed line shows the average debasement, or inflation, rate for the preceding five years — a naive projection of the inflation rate for the succeeding five years. You can see that for most years there is a fairly constant spacing between the two lines, reflecting investors' desire for a rate of return in real-dollar terms.

Figure 6.5.1
Value of the U.S. Dollar
(as measured by the Consumer Price Index)

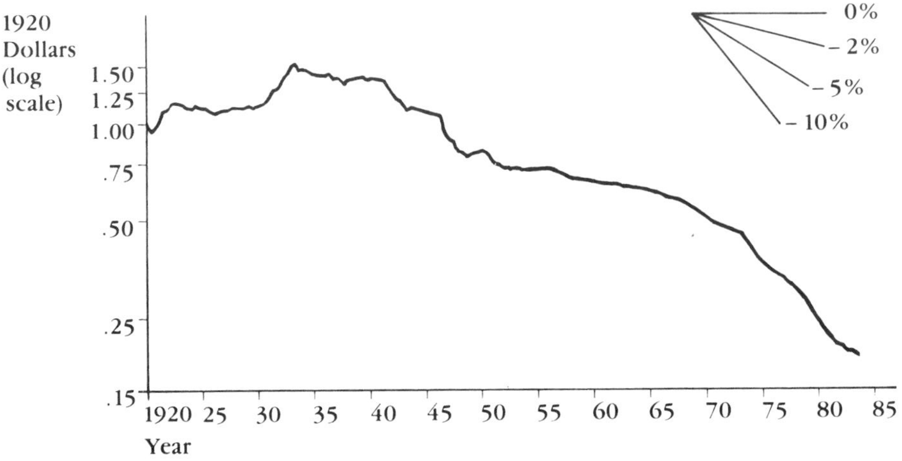

Figure 6.5.2
Short-Term Government Bond Yields vs. Five-Year-Average Inflation Rate

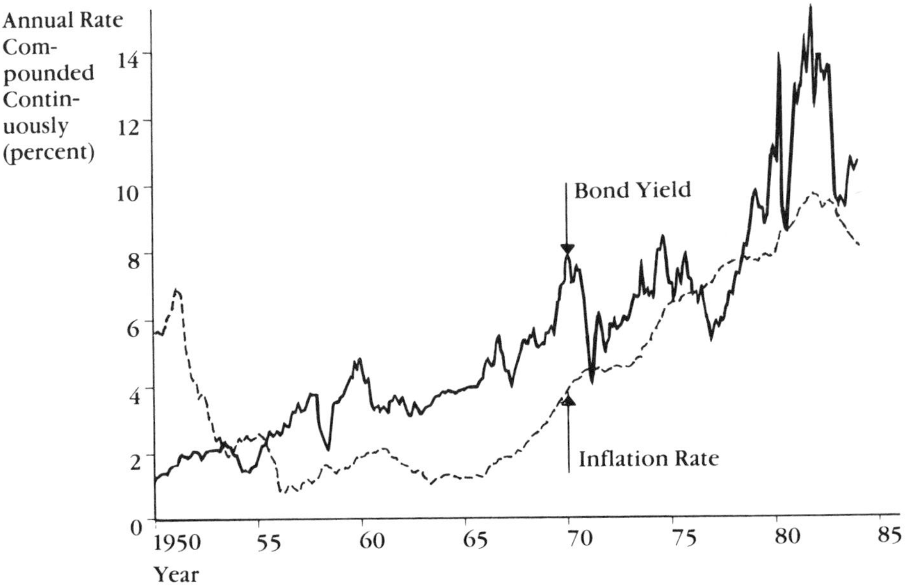

Now it is of course possible that an investor's projected rate of inflation will be too low, and that when he receives repayment of his loan he will find that he has realized a negative rate of return. But you can be sure that he will not allow such a state of affairs to continue forever: He will demand an even higher rate of return on his next loan or abandon the credit markets entirely and invest his money in precious metals or durable goods. Therefore, we may legitimately postulate that there is a real rate of return on risk-free debt (such as short-term U.S. Government bonds), and that this risk-free real rate of return is practically constant for all years. There are different real rates of return for different kinds of investments, owing to varying degrees of risk of default, but these differentials are also reasonably constant from year to year. The primary uncertainty with which we have to deal when we choose i for debt instruments is the uncertainty in the rate of inflation. Since, as stated above, we have no mathematical way to predict this rate, even for the very near future, we must simply make an educated guess. Once we have chosen our assumed rate on inflation β, then we can make a reasonable assumption as to the real rate of return on the pension fund (based on the kinds of investments the fund will make) and add the two rates together to produce the interest assumption for future investments, $\delta = log(1+i)$.

Where the fund has investments other than debt — for example, common stocks — it is somewhat more difficult to predict the real rate of return. Figure 6.5.3 shows the real value of an average share of common stock on the New York Stock Exchange (as reflected by the Standard & Poor's 500 stock index). Note that the real value of an average share in 1983 is about the same as in 1937 and in 1929, but inbetween there have been long periods of increase and decline. The real rate of return on common stocks is, it appears, anybody's guess.

Figure 6.5.3
Standard & Poor's 500-Stock Average
(in constant dollars)

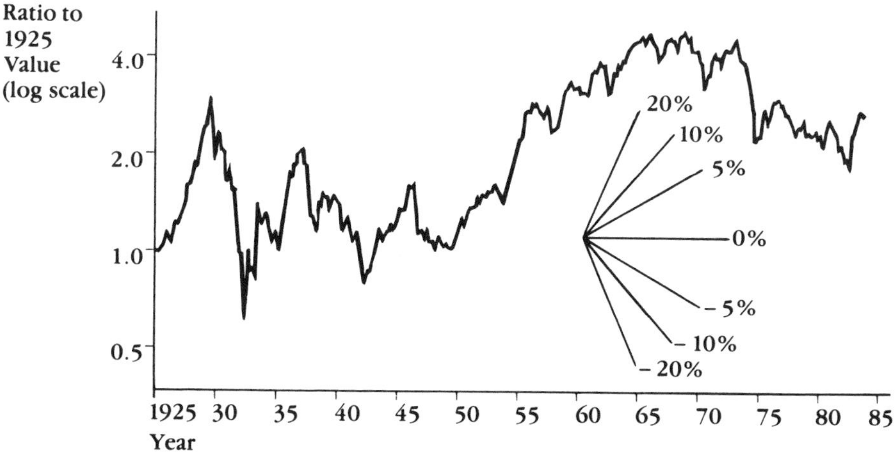

Since we have found it necessary to predict a real rate of return, and, at least on certain kinds of investments, we can predict it with a fair degree of confidence, why not simply ignore the rate of inflation and base our calculations of the present values, etc., on the *real* rate of return, expressing our answers in real dollars? The answer is that the absolute rate of inflation does not "cancel out" of both the asset and liability sides of our equations, and, that being the case, we must make our best estimate of the inflation rate — which for most of us will not be zero (see again Figure 6.5.1!).

To see that the ***absolute*** rate of inflation is critical, consider a plan covering at present only active employees, with benefits based on final pay (just before retirement), and suppose that the employer sees to it that wages always reflect inflation. Assume also that the real rate of return on the fund is maintained, so that inflation is immediately reflected in the value of the fund. Suppose further that the cost of the plan is determined under the entry-age-normal cost method, and that the assumptions incorporate a rate of inflation $b = e^{\beta} - 1$. Now if in a given year the actual inflation rate turns out to be $b + \Delta b$ — i.e., there is an ***acceleration*** in the rate of inflation — what are the consequences on the next valuation date?

(1) The new projected benefit is higher than the old by an amount ΔB, which is proportional to Δb, as you can see from equation (2.4.7); this gives rise to an increase in the accrued liability proportional to Δb.

(2) The realized interest rate i' is higher than i by Δb, so the interest gain is roughly equal to $\Delta b F_t$, as shown by equation (5.2.4).

(3) The difference, therefore, between (1) and (2) above represents an unexpected increase in the unfunded accrued liability — i.e., an *actuarial loss* — which is proportional to Δb.

If Δb is positive in some years and negative in others, gains will balance losses over time — the desired state of affairs. But if we deliberately understate b, particularly if we assume $b = 0$, then Δb will be positive in all years and losses will persist. In other words, the inflation rate b cannot be ignored unless it is explicitly assumed to be zero.

At the same time, we would be remiss if we chose i to reflect assumed inflation while ignoring the impact of inflation on the plan's *benefits*. If the benefit in the example of the preceding paragraph were a flat-dollar amount instead of a percentage of final pay, the accuracy of our cost determination would depend on whether or not that dollar amount was subject to periodic adjustment for inflation. In many such plans the dollar amount is adjusted for inflation, and if that fact is not recognized at the outset — and if, at the same time, there is an inflation component in the assumed interest rate — then, even if inflation proceeds at exactly the assumed rate, there will be periodic increases in the unfunded accrued liability, as the flat-dollar benefit level rises. These increases in unfunded are of course indistinguishable from other actuarial losses and will accumulate over the years. Many flat-dollar plans in the United States have fallen victim to the fallacy of projecting interest rates higher than the real rate of return (i.e., incorporating an inflation assumption implicitly) without reflecting the projected impact of inflation on benefit levels.* The result has been drastic underfunding of some of these plans and insolvency in some cases. Unfortunately, misguided laws and regulations often prevent the actuary from projecting ***benefits*** properly to reflect inflation, while insisting that he use a value of i higher than the real rate of return.

To review our discussion so far: We have seen that (a) the rate of return on future investments may be subdivided into an inflationary component and a real rate of return; (b) the real rate of return is predictable while the inflation rate is not; (c) the cost of the pension plan cannot be properly determined without explicitly recognizing inflation, both in the rate of return i and in future benefits (including, it should be added, any ***anticipated*** post-retirement adjustments in pension, whether or not these are explicitly provided for by the plan as written).

Note that the pension actuary looks on inflation somewhat differently than his counterpart in a life-insurance company. The life actuary is concerned with establishing reserves for ***fixed-dollar*** contracts; he is reluctant to predict too high an inflation rate for fear it will produce inadequate reserves. The pension actuary is generally not concerned with fixed-dollar contractual arrangements: Rather, he must anticipate the impact of inflation on the benefit payouts as well as the investment return. The life-insurance actuary, when he assumes any inflation at all, usually prefers to assume that it will persist for the near term at its current rate, but will taper off to nothing in the long term. This approach is conservative in his case. But the pension actuary would actually be *less* conservative if he made this assumption — unless he really thinks inflation will disappear. Furthermore, in view of the fact that no one (to the author's knowledge) has any way of successfully predicting inflation rates, there would appear to be little scientific justification for assuming anything about the future *changes* in these rates. The best we can do is assume a constant rate of inflation, and hope for the best.

If we thus assume a fixed rate of inflation for the future, then even if we expect the real rate of return to change for some reason (such as a shift in investment policy), we have no right to predict rates of return on ***future*** investments which vary from year to year. Therefore, the assumed rate of return should be constant for future investments. In most situations, this rate will also suffice for existing investments, so i can justifiably be taken as constant for all years. It might be, however, that we have a relatively certain future rate of return on existing assets (e.g., if we had a portfolio of bonds valued at amortized value) and we expect future rates of return to be higher. In such a situation we would be justified in using an assumed interest rate which varied with the passage of time, as old investments rolled over into the new rate. But in the ordinary case, we cannot improve on the assumption of a constant i.

---

*Robert C. Kryvicky, in his paper, "The Funding of Negotiated Pension Plans" (TSA XXXIV), discusses this phenomenon in detail using a computer model.

The salary scale, where there is to be one, should be expressed first in real-dollar terms and then combined with the assumed inflation rate. The first question, then, is will real rates of pay for the employees covered by a par-

Figure 6.5.4
Average Hourly Rate of U.S. Workers in Manufacturing Industries

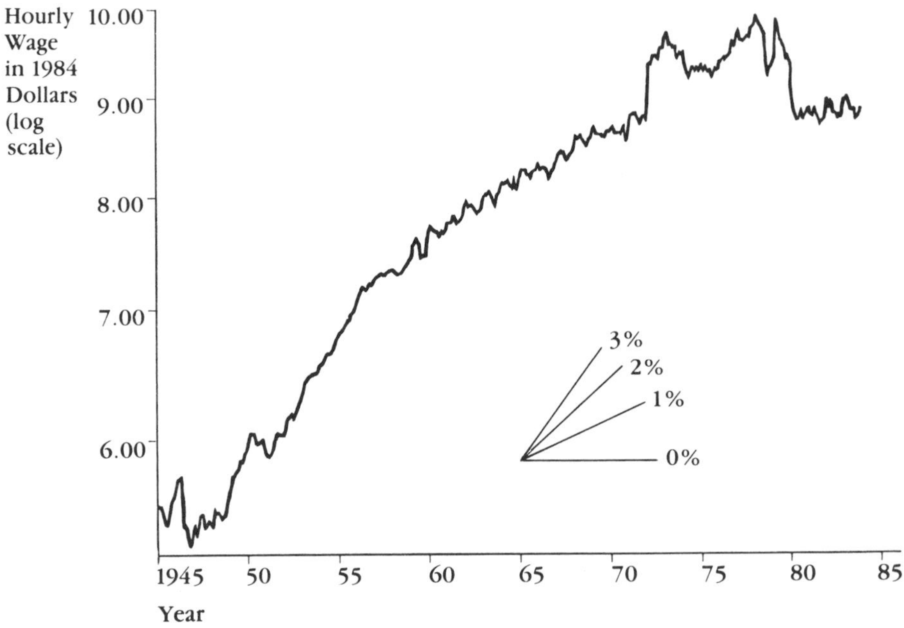

ticular plan increase or decrease? Figure 6.5.4 shows the behavior of the average hourly wage in manufacturing payrolls, as compiled by the U.S. Department of Labor. You can see that, generally speaking, American workers have had real wage gains of about 1½% per year over the last 40 years. Whether or not this will continue is an unanswerable question.

Whether real wage increases continue to be a normal feature of the economic scene is less important than the expected prosperity of the particular group of employees covered by the plan in question. Employees in a declining industry, for example, would not be expected to have real pay increases as high as those of employees of growing industries.

A subtle point, which is often overlooked, is that the salary scale attempts to measure the pay increases of employees who actually stay with the employer. In other words, the question answered by the salary scale is: Given that an employee stays until retirement, what will be his rate of salary increase? This means that the salary scale must not only reflect inflation and increases in standard of living, but must also reflect the policy of the employer with respect to merit and longevity increases. The stage of growth of the employer should also be considered, because employees of a young but rapidly growing enterprise will generally receive more frequent salary increases due to promotion in rank than will employees of a company which is not growing so quickly.

Sometimes, especially in very large employee groups, it is possible to express the policy of the employer with respect to salary increases in terms of rates which vary by age or length of service. In just as many situations, however, there is no discernible pattern, and a uniform rate of salary increase will serve just as well.

Exercises

6.5.1 Refer to the demonstration that the absolute rate of inflation affects pension cost. Does the argument hold if the unfunded is zero? (Answer: no; but explain why.)

6.5.2 Construct an argument similar to that of this section to show what would happen to the cost of the hypothetical plan if there were an acceleration Δb in the rate of inflation and the *aggregate,* rather than the entry-age-normal, cost method were used.

6.5.3 Show explicitly how the cost of a flat-dollar plan would behave if inflation proceeded at rate b, the assumed rate, but b was ignored when computing the cost under the entry-age-normal method. Use an argument modelled after the one in this section.

6.5.4 Show that under the individual entry-age-normal cost method an active employee's normal cost divided by his current salary is unchanged if both the force of interest and the "force of salary increase" (the instantaneous relative rate of increase in salaries) are changed by the same amount, provided $\ddot{a}_y^{(12)}$ remains constant. I.e., show that the normal cost depends on the *difference* between the (continuous) interest and salary-increase rates.

6.5.5 A plan provides a benefit of \$6 per month for each year of service and the normal cost is determined under the entry-age-normal cost method. Since it is probable that the \$6 will be increased as the dollar loses value, the actuary proposes to use an assumed interest rate of only 3% — what he believes to be the real rate of return on the pension fund. Is this procedure proper? Does your answer depend on the size of the unfunded? Would you change your answer if the cost method were different?

Chapter 7

Cost Methods Again

7.1 *Who Should Be Included?*

It almost goes without saying that any persons who are eligible (or potentially eligible, subject only to such contingencies as survival to a certain age) for a benefit from the plan should be included in the valuation. Such persons might be actual pensioners, survivors of deceased pensioners, terminated employees with "vested" rights to deferred benefits — even employees transferred to, say, another division of the employer or to another classification of employment, but who might eventually receive some kind of benefit if they remain employed. Because such "inactives" have no normal costs (as we saw in section 2.10), their respective accrued liabilities are equal to the present values of their respective future benefits; so the unfunded accrued liability of the plan as a whole would be understated if their individual accrued liabilities were not recognized. An exception to the foregoing rule is where benefits have been purchased from an insurance company on a nonparticipating basis, so that the present value of future benefits (i.e., the accrued liability) is exactly equal to the assets on hand. In this case both assets and accrued liabilities may be ignored without affecting the unfunded of the plan as a whole.

The more difficult question is which *active employees* to include — and what do we mean by "active employee"? Although we began using the term in section 2.1, where we defined the set $\mathbf{A}_t$ as the set of persons over whose active working lifetimes the cost of pensions are to be accrued, we did not then stop to examine all of the complexities of this seemingly simple definition. Now it is time to do so.

To see that, in general, the definition of $\mathbf{A}_t$ is not trivial, consider the following hypothetical cases:

Example 1 — Multidivisional Corporation

A large corporation has many separate divisions, only one of which is covered under the plan in question. Should we include the employees of *all* of the divisions of the corporation (using in our valuation assumed probabilities of transfer to and from the covered division)? Or, should we let $\mathbf{A}_t$ comprise only employees working at the division in question (in which case we would treat employees who transferred to another division as having terminated, and employees transferring into the division as new entrants)?

Example 2 — Contributory Plan

Participation in a contributory plan is usually voluntary, and there is usually a waiting period for participation. The question is, should we include all employees *potentially* eligible to elect to participate? If so, then we need to take into account the probability of a nonparticipating employee's joining the plan, as well as the probability that an employee already participating will cease to participate. Or, should we include in $\mathbf{A}_t$ only those employees who are actually participating in the plan on the valuation date?

Example 3 — Industrywide Union Plan

In the U.S.A., these are called "multiemployer" plans. Suppose we have one covering all of the carpenters working within the jurisdiction of a particular local union. In this case there is not just one employer, but several: all of the contractors in the area who employ carpenters and who have agreed to participate in the plan. Each employer contributes a certain amount per hour for each of the carpenters he employs. Each employer has also employees who are not covered: supervisors, for example, or other tradesmen. Who should be in $\mathbf{A}_t$ in this case? All carpenters in the district, whether or not currently employed in their trade? All employees of the participating employer? (The answer to that one is obviously "no" — which shows ironically how inadequate our original definition of $\mathbf{A}_t$ was!) Only those carpenters who are currently working in the district?

Example 4 — Social Security (U.S.A.)

The cost of the Old-Age Insurance (Social Security) program in the U.S.A. is not determined in a "proper" manner, as defined in section 2.11, but there is no conceptual reason why it could not be; if we wanted to determine its cost, we should have to begin by defining set $\mathbf{A}_t$. The program is funded by a payroll tax on all covered workers (not all workers in the country are covered). For those persons who hold covered jobs, whether or not they are citizens of the U.S.A., participation is mandatory. So who should comprise the set $\mathbf{A}_t$? All workers in the U.S.A, (because any one of them might change jobs and become covered, even if he is not now in covered employment)? All workers in covered employment? All residents of the U.S.A. who are of working age, even though not now employed? All residents of the U.S.A., even those under working age?

You can see that the question of defining $\mathbf{A}_t$ is not always straightforward. What we need to discover is a general approach to the question, so that no matter with what complex situation we are confronted, we can proceed directly to a correct definition.

Even when we have a satisfactory definition of $\mathbf{A}_t$, we shall need to address two variant procedures: The first is what is called a "funding exclusion"; the second is the use of "open-group" computer models.

A "funding exclusion" is the arbitrary exclusion from the valuation of a subset of $\mathbf{A}_t$, using an age/service criterion. For example, all employees under age 25 or with less than one year of service might be ignored for valuation purposes. This technique is often used in contributory and individual-policy plans, and sometimes in other plans, as an allowance for employee turnover. Is it legitimate to use a funding exclusion? If so, when? If not, why?

While a funding exclusion is an arbitrary *shrinking* of $\mathbf{A}_t$, an open-group model is an expansion of it. We have heretofore dealt with the set $\mathbf{A}_t$ as a closed cohort of employees, recognizing new entrants only as they occur (see section 2.7). This means that when we computed, say, present value of future benefits, we computed it only for the employees now on hand; likewise with present value of future salaries. But is this realistic? Some might say that in determining pension cost we necessarily assume that the employer is a going concern, and that the present value of future benefits and present value of future salaries should be computed over *all* future active employees — not only those now employed, but also their successors after they leave employment, and the successors of the successors, *ad infinitum*. What about this claim? Have we defined $\mathbf{A}_t$ too narrowly?

Importance of the Normal Cost

The key to the questions raised above is a thorough understanding of the normal cost. So before attempting any answers, we shall pause for a moment to review and fortify the fundamental logic of actuarial cost methods.

Under each of the methods studied in Chapter 2, there is, for each *individual* member of set $\mathbf{A}_t$, a unique and unambiguous normal cost. This is true even for so-called "aggregate" methods. Table 7.1.1 summarizes the definition of normal cost under each of the methods. It will be worth your while to study this table carefully before reading on, and especially to review each of the back-references cited. Note the similarity of the normal costs under each of the projected-benefit cost methods and the uniqueness of the unit-credit.

Table 7.1.1
Summary of Normal-Cost Definitions

Cost Method	*Normal Cost for Employee j*	*Back-references*
Unit-credit	$NC_t^j = \Delta AB_t^j \frac{D_y}{D_x} \ddot{a}_y^{(12)}$ + *PV of ancillary benefits attributable to* ΔAB_t^j	equations (2.2.4) (3.2.8) (4.2.13)
Entry-age-normal (individual)	$NC_t^j = \underbrace{\frac{PVFBW_t^j}{PVFSW_t^j}}_{U_t^j} \cdot S_t^j$	equations (2.4.5) (3.3.4) (3.5.3) (4.4.1) (4.4.2)
Entry-age-normal (aggregate)	$NC_t^j = \underbrace{\frac{\sum_{\mathbf{A}_t} PVFBW_t^j}{\sum_{\mathbf{A}_t} PVFSW_t^j}}_{U_t} \cdot S_t^j$	equation (2.8.8); exercise 2.8.3
Individual-level-premium	$NC_t^j = \underbrace{\frac{PVFB_t^j - AL_t^j}{PVFS_t^j}}_{U_t^j} \cdot S_t^j$	equations (2.5.2) (2.5.14) (2.5.15) (2.5.18); exercise 3.4.2
Frozen-initial-liability; Attained-age-normal; Aggregate	$NC_t^j = \underbrace{\frac{\sum_{\mathbf{A}_t} PVFB_t^j - AL_t}{\sum_{\mathbf{A}_t} PVFS_t^j}}_{U_t} \cdot S_t^j$	equations (2.6.4) (2.8.4) (2.9.1) (2.9.5); exercises 3.5.3 4.4.4 4.4.5

The normal cost is the embodiment of our cardinal premise that the cost of each person's pension should be recognized during his working years. Under the individual cost methods, the present value of an individual's future benefits exactly equals the present value of his future normal costs, when he enters the plan. Under the aggregate methods, this is not generally true, because the sum of the individual normal costs is adequate only *in aggregate* to fund the benefits at retirement: The restriction that each person's normal cost be the same percentage of his salary means that for some employees the normal cost will be more than sufficient to fund their pensions, and for others less than sufficient (see exercise 2.6.6). In other words, under aggregate methods the pension cost is spread over the average (rather than the individual) working lifetimes of active employees taken as a group, with the consequence that the aggregate methods cannot be used indiscriminately (remember exercise 2.9.5?).

Under each of the cost methods it is also possible to define a "gain" in such a way that the following equation holds true

$$UAL_{t+1} = (UAL_t + NC_t)(1 + i) - (C + I_C) - Gain \ . \tag{7.1.1}$$

A review of Chapter 2 should convince you that in each case the term "gain" (which for aggregate methods is not in this case equal to zero — as you will see in exercise 7.1.3) is a random variable with mean zero. In other words, if it were possible to turn back the clock at the end of a given year and let the year happen all over again, the gain would be different due to the random nature of deaths, terminations, etc. To say that the mean of this random variable is zero is simply to say that we have presumed our assumptions correct (otherwise we should revise them). In section 6.2 we saw that the distribution of this random variable was quasi-Poisson.

Now if we looked at the normal cost and the accrued liability after rerunning the year, we would find that they were exactly the same as before — because they were strictly deterministic quantities calculated on the valuation date. I.e., the normal cost and accrued liability are *not* random variables. The accrued liability is, as we emphasized in section 2.2 and later, simply a benchmark number representing the ideal fund balance at any given time. The normal cost is the secular increase in the accrued liability (remember exercises 2.2.4 and 2.3.3?), or, in other words, is a balancing item to make "gain" a stationary random variable, as you can see by equation (7.1.1).

As to the initial unfunded accrued liability, if any, it is simply an asset in the form of a promissory note from the employer, giving rise to extra contributions in the form of amortization payments — but in any case a transitional component of the overall pension cost.

Therefore, the normal cost truly is normal: The gain fluctuates randomly around a mean of zero and the amortization of the initial unfunded is just a temporary cost adjustment used to make the transition between the zero pension cost recognized before the plan was in effect, and the ultimate plan cost. The normal cost is therefore the central feature of the cost method being used, because it expresses the logical premises of the method (as we saw in Chapter 2) and it shows exactly how the cost of each *person's* pension is to be spread over time.

Natural Definition of $\mathbf{A}_t$

The cost of a pension plan is not just an idle abstraction, created by actuaries for their own amusement. Rather, the only reason for going to the trouble of figuring out how to compute it (deciding on a cost method, choosing assumptions, etc.) is so that some *accountable entity* — the employer in the typical case — can actually charge its books with the proper cost of the pension promise it has made. In the case of plans which are required to fund in full the actuary's computed cost, the accounting entries are simple: The employer debits pension expense and credits cash. On the other hand, when the full cost of the plan is not funded (as, for example, in the case of book-reserve plans, or funded plans where the employer defers a contribution) the accounting entries can get more complicated, because the pension-expense account bears interest at the assumed rate. Whatever the accounting details, the pension cost is a number which someone needs to know in order to make bookkeeping entries.

The pension-expense account of the employer (or other sponsoring entity) is intended to be matched against the revenues produced by the "asset" (in this case the employee). That expenses should match revenues in a reasonable way is a basic accounting principle. In the case of the multiemployer plan (Example 3, above), the situation is a little bit different. There, the employer's pension expense is simply his contribution to the fund, which is determined by the formula promulgated by the jointly administered pension trust. In this case, it is the trust, not the employer, which is interested in matching properly the pension cost to the contribution-assessment formula. In the case of Social Security (Example 4) the pension cost is of interest more to the public than to the employer, because the former must (or should) compare that cost, expressed as a percentage of taxable payroll, to the payroll-tax rate.

When we view the pension cost as an accounting entry — something very tangible — and bear in mind with what revenues we intend to match it, we find that the definition of $\mathbf{A}_t$ follows naturally, as we can see by returning to our examples.

Example 1 — Multidivisional Corporation

The set $\mathbf{A}_t$ should comprise only the employees of the division which is covered by the plan, and no others, because the cost of the plan is to be matched against the revenues of that division. The employees of that division produce the revenue from which earnings are derived, so they should each bear a normal cost. To charge a normal cost to any other employee of the corporation would be like charging one division for the cost of machinery purchased by and used by another division, which does not make any accounting sense.

Example 2 — Contributory Plan

The contributory plan is not quite as simple a case. On one hand, if every employee (for practical purposes) eventually participates, then it should be treated no differently from any other kind of plan.

On the other hand, if the employer views his pension expense as *matching* the employees' contributions, then it is proper for him to define $\mathbf{A}_t$ as the set of all employees who actually participate in the plan. Under this view, the revenue which is to be matched is the employee contributions to the plan, rather than their share of the employer's gross sales. The philosophy of the typical employer who installs a contributory plan is that he does not wish to bear the cost of a plan for any employee who is unwilling to share the burden; under that philosophy, the set $\mathbf{A}_t$ rightly excludes nonparticipating employees.

Example 3 — Multiemployer Plan

The purpose of the pension cost under the multiemployer plan is to determine the employer contribution rate (usually expressed in cents per hour). Therefore, we should include in $\mathbf{A}_t$ only the employees whose hours will be charged with the contribution rate: I.e., $\mathbf{A}_t$ should comprise only those carpenters covered by the plan who are *actually working* for a participating employer on the valuation date. The contingency that they may cease to work after the valuation date is irrelevant to the definition of $\mathbf{A}_t$, because that is to be allowed for in the service table.

Example 4 — Social Security

Because the purpose to which the pension cost is to be put is to test the adequacy of the payroll tax, the set $\mathbf{A}_t$ should comprise only workers who are in covered employment on the valuation date. No other resident of the U.S.A. should bear a normal cost, because no such person is paying payroll taxes: The expense (pension cost) must be matched to the revenue (payroll taxes).

Note that we cannot *deduce* anything about the definition of $\mathbf{A}_t$ using the logic of prior chapters. All of that logic has rested at least in part on the hypothesis that $\mathbf{A}_t$ is well defined; we cannot expect the logic to shed light on the hypothesis. Rather, the definition of $\mathbf{A}_t$ is dictated in every case by (1) the existence of an individual normal cost for each "active employee" and (2) the *accounting purpose* to which the pension cost is intended to be put — i.e., the revenue which it is supposed to match.

Funding Exclusions

A "funding exclusion" (which should more properly be called a "costing exclusion" because we are not restricting our deliberations to those pension plans which are actually funded, in the sense of having a trust or separate funding agency), is a deliberate exclusion from the valuation of a subset of $\mathbf{A}_t$ — after $\mathbf{A}_t$ has been defined naturally in the manner described above. When we employ a funding exclusion, we arbitrarily define the normal cost of each member of the excluded subset as zero. Why would we want to do such a thing?

Rather than answer the question in abstract, let us return to Example 2 above, the contributory plan. As before, we let $\mathbf{A}_t$ represent the set of all "active employees" whether or not they are now participating in the plan. Let us introduce a new symbol $\mathbf{M}_t$, to represent the subset of $\mathbf{A}_t$ consisting of actual members of the plan. Suppose we decided *not* to exclude the members of set $\mathbf{A}_t - \mathbf{M}_t$ from our valuation, but rather to include all members of $\mathbf{A}_t$. When we set up our service table, we must allow somehow for the probability that an employee in the set $\mathbf{A}_t - \mathbf{M}_t$ will, when he becomes eligible, actually decide to join the plan and make contributions — i.e., to enter set $\mathbf{M}_t$. One approach would be to set up a service table for the set $\mathbf{A}_t - \mathbf{M}_t$ (the nonmembers) which would contain the probability of leaving that set and entering $\mathbf{M}_t$. Then we would have to set up a *secondary* service table for set $\mathbf{M}_t$, to represent the probability of leaving $\mathbf{M}_t$ given that one has entered it. With these primary and secondary service tables we could then compute the present value of future retirement pensions as an "ancillary benefit", as described in section 4.7.

All this makes for quite a messy valuation which, although it could be done by computer nowadays, would have been laughably difficult before the computer era (the author is not aware of any contributory plans which were or are valued in this manner). When we add to this practical difficulty the argument that the employer's cost should properly be matched against employee *contributions* rather than *wages,* the case for a funding exclusion of the set $\mathbf{A}_t - \mathbf{M}_t$ is overwhelming. In short, when valuing a contributory plan we must, as a practical matter, use $\mathbf{M}_t$ rather than $\mathbf{A}_t$ as the set of "active employees".

There are other practical situations which virtually mandate the use of a funding exclusion. For example, when we have a plan funded exclusively by a group deferred-annuity contract and where we are using the "default" cost method of letting the insurance premiums less dividends be our cost for the year (as discussed in section 5.4), we are in fact using a funding exclusion — because such contracts normally have a waiting period before annuity purchases begin.

Another such situation is when we have a "split-funded" plan, as discussed in section 5.5. We saw that it is necessary for practical purposes to use the "two-plan" approach to determine the normal cost. Since here, too, policies are purchased only for employees who have survived the waiting period (an attempt to lower the lapse rate and reduce administrative expense) we can see from equation (5.5.6) that $\mathbf{A}_t$ has to be defined as the set of all persons on whom the employer is paying insurance premiums. Of course, the "two-plan" approach was itself a compromise, but having made that compromise we are forced into yet another.

If we find it conscionable to use a funding exclusion in the examples cited above, why can we not simply use it whenever we like? The answer is that we can, with limitations.

An extreme form of funding exclusion would be to define $\mathbf{A}_t$ as the set of all employees who are about to retire in the coming year, and to exclude all other employees. This approach actually has been used, although it is now almost completely obsolete; it is called *terminal funding*. Under this "cost method" you simply set up a reserve for each employee in the year he retires, equal to the present value of his pension. The terminal-funding approach, however, has many of the vices associated with pay-as-you-go funding (see section 2.1).* Somewhere between the extremes of no funding exclusion and terminal funding we must draw the line; but where? Sometimes the line is drawn by governmental regulation or by rules of accounting bodies, but in many cases it is left to the judgment of the actuary.

When you are called upon to make such a judgment, remember that a funding exclusion implies there is no normal cost borne by any excluded employee. If the excluded employee has a wage cost to the employer, why does he not also have pension cost, given that he is just as likely as any other employee in his class to get a pension?

If you decide to use a funding exclusion, beware of the plan covering a group of relatively new employees. If you determine the pension cost by excluding, say, all employees with less than a year of service, you are in essence assuming that the probability of termination of employees in their first year of employment is 100% (see exercise 7.1.6). When you make the subsequent valuation, you may discover that a large number of employees has survived the exclusion period and entered the set $\mathbf{A}_t$ (as you have defined it), and that the cost has jumped drastically. In the usual situation (no funding exclusion) it is not taken as a bad reflection on your determination of this year's cost if a lot of new entrants appear in a subsequent year — both the wage costs and the pension costs appear at the same time. But if you have used a funding exclusion, the changes in the two are out of phase.

If you are using the entry-age-normal cost method, the definition of "entry age" would be changed if a funding exclusion were introduced: Rather than being age at hire, entry age would be the age at entry into $\mathbf{A}_t$.

Note that if two actuaries perform a valuation on the same plan on the same date, and if both use the same actuarial cost method, but one uses a funding exclusion and the other does not, then they are not using the cost method in the same way. The actuary who does not use the funding exclusion is distributing the cost of each employee's pension over his entire period of employment, whereas the other actuary is distributing it over a shorter period. In section 5.1 we noted that the definition of "assets" is an integral part of the cost method; the use of a funding exclusion is likewise a modification of the cost method.

Open-Group Models

Suppose we are at time zero, and that we have decided on the definition of set $\mathbf{A}_0$ and chosen our actuarial assumptions in accordance with Chapter 6. If

*Of course, we have to distinguish between *cash outlay* and pension *expense*. It would be quite defensible (when permitted by law) to assess pension expense using no funding exclusion, but to make cash contributions on a terminal-funding basis. The vice lies in using terminal funding or pay-as-you-go as cost methods.

each member is to get an annual pension B^j commencing at age y, we can compute the present value of future benefits as follows:

$$PVFB_0 = \sum_{\mathbf{A}_0} \frac{D_y}{D_x} B^j \ddot{a}_y^{(12)} . \qquad (7.1.2)$$

which can be transformed into

$$PVFB_0 = \sum_{\mathbf{A}_0} \sum_{t=y-x}^{\infty} \underbrace{v^t}_{\text{interest discount to time zero}} \; \underbrace{{}_tp_x B^j}_{\text{expected benefit payment at time } t} . \qquad (7.1.3)$$

This shows that when we do the simple calculation of equation (7.1.2) we are implicitly projecting a series of *expected* benefit payments into the future, and discounting each of those payments back to the present using the assumed interest rate. If we summed the expected future benefit payments by year of payment we could plot them on a graph to produce a curve like that of Figure 7.1.1. Note that eventually the *expected* benefit payments vanish, as probability of payment approaches zero. This occurs because our set $\mathbf{A}_0$ is a closed cohort.

Of course, we do not really think there will be no new entrants. Rather, we expect future benefit payments to follow a pattern like that of Figure 2.1.1. Figure 7.1.2 shows, superimposed, the curves of Figures 2.1.1 and 7.1.1, from which it is obvious that the difference between the two curves in the later years is attributable to the benefits paid to persons hired after time 0: i.e., to future new entrants.

For many purposes, it would be useful to know the shape of the solid line in Figure 7.1.2 — the expected cash benefit payments made each year into the

Figure 7.1.1
Expected Benefit Payments for Set $\mathbf{A}_0$

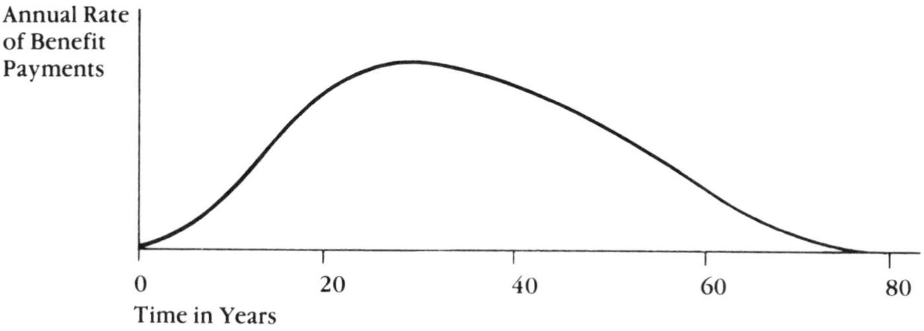

Figure 7.1.2
Annual Rate of Benefit Payment for Open Group (solid) and Closed Group (dashed)

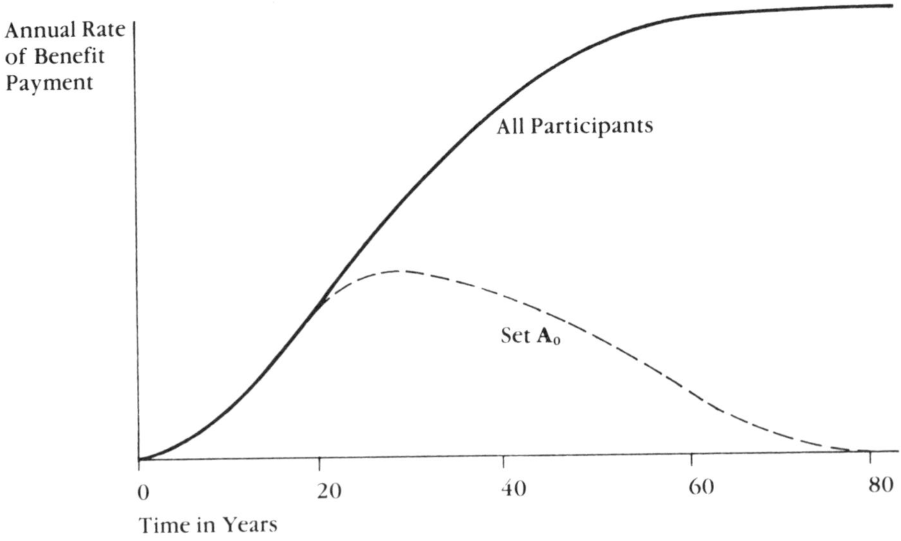

future. If, for example, the plan were not funded but simply paid out of the employer's current income, such a projection would allow him to anticipate his expenditures. Or, for another example, if an employer had budgeted 10% of payroll for pensions, he could match the projected contributions in each year to the projected cash outflow, and work up a year-by-year projection of the fund assets, which might help him in setting his investment policy (or warn him of impending insolvency!). To get the curve, however, we must go beyond our regular calculations and anticipate future new entrants.

One way to do this is to interpret the q's of the service table as *rates* of decline rather than *probabilities* of decline. Then we can make our projections year by year, replacing the persons leaving the group by persons (or fractional persons) presumed to be hired in their stead. We can even embellish our model by assuming a rate of replacement — perhaps a rate greater than unity while the company is young and growing, and less than or equal to unity when it reaches maturity. In so doing, we create what is properly called a *dynamic model:* one in which there exist "level" variables (numbers and total salaries of active employees, for example), and "rate" variables (such as the rates of termination of employment) — *and* where there are "feedback loops" between the rate variables and level variables. In our case, the feedback occurs (for example) as the mortality rates change due to increasing age, and as replacement rates respond to the size of the group.

Dynamic models are a fascinating study in themselves,* but outside the scope of this book, and we must move on.

The dynamic model we have just described is a *deterministic* one because we have interpreted the q's as rates rather than probabilities. It is, of course, also possible to construct a dynamic *stochastic* model, similar to the Monte Carlo experiment of section 6.2, but substantially more complex! If we use a stochastic model we cannot get sharp curves as in Figure 7.1.2, but only curves showing confidence intervals, which might look something like Figure 7.1.3. Our purpose, however, is not to get into the details of model-building, but rather to ask whether these dynamic models can be used to determine pension cost.

Figure 7.1.3
Typical Benefit-Payment Projection by Stochastic Model

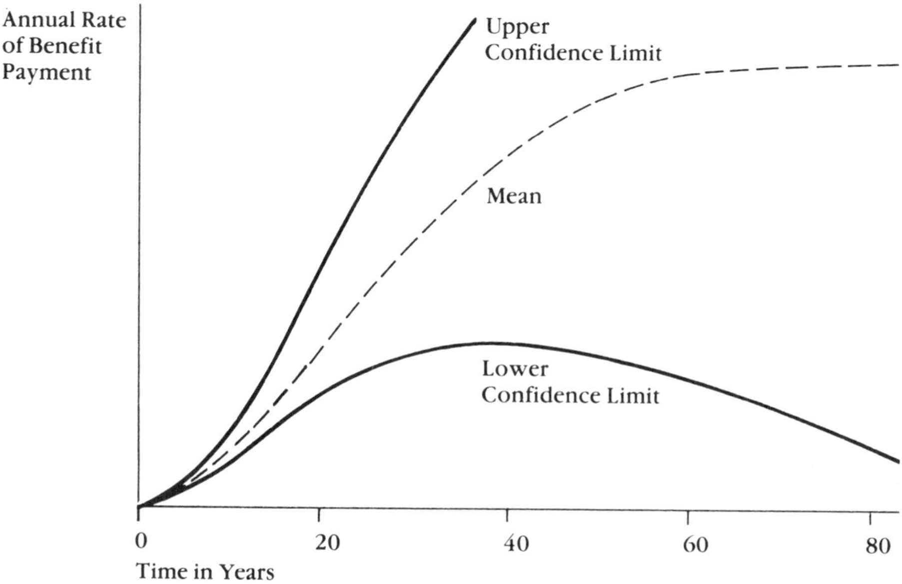

Suppose we have a plan whose cost we are determining in the usual way using the aggregate cost method. We thus determine a normal-cost rate U (see Table 7.1.1), the fraction of pay which we will assess as the pension cost for the current year. Now we know from sections 2.7 and 2.9 that new entrants as they occur will change the value of U in future years. Our ability to construct a dynamic model shows that it is possible to make assumptions about the quantity and demography of new entrants in future years, so if we simply

*A pioneer in the development of dynamic models is Jay Forrester, whose book, *Principles of Systems* (MIT Press, Cambridge, Massachusetts), is an excellent starting point if you wish to investigate this subject further.

made use of such assumptions right now, we could project the future increases or decreases in U. Then, we could average out the projected future changes in U and arrive at a new value of U which would remain constant indefinitely. This approach would not produce, in general, the same value of U as the regular aggregate cost method, but a different value which takes into account future new entrants. Let us call this "cost method" the *open-group aggregate method.*

The open-group aggregate method has some good uses. For example, given a plan which has always been funded on a pay-as-you-go basis, use of it will give the lowest possible level percentage of salary which will maintain long-term solvency (assuming of course that the new-entrant and other assumptions are correct). But is the cost produced by the open-group aggregate method (i.e., the modified U multiplied by this year's covered payroll) a proper pension cost for this year?

Under the regular aggregate method, we compute the unit normal cost using an equation of the following form

$$U = \frac{PVFB - F}{PVFS}, \tag{7.1.4}$$

where *PVFB* and *PVFS* are the present value of future benefits and salary, respectively, computed on the closed group $\mathbf{A}_0$ only. If we wanted to use the open-group method we would have to add $PVFB'$ to $PVFB$, where $PVFB'$ is the present value of future benefits payable to persons who are not yet employees — i.e., the present value of all future benefits between the solid and dashed lines of Figure 7.1.2. This is a finite number because even though future benefits may increase indefinitely, the action of the interest discount makes the series converge.* Likewise, we would have to add a term $PVFS'$ to *PVFS* to compute our new unit normal cost, U^{OG} as follows:

$$U^{OG} = \frac{PVFB + PVFB' - F}{PVFS + PVFS'}. \tag{7.1.5}$$

If we now invoke equation (2.6.9) we can write:

$$U^{OG} = U + \frac{PVFB' - U \cdot PVFS'}{PVFS + PVFS'}. \tag{7.1.6}$$

which reduces to

$$(U^{OG} - U)PVFS = \underbrace{PVFB' - U^{OG} \cdot PVFS'}_{\substack{\textit{accrued liability}\text{ now} \\ \textit{for future new entrants}}} \equiv AL'. \tag{7.1.7}$$

---

*Assuming that benefits are expressed in inflation-adjusted currency units and that we are assuming a positive real rate of return.

The significance of equation (7.1.7) is that the additional accrued liability attributable to the future new entrants is proportional to the difference $U^{OG} - U$. From this fact we can make the following deductions:

Case 1. $AL' = 0$

If this is so, the whole effort of projecting new entrants is wasted, because the open-group method produces the same cost as the closed-group, and the question of the validity of the open-group method is moot.

Case 2. $AL' > 0$

From equation (7.1.7) we see that this is true if and only if $U^{OG} > U$. This means that for the present year we would charge a higher cost under the open-group approach than under the closed-group, presumably because we anticipate future losses on account of new entrants. Note that U is a function of the present active group $\mathbf{A}_0$, but the excess $U^{OG} - U$ is not. This means that we are making an expense charge this year for employees not yet hired — which is just as invalid as taking a depreciation charge this year for a machine not yet acquired (a good analogy, because the pension may be thought of as arising from a sinking fund built up from "depreciating" the employee).

Case 3. $AL' < 0$

This can be so only if $U^{OG} < U$, which means that we are lowering this year's cost on the ground that we will hire, in future years, employees for whom we will charge normal costs generally in excess of those required to fund their individual pensions (taking each cohort of new entrants respectively). In other words, we intend to overcharge future generations of employees so that we can undercharge the present one.

In both cases 2 and 3 above, we are obviously shifting pension cost from one generation to another — in direct violation of our axiomatic definition of "proper" cost recognition as set forth in section 2.1. You can of course get around this logic by going back and rejecting the axiom, but that is to beg the question and reject actuarial cost methods (in our sense of the term) entirely. Therefore, we can say categorically that open-group methods, to the extent that they produce cost results for this year different from their closed-group counterparts — are not legitimately applied to *determine* pension cost.

Exercises

7.1.1 Referring to Table 7.1.1 —

(a) In the equation for FIL, AAN, and aggregate, what does the symbol AL_t stand for in each case? Is it the same for all three cost methods?

(b) Does equation (3.2.8) fit the general format? What about equation (2.4.5)? What about (3.3.4)?

7.1.2 Make up a companion to Table 7.1.1, showing the formulas for computing the accrued liabilities at time t under each cost method. Under which methods can the accrued liability be unambiguously ascribed to individual members of set $\mathbf{A}_t$?

7.1.3 Show how to define the "gain" under the aggregate cost method in terms of a redefined accrued liability, in such a way that equation (7.1.1) is satisfied. (Hint: Remember the general formula for accrued liability, and refer back to equation (2.9.8).)

7.1.4 Consider the following definition: An *individual* cost method (as opposed to an aggregate one) is a cost method under which the normal cost for employee j depends solely on that employee's own attributes. Does the frozen-initial-liability method fit this definition? What about the aggregate cost method? Is the proposed definition a good one?

7.1.5 In this section we noted that the probability distribution of "gain" in equation (7.1.1) has a "quasi-Poisson" distribution. Are there any circumstances under which it might have a pure Poisson distribution?

7.1.6 Assume that we are doing a valuation using a funding exclusion. Show *algebraically* that the present value of future benefits using the funding exclusion is the same as the present value of future benefits computed without the funding exclusion, if and only if $p_x = 0$ for all members of the excluded subset. Does the same result hold true for the present value of future salaries? Prove it.

7.1.7 Under the frozen-initial-liability method, how must we define "covered payroll" in order that the normal cost computed using a funding exclusion be exactly equal to the normal cost computed without a funding exclusion but using $q_x = 1$ in the service table for members of the excluded subset?

7.1.8 Consider the normal cost under the entry-age-normal cost method for employee j. Suppose that w represents j's age at hire, that $q_w = 90\%$ in the service table, and that we define j's entry age to be w. If j survives the first year, his accrued liability will be what multiple of his normal cost if $i = 10\%$? (Answer: 11.)

7.1.9 Two simultaneous valuations are to be done using the entry-age-normal cost method for both. The first valuation will be based on all active employees and the second will exclude employees with less than one year of service on the valuation date. Let w represent the age at hire. In the first valuation we define the entry-age to be w and we compute the normal cost for each individual as NC_t^j, in accordance with Table 7.1.1. In the second valuation we define the entry age as $w+1$, and compute a new normal cost $NC_t^j + \Delta NC_t^j$. If $\mathbf{B}_t$ is the set of all employees with less than one year of service at time t and $\mathbf{A}_t' = \mathbf{A}_t - \mathbf{B}_t$,

(a) write an equation for ΔNC_t^j $(j \epsilon \mathbf{A}_t')$.

(b) show that the total normal costs are the same under both valuations if and only if

$$\sum_{\mathbf{B}_t} NC_t^j = \sum_{\mathbf{A}_t} \Delta NC_t^j . \tag{7.1.8}$$

7.1.10 Suppose we had the same situation as in exercise 7.1.9, but that in the second valuation (the one with the funding exclusion) we continued to define entry age $= w$. Suppose furthermore that during the year $(t, t+1)$ the actual number of employees surviving their first year of employment is exactly equal to the number expected by the service table. Show that the actuarial loss, computed at time $t+1$ for the previous year, on account of this experience will be exactly $(1+i)\sum_{\mathbf{B}_t} NC_t^j$. Note that this implies that the mean actuarial gain for the year cannot be equal to 0. What does this fact tell us about the proper definition of entry age?

7.1.11. Assume that we are doing a valuation using a funding exclusion of all employees with less than a year of service. Suppose further that we are using the unit-credit cost method. Show that the mean or expected actuarial gain is 0 if and only if there are no benefits accrued by employees during their first year of employment.

7.2 *More Unit Credit*

Among the cost methods we have studied so far, unit-credit is something of an oddity, in that its accrued liability (for a "pure" pension plan with no ancillary benefits) depends not just on the ultimate pension at retirement, but also on the manner in which that pension "accrues" over time. The method was originally designed to be used with "career-pay" plans (e.g., the one described in exercise 4.4.1), under which there is a "unit-benefit" formula, which tells how to compute the pension to be credited each year, and the accrued benefit is the sum of previously earned unit benefits. It is also possible, however, to use the unit-credit cost method on a "final-pay" plan — for example, one providing a pension of 50% of the last three years' average pay — but in order to do so we have to specify what we mean by "accrued benefit". It is not absolutely necessary in a final-pay plan that there be an "accrued benefit" formally defined as such, although nowadays with minimum vesting requirements imposed by law in most countries, there has to be such a definition in order to implement the law.

The purpose of this section will be, first, to clean up our discussion of the unit-credit method as used with a career-pay plan and, second, to attack the much larger problem of using the method on final-pay plans.

Under a career-pay plan the accrued benefit of employee j progresses from year to year as follows:

$$AB^j_{t+1} = AB^j_t + UB^j_t \tag{7.2.1}$$

where UB^j_t is a function of j's salary for the year t to $t+1$. For most career-pay plans we do not actually know at time t precisely what UB^j_t will be, because we don't know what j's pay for the year will be — how much overtime he will work, whether he will quit during the year, etc. — so we generally compute the normal cost using an estimated unit benefit, $\widetilde{UB}^j_t$:

$$NC^j_t = \widetilde{UB}^j_t \frac{D_y}{D_x} \ddot{a}_y^{(12)} . \tag{7.2.2}$$

Remember that before now we have been assuming just the opposite — that we know in advance what the unit benefit (which we called ΔB in equations (2.2.4), (3.2.7), and ΔAB in equation (4.2.13)) will be.

The approximation (7.2.2) is tantamount to assuming that the accrued liability at time $t+1$, AB^j_{t+1}, will be the same as

$$\widetilde{AB}^j_{t+1} \equiv AB^j_t + \widetilde{UB}^j_t . \tag{7.2.3}$$

Of course, in general it is not, so we get a gain for the year equal to

$$\sum_{A_t \cap A_{t+1}} (\widetilde{UB}^j_t - UB^j_t) \frac{D_y}{D_{x+1}} \ddot{a}_y^{(12)}$$

(exercise 7.2.1) — a component which did not appear, for example, in equation (2.2.7) because we were assuming we knew exactly what the unit benefit would be.

To illustrate with a concrete example, suppose the unit benefit were defined as 1% of actual pay received each year and that we estimated the unit benefit by

$$\widetilde{UB}_t^j = .01\, S_t^j \tag{7.2.4}$$

(where S_t^j is the annual *rate* of pay at time t); then

$$UB_t^j = .01 \int_t^{t+1} S_u^j\, du\ , \tag{7.2.5}$$

and the gain on account of this estimate would be

$$\sum_{\mathbf{A}_t \cap \mathbf{A}_{t+1}} .01\left(S_t^j - \int_t^{t+1} S_u^j\, du\right) \frac{D_y}{D_{x+1}}\, \ddot{a}_y^{(12)} \approx \sum_{\mathbf{A}_t \cap \mathbf{A}_{t+1}} .01 \cdot \frac{1}{2}\left(S_t^j - S_{t+1}^j\right) \frac{D_y}{D_{x+1}}\, \ddot{a}_y^{(12)}\ , \tag{7.2.6}$$

where we have estimated the integral by the trapezoidal rule. This gain is usually negative because j's salary increases each year. The important point, however, is that the amount of the gain is of the same order of magnitude (relative to salary) each year and not cumulative. Furthermore, we could minimize this gain (or loss) by a more sophisticated estimate of UB_t .

Now the same cannot be said if we are dealing with a final-pay plan. Suppose that the retirement pension was equal to 1% of the *final year's* pay for each year of service. The accrued benefit under such a plan is commonly defined in terms of current pay, rather than some artificial projection of pay at retirement:

$$AB_t^j \equiv .01\underbrace{\left(\int_{t-1}^{t} S_u^j\, du\right)}_{\substack{\textit{previous}\\ \textit{year's pay}}}\underbrace{(x - w)}_{\substack{\textit{years of}\\ \textit{service}\\ \textit{at time t}}}\ . \tag{7.2.7}$$

This means that the "unit benefit" is effectively

$$\Delta AB_t^j = AB_{t+1}^j - AB_t^j = .01\left[(x - w + 1)\int_t^{t+1} S_u^j\, du - (x - w)\int_{t-1}^{t} S_u^j\, du\right]$$

$$= AB_t^j \frac{\int_t^{t+1} S_u^j\, du}{\int_{t-1}^{t} S_u^j\, du} + .01\int_t^{t+1} S_u^j\, du - AB_t^j\ . \tag{7.2.8}$$

So if j's actual pay increased by a fraction r from one year to the next, i.e.,

$$1 + r \equiv \frac{\int_t^{t+1} S_u^j \, du}{\int_{t-1}^{t} S_u^j \, du} \,, \tag{7.2.9}$$

then

$$AB_{t+1}^j = AB_t^j(1+r) + .01 \int_t^{t+1} S_u^j \, du \,. \tag{7.2.10}$$

In other words, under a final-pay plan the accrued benefit does not stand still while we add the unit benefit to it, as it does with a career-pay plan (equation (7.2.1)). Rather, it grows, not only by adding 1% of current pay, but also by a percentage of its previous value. So if we followed past practice of estimating the next year's pay by the annual *rate* at time *t* we would define

$$\widetilde{UB}_t^j = r \cdot AB_t^j + .01\, S_t^j \,. \tag{7.2.11}$$

Then *j* 's normal cost would be equal to the career-pay normal cost (equation (7.2.2)) *plus* an additional component, $r(x-w)(\int_{t-1}^{t} S_u^j \, du) \frac{D_y}{D_x} \ddot{a}_y^{(12)}$, which is proportional to prior service. The additional component starts out small but grows large as *j* approaches retirement — so we get not only the normal geometric increase in normal cost due to an application of the factor D_y/D_x (exercise 2.2.2) but also an additional acceleration due to the fact that the accrued liability increases in proportion to current pay.

The method we have been describing is what we may call the "natural" unit-credit cost method, where the accrued liability is defined by the actual accrued benefit under the terms of the plan. This method can work well enough with a career-pay plan — provided the plan is not updated for inflation — but it results in much "back-loading" of pension costs when used with a final-pay plan whose accrued benefit is defined as a percentage of current pay multiplied by prior service. For this reason the "natural" approach is almost never used with such plans (and indeed is prohibited in the U.S. by IRS regulation).

An obvious way around the incompatibility of natural unit-credit to final-pay plans is first to project the ultimate retirement pension, using a salary scale and other assumptions, and then to redistribute that benefit over the employee's career, to produce a hypothetical pattern of benefit accrual which is not related to the actual pattern prescribed by the plan. This approach is called the ***projected unit-credit*** cost method, to distinguish it from the regular or natural unit-credit method. Let us see how this approach might work with our hypothetical final-pay plan.

Before we can use this method, we need to sharpen up our terms a bit. Assume that *j* 's salary remains constant at S_t^j all year every year, that he is aged exactly *x* years at time *t*, and that our salary scale is represented by the set of indices $\{s_z | z = x, \ldots, y\}$. Also assume that j was hired at exact age w and is assumed to retire at age y. Then we can express his projected benefit as

$$B_t^j(y) = .01\,(y-w)\,\frac{s_{y-1}}{s_x}\,S_t^j\,. \tag{7.2.12}$$

In order to use the projected unit-credit method we want to prorate this projected benefit in some way. For example, we could prorate the benefit in direct proportion to service:

$$\textit{Hypothetical accrued benefit} = B_t^j(x) = B_t^j(y)\,\frac{x-w}{y-w} = .01\,\frac{s_{y-1}}{s_x}\,S_t^j\,(x-w) \tag{7.2.13}$$

and

$$\textit{Hypothetical unit benefit} = \Delta B_t^j(x) = B_t^j(y)\,\frac{1}{y-w} = .01\,\frac{s_{y-1}}{s_x}\,S_t^j\,. \tag{7.2.14}$$

Note that the hypothetical unit benefit is usually larger than the actual one (equations (7.2.8) and (7.2.11)) because it applies the 1% factor to the final year's pay. It follows that the accrued liability and normal cost for j can be expressed as

$$AL_t^j = B_t^j(x)\,\frac{D_y}{D_x}\,\ddot{a}_y^{(12)}\,, \tag{7.2.15}$$

and

$$NC_t^j = \Delta B_t^j(x)\,\frac{D_y}{D_x}\,\ddot{a}_y^{(12)}\,. \tag{7.1.16}$$

The four equations (7.2.13)–(7.2.16) express the application of the projected unit-credit method using what we shall call *linear proration* of the projected benefit.

Another approach to prorating the ultimate benefit is to assume that $B_t^j(y)$ is arrived at by some hypothetical career-pay formula providing a fraction p^j of salary for each year of service since hire (obviously a different percentage for each employee):

$$B_t^j(y) = \sum_{z=w}^{y-1} p^j S_t^j \frac{s_z}{s_x} = .01\,(y-w)\,S_t^j\,\frac{s_{y-1}}{s_x}\,. \tag{7.2.17}$$

Solving for p^j, we get

$$p^j = .01\,(y-w)\,\frac{s_{y-1}}{\sum_w^{y-1} s_z}\,. \tag{7.2.18}$$

Then the "accrued benefit" for cost purposes becomes

$$B_t^j(x) = \sum_{z=w}^{x-1} p^j S_t^j \frac{s_z}{s_x} = .01\,(y-w)S_t^j\,\frac{s_{y-1}}{s_x}\,\frac{\sum_w^{x-1} s_z}{\sum_w^{y-1} s_z}$$

$$= B_t^j(y)\,\frac{\sum_w^{x-1} s_z}{\sum_w^{y-1} s_z}\;. \tag{7.2.19}$$

and

$$\Delta B_t^j(x) = B_t^j(y)\,\frac{s_x}{\sum_w^{y-1} s_z}\;. \tag{7.2.20}$$

With the foregoing two equations plugged in to (7.2.15) and (7.2.16) we have a different application of the projected unit-credit method due to this "career-pay-mimic" proration method.

In general, we can choose any proration function $f(x)$ such that $f(w)=0$, $f(y)=1$, and $f'(x)>0$; then simply *declare* that the accrued benefit for cost purposes is

$$B_t^j(x) = f(x)B_t^j(y)\;. \tag{7.2.21}$$

For example, for linear proration we would have $f(x) = \dfrac{x-w}{y-w}$ and for CPM proration $f(x) = \sum_w^{x-1} s_z \Big/ \sum_w^{y-1} s_z$. No matter what function is chosen, we can write

$$NC_t^j = \Delta f(x)B_t^j(y)\,\frac{D_y}{D_x}\,\ddot{a}_y^{(12)}\;. \tag{7.2.22}$$

Note that if the salary scale is correct there will be no gain or loss due to salary increases using this definition of normal cost — no matter how we define $f(x)$ (exercise 7.2.2). Therefore, $\Delta f(x)$ controls the definition of normal cost under the projected unit-credit method.

We can generate a third proration method by choosing $f(x)$ such that the normal cost remains a level percentage of pay; i.e.,

$$NC_t^j = \Delta f(x)B_t^j(y)\,\frac{D_y}{D_x}\,\ddot{a}_y^{(12)} = B_t^j(y)\,\frac{D_y}{D_x}\,\ddot{a}_y^{(12)}\,\frac{{}^sD_x}{{}^sN_w - {}^sN_y}\;. \tag{7.2.23}$$

Then

$$\Delta f(x) = \frac{{}^sD_x}{{}^sN_w - {}^sN_y} \;\Rightarrow\; f(x) = \frac{{}^sN_w - {}^sN_x}{{}^sN_w - {}^sN_y}\,, \tag{7.2.24}$$

which makes the accrued liability exactly the same as if it were computed under the entry-age-normal cost method! (See exercise 7.2.3.) Let us call this proration method the "EAN-equivalent".

You are now getting the point: The projected-unit-credit cost method can be anything we want it to be, depending (for a given set of assumptions) only on our choice of $f(x)$. And it is not necessary to restrict the method to final-pay plans; we can use it on career-pay plans, too. If we consider "natural" unit-credit as a special case of projected unit credit — where the accrued benefit for cost purposes is equal to the *actual* accrued benefit — then we can state the general proposition that unit-credit is not a distinct cost method at all, but rather a family of methods with different characteristics which depend on the proration function $f(x)$. In other words, unit-credit is more a way of *looking at* pension cost than a way of defining it.

Remember from section 7.1 that the normal cost expresses the philosophy of any cost method with respect to the distribution of the value of an employee's pension over his working lifetime. We have seen that under the unit-credit method the proration function controls the normal cost through equation (7.2.22). Let us now compare the normal costs (for our hypothetical final-pay plan) under the several proration methods we have looked at, as a percentage of j's salary, assuming that all assumptions are exactly realized over his whole career.

If the salary scale has always worked out, j's actual accrued benefit at time t (the valuation date) is

$$B_t^j(x) = .01\,(x-w)S_t^j\,\frac{s_{x-1}}{s_x}\,, \tag{7.2.25}$$

and his projected benefit at age y is

$$B_t^j(y) = .01\,(y-w)S_t^j\,\frac{s_{y-1}}{s_x}\,. \tag{7.2.26}$$

Therefore, the proration function for the *natural* unit-credit method is (for this plan and this employee)

$$f(x) = \frac{B_t^j(x)}{B_t^j(y)} = \frac{x-w}{y-w}\,\frac{s_{x-1}}{s_{y-1}}\,, \tag{7.2.27}$$

so that

$$\begin{aligned}\Delta f(x) &= \frac{x+1-w}{y-w}\,\frac{s_x}{s_{y-1}} - \frac{x-w}{y-w}\,\frac{s_{x-1}}{s_{y-1}}\\ &= \frac{(x-w)(s_x - s_{x-1}) + s_x}{(y-w)s_{y-1}}\,.\end{aligned} \tag{7.2.28}$$

Note that for our sample plan equation (7.2.22) becomes

$$NC_t^j = \Delta f(x)(.01)(y-w)S_t^j \frac{s_{y-1}}{s_x} \frac{D_y}{D_x} \ddot{a}_y^{(12)},$$

or

$$\frac{NC_t^j}{S_t^j} = \underbrace{\Delta f(x)(.01)(y-w)\frac{s_{y-1}}{s_x}}_{\substack{\textit{hypothetical}\\ \textit{unit benefit}\\ \textit{as \% of pay}}} \cdot \underbrace{\frac{D_y}{D_x}\ddot{a}_y^{(12)}}_{\textit{PV factor}}. \qquad (7.2.29)$$

With this equation we can assemble all the formulas in Table 7.2.1 (exercise 7.2.4). Notice the terms representing the hypothetical unit benefit in each case.

Table 7.2.1
Normal-Cost as a Fraction of Salary for Various Proration Functions

Proration Method	$f(x)$	$\Delta f(x)$	NC_t^j/S_t^j *(equation (7.2.29))*
Natural	$\frac{(x-w)s_{x-1}}{(y-w)s_{y-1}}$	$\frac{(x-w)(s_x-s_{x-1})+s_x}{(y-w)s_{y-1}}$	$.01\left[(x-w+1) - (x-w)\frac{s_{x-1}}{s_x}\right]\frac{D_y}{D_x}\ddot{a}_y^{(12)}$
CPM	$\sum_w^{x-1} s_z \Big/ \sum_w^{y-1} s_z$	$s_x \Big/ \sum_w^{y-1} s_z$	$\frac{.01(y-w)s_{y-1}}{\sum_w^{y-1} s_z}\frac{D_y}{D_x}\ddot{a}_y^{(12)}$
Linear	$\frac{x-w}{y-w}$	$\frac{1}{y-w}$	$.01\frac{s_{y-1}}{s_x}\frac{D_y}{D_x}\ddot{a}_y^{(12)}$
EAN-equivalent	$\frac{{}^sN_w-{}^sN_x}{{}^sN_w-{}^sN_y}$	$\frac{{}^sD_x}{{}^sN_w-{}^sN_y}$	$.01\frac{s_{y-1}}{s_x}\frac{y-w}{\frac{{}^sN_w-{}^sN_y}{{}^sD_x}}\frac{D_y}{D_x}\ddot{a}_y^{(12)}$

To breathe some life into these formulas, let us work up a numerical example. Assume that employee j was hired at age 30, and that he is retiring at age 65. Assuming also that salaries increase at 6% a year and that interest on the fund is credited at 7%. Take $\ddot{a}_{65}^{(12)} = 9.0$. Because we are using the unit-credit method, if we assume that the accrued benefit is fully vested (and that the value of it is paid at death) we can ignore the service table, as we saw in section 4.2. Then the ratios of normal cost to salary from Table 7.2.1 can be simplified to

Table 7.2.2

Proration Method	NC_t^j / S_t^j
Natural	$\frac{.09}{(1.07)^{65-x}}\left(x - 29 - \frac{x-30}{1.06}\right)$
CPM	$\frac{.2050}{(1.07)^{65-x}}$
Linear	$.0849\left(\frac{1.07}{1.06}\right)^{-(65-x)}$
EAN-equivalent	.07138

The functions of Table 7.2.2 are graphed in Figure 7.2.1.

Figure 7.2.1 gives rise to a number of inferences and observations, such as the following:

- The linear proration method is very close to the EAN-equivalent. In fact it would be identical if the assumed salary increase rates and interest rates were the same (remember exercise 2.4.1).
- As i exceeds r, the curve of the linear proration method tilts more upward from the level line of the EAN-equivalent.
- The natural and CPM methods are similar: They would be exactly the same if we were dealing with a career-pay plan. In other words, the CPM curve also represents the cost curve of a career-pay plan valued on natural unit credit.
- The EAN-equivalent method does not distribute the total pension cost over service in level dollars, but as a level percentage of payroll (in this case 7.1%), so all the other methods have not only costs that increase with increasing age (or time) but costs that increase more rapidly than payroll. For example, the natural-unit credit starts out at 0.8% of salary at age 30 and winds up at 25% at age 64. With CPM the percentages are 1.9% initially and 19% at age 64, so even if the plan were career-pay, the unit-credit method would still show accelerating costs with the passage of time.
- If a service table were introduced into the example it would exacerbate the differences between the curves rather than ameliorate them.
- Unless the plan's definition of accrued benefit is such that the accrued benefit is always greater than or equal to the EAN-equivalent accrued benefit, then the EAN accrued liability will always exceed that under the unit-credit method, because the accrued liability is equal to the actuarial present value of prior normal costs.

- The normal cost for the entire set $\mathbf{A}_t$ might remain a constant percentage of covered payroll under any of the proration methods we have looked at. But, except under the EAN-equivalent this could happen only if there were a constant influx of new entrants — a point first made in section 2.3, but which bears repeating. If the flow of new entrants stops the cost will rise as the group ages.
- Current tax regulations in the U.S.A. prohibit the use of natural and CPM proration methods on final-pay plans for purposes of meeting minimum funding standards. Since natural unit-credit used on a career-pay plan is theoretically indistinguishable from projected unit credit with CPM proration on a final-pay plan (providing the same benefits), the former should be prohibited too; but it is not because the language of Internal Revenue Code specifically authorizes the use of the natural unit-credit method.
- If you accept the proposition that the pension cost for employee *j* should remain level as a percentage of his salary, you must (a) reject the natural unit-credit method in all circumstances, and (b) reject the projected unit-credit method in all circumstances except where the EAN-equivalent proration method is used — in which case you are simply using the EAN method.

Figure 7.2.1
Projected-Unit-Credit Normal Costs under Four Proration Functions

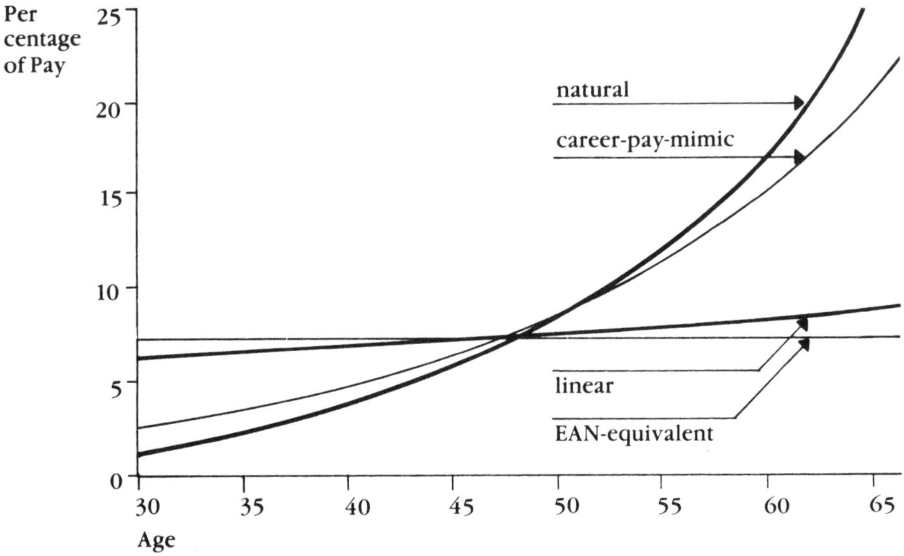

Exercises

7.2.1 Retrace the derivation of equation (2.2.7), assuming that the normal cost is computed using an estimated unit benefit rather than the actual one, and verify the expression shown in the text for the additional gain term which is generated.

7.2.2 Prove that under the projected unit-credit method any proration function which conforms to the limitations set forth in the text will "work", in the sense that if the salary increase and other assumptions work out, no loss on account of salary increases will result.

7.2.3 Show that the EAN-equivalent proration method is truly equivalent to entry-age-normal, by showing that the accrued liability and normal cost are the same as for entry-age-normal.

7.2.4 Show that each of the expressions in Table 7.2.1 is correct, by (a) showing that the expression for $f(x)$ is correct, then (b) deriving Δf, then (c) applying equation (7.2.29).

7.2.5 Using the same assumptions as in the text, verify that each of the expressions in Table 7.2.2 is correct.

7.2.6 Show that, assuming no ancillary benefits and an arbitrary definition of "accrued benefit", the general definition of the normal cost under the unit-credit method (for employee j) is

$$NC_t^j \equiv AL_{t+1}^j \frac{D_{x+1}}{D_x} - AL_t^j \,. \tag{7.2.30}$$

7.3 *More Individual Level Premium*

In section 2.5 we remarked that individual-level-premium is a cost method particularly suited to small plans, where the projected benefits of participants may vary widely — because under the ILP method each *person's* projected benefit is funded over his own career; whereas with entry age normal, for example, a considerable portion of the present value of his benefit may reside in the initial accrued liability. ILP, you will recall, does not treat changes in projected benefits as gains or losses, but provides for them explicitly by increments in the normal cost. There is, however, still an actuarial gain under ILP (see equation (2.5.12)), and that gain must be amortized in some manner in order to arrive at the cost of the plan.

In section 7.1, we remarked that the actuarial gain is a *random variable* with mean zero, and that, therefore, the sum of gains and losses over a period of several years can be expected (statistically) to be zero. With a small plan, however, there is often not enough statistical base (number of employees) nor sufficient homogeneity in benefits or salaries to assure that statistical expectations will be borne out. It is often desirable, therefore, not only to put unexpected changes in projected benefit into the normal cost, but to put all other gains and losses there as well. When we do that in connection with the ILP cost method we actually create a new cost method which is called, incongruously, the *individual-aggregate* method. Although the individual-aggregate (I/A) method is really a variety of ILP, it has some special properties: For example, both assets and pension cost are at all times completely allocated to active participants — a feature which makes it particularly attractive to small employee groups, where there is strong emphasis on individual cost-accounting.

If we decide to amortize the accumulated gains and losses under ILP over the *average* future working lifetimes of the active participants (rather than allocating the gains and spreading them specifically over each person's lifetime) we arrive at the related cost method called the *modified-aggregate,* under which ILP normal costs replace salaries in the formula for the aggregate normal cost. In spite of its name, the modified-aggregate (M/A) method is more closely related to ILP and I/A than to *the* aggregate cost method.

Not only will we learn about two new very useful cost methods in this section but we shall also have occasion to examine more closely what we mean by "aggregate" and "individual" cost methods, and to sharpen our understanding of cost methods generally; because while the I/A and M/A methods are relatively simple to use in practice, their inner workings are complex.

For this section, let us return to our pure pension plan of Chapter 2 — free of ancillary benefits of all kinds — where we assume that pensioners are removed from the plan by annuity purchase or lump-sum distribution. Then we can use the set relationship of equation (2.7.1) to express the movement of employees through the plan.

Under the I/A method we treat each active participant at time t as though he were a sole employee with his own separate fund F_t^j (where, of course, the individual funds add up to the actual fund F_t). We look separately at each of these one-person plans and define the annual pension cost payable at time t using the *aggregate* cost method:

$$C_t^j = \frac{PVFB_t^j - F_t^j}{PVFS_t^j} S_t^j . \tag{7.3.1}$$

We then determine the total cost C_t as the sum of the individual costs. (The terms in equation (7.3.1) have the same definitions as in section 2.9.) The name "individual-aggregate" derives from the fact that we do an "aggregate" valuation for each individual (see equation (2.9.5) and Table 7.1.1).*

---

*Of course, when you have a one-person plan, and you stipulate that his pension is to be funded over his working lifetime, you have already specified the aggregate cost method.

Actually, C_t may be called the "normal cost" under the I/A method, but we shall for most of this chapter continue to refer to it by the symbol C_t (rather than NC_t), so as to reserve NC_t for the normal cost under the ILP method. Similarly, the symbols AL_t, UAL_t, G_t, and so forth, will stand for quantities computed under the ILP method.

Note that at time 0, when the plan begins, we have $F_0 = 0$ and $C_0 = NC_0$ — i.e., the I/A method and the ILP method produce exactly the same results. Also note that you can't use equation (7.3.1) without first having allocated the assets to individuals. Finally, note that the I/A method is not really an "aggregate" cost method — if you define an "individual" cost method to be one under which the normal cost of any particular employee is independent of those of the other employees, and, conversely, an "aggregate" cost method to be one under which the normal cost of any employee depends on the characteristics of other employees. (See exercises 7.1.4 and 7.3.2 for further discussion of this matter.)

Now, the accrued liability under the I/A method is identical to the fund balance F_t, and it will prove convenient for us to express F_t^j in terms of its counterpart AL_t^j (the accrued liability under the ILP method) as follows:

$$F_t^j = AL_t^j - \underbrace{(AL_t^j - F_t^j)}_{UAL_t^j} = AL_t^j - UAL_t^j , \tag{7.3.2}$$

from which we see that allocation of F_t is tantamount to allocation of UAL_t. Furthermore, we have by definition $UAL_0 = 0$ and

$$UAL_t = (UAL_{t-1} + NC_{t-1})(1+i) - C - I_C - G_t \qquad \textit{for } t>0 , \tag{7.3.3}$$

where G_t is the actuarial gain for the year just past. We shall now make the assumption that the cost of the plan determined under I/A method is "contributed" effectively at time t so that

$$C + I_C = C_t(1+i) . \tag{7.3.4}$$

This relation can be made to hold simply by appropriately defining F_t: i.e., by including any over- or underpayments as receivables or advance contributions. This assumption allows us to write (7.3.3) as

$$UAL_t = (UAL_{t-1} + NC_{t-1} - C_{t-1})(1+i) - G_t . \tag{7.3.5}$$

Then, from equations (7.3.1) and (7.3.2) we can deduce

$$C_t \equiv \sum_{\mathbf{A}_t} \frac{PVFB_t^j - F_t^j}{PVFS_t^j} S_t^j = \sum_{\mathbf{A}_t} \frac{PVFB_t^j - AL_t^j + UAL_t^j}{PVFS_t^j} S_t^j$$

$$= \sum_{\mathbf{A}_t} \left(\frac{PVFB_t^j - AL_t^j}{PVFS_t^j} + \frac{UAL_t^j}{PVFS_t^j} \right) S_t^j = \sum_{\mathbf{A}_t} \frac{PVFNC_t^j}{PVFS_t^j} S_t^j \left(1 + \frac{UAL_t^j}{PVFNC_t^j}\right);$$

(7.3.6)

or, more concisely,

$$C_t = \sum_{\mathbf{A}_t} C_t^j = \sum_{\mathbf{A}_t} NC_t^j (1 + \lambda_t^j) \quad \textit{where}\; \lambda_t^j = \frac{UAL_t^j}{PVFNC_t^j}.$$

(7.3.7)

Substituting (7.3.7) into (7.3.5), we get

$$UAL_t + G_t = \left(UAL_{t-1} + NC_{t-1} - \sum_{\mathbf{A}_{t-1}} (1 + \lambda_{t-1}^j) NC_{t-1} \right)(1+i)$$

$$= \sum_{\mathbf{A}_{t-1}} \left(\lambda_{t-1}^j \, PVFNC_{t-1}^j + NC_{t-1}^j - NC_{t-1}^j - \lambda_{t-1}^j \, NC_{t-1}^j \right)(1+i)$$

$$= \sum_{\mathbf{A}_{t-1}} \lambda_{t-1}^j \, \widetilde{PVFNC}_t^j$$

where $\widetilde{PVFNC}_t^j = (PVFNC_{t-1}^j - \mathrm{NC}_{t-1}^j)(1+i)$ for $j \in \mathbf{A}_{t-1}$.

(7.3.8)

If we define $\lambda_{t-1}^j = 0$ for $j \in \mathbf{N}$, we can write

$$\sum_{\mathbf{A}_t} UAL_t^j + G_t = \sum_{\mathbf{A}_t} \lambda_{t-1}^j \, \widetilde{PVFNC}_t^j + \sum_{\mathbf{R}+\mathbf{T}} \lambda_{t-1}^j \, \widetilde{PVFNC}_t^j \qquad (7.3.9)$$

or,

$$\sum_{\mathbf{A}_t} \lambda_t^j \, PVFNC_t^j = \sum_{\mathbf{A}_t} \lambda_{t-1}^j \, \widetilde{PVFNC}_t^j - \Gamma_t$$

where

$$\Gamma_t = G_t - \sum_{\mathbf{R}+\mathbf{T}} \lambda_{t-1}^j \, \widetilde{PVFNC}_t^j.$$

(7.3.10)

If Γ_t is allocated in some way to individual members of A_t, so that $\Gamma_t = \sum_{\mathbf{A}_t} \Gamma_t^j$, then (7.3.10) implies, for $j \in \mathbf{A}_t$,

$$\lambda_t^j = \frac{\lambda_{t-1}^j \, PV\widetilde{FNC}_t^j - \Gamma_t^j}{\mathrm{PVFNC}_t^j}$$

(7.3.11)

Γ_t may be thought of as the "actuarial gain" under the I/A method, because it is the amount by which the unfunded is "unexpected".

In actual practice, the I/A method is usually applied by allocating the *assets* in some fashion and then using equation (7.3.1) to determine the individual costs. But for purposes of our discussion it will be enlightening to consider an equivalent application of the method based on allocation of the *gains,* as follows. At time 0 — when the plan has just started — you do your I/A valuation the same as under ILP. Then at any time $t>0$, you

(1) do the ILP valuation in the normal way to determine $\{NC_t^j\}$ and $\{AL_t^j\}$ for $j \in \mathbf{A}_t$ (see section 2.5 if you have forgotten how to do this);

(2) allocate the I/A actuarial gain from the previous year using your gain-allocation method (as yet unspecified) and update the loading factor for each employee using equation (7.3.11);

(3) compute the individual "aggregate costs" by equation (7.3.7).

Now the only missing ingredient for a complete description of the individual-aggregate cost method is a gain-allocation procedure. Let us emphasize right at the start that there is no single right way to allocate gains: Pension plans and their sponsors vary widely and there may be a number of reasons for allocating gains (or losses) one way or another. However, a discussion of the subject for the "typical" case will get you started.

The "gain" we are interested in allocating is of course the gain computed under the I/A cost method, so we can use equations (2.5.12) and (7.3.10) to get

$$\Gamma_t = \underbrace{I - iF_{t-1} - I_C + I_P}_{\textit{investment gain}} + \underbrace{\sum_{\mathbf{T}} \tilde{F}_t^j - \sum_{\mathbf{A}_{t-1}} q_{x+t-1} \, AL_t^j}_{\textit{termination gain}} + \underbrace{\sum_{\mathbf{R}} \tilde{F}_t^j - P - I_P}_{\textit{retirement gain}}$$

where $\tilde{F}_t^j = AL_t^j - \lambda_{t-1}^j \, PV\widetilde{FNC}_t^j$.

(7.3.13)

As we have said earlier, Γ_t is just as likely to be positive as negative, because we have presumed that i and the service table were chosen so as to represent the means of their respective distributions, and because we have chosen the assumed retirement age y in such a manner as to minimize retirement gains. So it is important to recognize that allocating the actuarial gain is *not* the same as allocating surplus in a mutual life insurance company — because in the pension case we are allocating deficits as often as surplus.

Actuaries involved with allocating surplus to individual life insurance policies in a mutual company have developed the so-called "contribution theory", which says that surplus should be allocated by source. For example, policies with the largest reserves should receive the largest share of investment gains; and policies with the largest expected claims should get the largest share of underwriting gains (due to death claims lower than anticipated). This theory rests on the assumption that there will be positive surplus — i.e., that the mortality and interest assumptions (and expense assumptions in the case of an insurance company) are chosen so as nearly always to produce gains rather than losses. Thus, while the problem of allocating gains and losses in a pension plan looks similar to the problem of allocating surplus to life insurance policies, the two are fundamentally different.

To see this difference, suppose we have consistent investment gains under our hypothetical pension plan. Since we are providing a defined amount of pension at age y for employee j, if we follow "contribution theory" and allocate investment gains in proportion to j's accrued liability, we cause his normal cost (as a percentage of salary) to decrease each year, rather than remain level. If the gains were large enough, they might cause j's accrued liability to exceed the present value of his benefits at some time before retirement, making his normal cost negative. Further investment gains would only make the situation worse. So for our purposes, allocating investment gains in proportion to accrued liability is not necessarily the best approach.*

The actuarial gain that we want to allocate, whether positive or negative, is not a "surplus" which belongs to a particular individual or generation which gave rise to it, but is rather a statistical aberration which belongs to the plan as a whole. Since the gain is a random variable with mean zero, those employees with the longest potential future service will have the greatest likelihood of having gains balance losses (i.e., they will be taking a larger sample from the distribution of the random variable). Conversely, those employees with the shortest times left have relatively less chance of having gains and losses balance each other out. Therefore, it makes sense to allocate larger portions of the total gain to those with the longest periods of future service. Likewise, those employees with larger salaries in general will have larger accrued

---

*But if employee j's benefit depended on the assets allocated to his account, the gains would *have* to be allocated proportionally to accrued liability; such plans, however, are largely obsolete in the United States except when funded entirely through individual insurance policies.

liabilities (because we have hypothesized a plan based on salary) so the allocation of gains should also be proportional to salary. These two requirements suggest an allocation in proportion to the present value of future normal costs: The normal cost is proportional to salary and its present value takes into account the future working lifetime.

Therefore, let us see what happens if we use the I/A cost method with the following gain-allocation method:

$$\Gamma_t^j \equiv \frac{\Gamma_t}{PVFNC_t} PVFNC_t^j . \tag{7.3.14}$$

You will recall that in equation (7.3.11) we did not define the term Γ_t^j ; now that we have a definition we can rewrite that equation as follows:

$$\lambda_t^j = \frac{\lambda_{t-1}^j \, PV\widetilde{FNC}_t^j - \dfrac{\Gamma_t}{PVFNC_t} PVFNC_t^j}{PVFNC_t^j}$$

$$= \frac{\lambda_{t-1}^j \, PV\widetilde{FNC}_t^j}{PVFNC_t^j} - \underbrace{\frac{\Gamma_t}{PVFNC_t}}_{\textit{constant for all employees}} . \tag{7.3.15}$$

Note that equation (7.3.15) implies that new entrants (for whom $\lambda_{t-1} \equiv 0$) will have some positive or negative amount of assets allocated to them the moment they are included in the valuation. This is not necessarily bad, but could be a problem in extreme circumstances, such as those of exercise 7.3.7. (Remember that since benefits do not depend on F_t^j the gain-allocation method does not affect the *benefits* payable to any particular person unless the plan as a whole is insolvent.)

Note also that if we are not using a service table and the projected benefit does not change, the factor of λ_{t-1}^j in equation (7.3.15) is exactly 1, so $\lambda_t^j = \lambda_{t-1}^j$ − constant. This means that all employees hired in the same year would have the same loading factor, because it would start out at zero and then be adjusted by a constant each year.

Thus it would not require a great leap of imagination simply to declare a *constant* loading factor for *all* employees. After all, we would not thereby change the underlying ILP normal cost, but only the portion of the current unfunded to be allocated to a particular employee. When we do so, we are led directly to the *modified-aggregate* cost method, as we shall now see.

First, note that if the loading factor is a constant, equation (7.3.7) implies

$$UAL_t \equiv \sum_{\mathbf{A}_t} \lambda_t^j PVFNC_t^j = \lambda_t \sum_{\mathbf{A}_t} PVFNC_t^j , \tag{7.3.16}$$

or,

$$\lambda_t = \frac{UAL_t}{PVFNC_t} , \tag{7.3.17}$$

the "aggregate" analogue of equation (7.3.7). The cost of the plan at time t then becomes

$$\begin{aligned} C_t &\equiv (1 + \lambda_t) NC_t \\ &= \left(1 + \frac{UAL_t}{PVFNC_t}\right) NC_t = \frac{PVFNC_t + AL_t - F_t}{PVFNC_t} NC_t \\ &= \frac{PVFB_t - AL_t + AL_t - F_t}{PVFNC_t} NC_t \\ &= \frac{PVFB_t - F_t}{PVFNC_t} NC_t , \end{aligned} \tag{7.3.18}$$

which may be written in more detail as follows:

$$C_t^{M/A} = \frac{PVFB_t - F_t}{\sum_{\mathbf{A}_t} NC_t^j \dfrac{{}^sN_{x+t} - {}^sN_y}{{}^sD_{x+t}}} \cdot \sum_{\mathbf{A}_t} NC_t^j . \tag{7.3.19}$$

This is the definition of the normal cost under the M/A method. The normal cost under the *aggregate* cost method can be written in a similar fashion, from equation (2.9.5):

$$C_t^{AGG} = \frac{PVFB_t - F_t}{\sum_{\mathbf{A}_t} S_t^j \dfrac{{}^sN_{x+t} - {}^sN_y}{{}^sD_{x+t}}} \cdot \sum_{\mathbf{A}_t} S_t^j . \tag{7.3.20}$$

So the modified-aggregate cost of the plan is similar in form to the regular aggregate cost, except that the salaries of each of the participants have been replaced in each case by the ILP normal costs — hence the term *modified* aggregate.

One big advantage of the M/A over the I/A method is that you can apply it without having to allocate assets — or gains — beforehand (compare equation (7.3.18) to equation (7.3.1)). Nevertheless, by stipulating that the loading factor be constant for all employees we *imply* the asset allocation:

$$F_t^j = AL_t^j - \lambda_t PVFNC_t^j . \tag{7.3.21}$$

Note also that the M/A method, like the I/A, produces the same cost as ILP in the first year of operation.

In summary, to perform an actuarial valuation under the modified-aggregate cost method you need only proceed as follows:

(1) Do the regular ILP valuation;

(2) Sum the individual values NC_t^j and $PVFNC_t^j$;

(3) Plug these into equation (7.3.18) to get the cost (you have already computed individual values of $PVFB_t^j$ to get the ILP normal costs via equation (2.5.17)).

Therefore, if the gain allocation of equation (7.3.14) is acceptable, you will save some work by using the modified-aggregate instead of the individual-aggregate cost method, and get practically the same results. Remember, though, that each year's gain is amortized over the average future working lifetime of employees — weighted by salary, not by ILP normal cost (as you will see in exercise 7.3.5(c)). Therefore, a large loss just before the retirement of a key employee might present solvency problems for the plan as a whole (see exercise 7.3.7).

Until now we have reserved the terms "normal cost", "accrued liability", etc., to refer to the ILP method; but now that we have defined the I/A and M/A methods as cost methods in their own rights, it is appropriate to summarize the definitions of those terms for each of the three cost methods independently, as in Table 7.3.1.

Exercises

7.3.1 Show that under the I/A cost method

$$F_t^j = AL_t^j - \lambda_t^j PVFNC_t^j . \tag{7.3.22}$$

7.3.2 In this section we suggested two possible criteria for distinguishing "individual" cost methods from "aggregate" ones. Which of the following criteria are *sufficient* to distinguish an individual cost method from an aggregate cost method?

(a) (Under an individual cost method) j's accrued liability can never be negative.

(b) j's normal cost would be unchanged if no other employees were present.

(c) j's total pension cost (normal cost plus amortization of current unfunded) is entirely covered by his own normal costs before he retires, regardless of actuarial gains and losses.

Table 7.3.1

	Individual Level Premium	*Individual Aggregate*	*Modified Aggregate*
Normal Cost	$\sum_{A_t} \frac{PVFB_t^j - AL_t^j}{PVFS_t^j} S_t^j$	$\sum_{A_t} \frac{PVFB_t^j - F_t^j}{PVFS_t^j} S_t^j$	$\frac{PVFB_t - F_t}{PVFNC_t} NC_t$
Accrued liability	$\begin{cases} 0\,;\, t=0 \\ \sum_{A_t}(AL_{t-1}^j + NC_{t-1}^j)\frac{D_{x+t-1}}{D_{x+t}}\,;\, t>0 \end{cases}$	$\sum_{A_t} F_t^j$; *allocation arbitrary*	F_t
Unfunded accrued liability	$AL_t - F_t$	0	0
Total pension cost at time t	$NC_t + \frac{UAL_t}{\ddot{a}_{\overline{n}\vert}}$ *n arbitrary*	*Same as normal cost (line 1); e.g.* $NC_t + \sum_{A_t} \frac{NC_t^j}{PVFNC_t^j} UAL_t^j$ *for the asset-allocation method discussed in the text.*	*Same as normal cost (line 1):* $NC_t + \frac{NC_t}{PVFNC_t} UAL_t$

Note: The symbols NC_t, AL_t, etc., refer to ILP throughout the table.

(d) The accrued liability is not equal to current assets, except by accident.

(e) The actuarial gain can be determined without computing the current normal cost.

Try each of these criteria on all of the cost methods so far studied (you can use Table 7.1.1 and exercise 7.1.4 to refresh your memory). Can we classify cost methods by these two categories unambiguously?

7.3.3 Prove that assets are implicitly allocated to employees under the M/A method by equation (7.3.21). Can any employee have *negative* assets?

7.3.4 Derive the following recursion relation for the loading factor λ_t under the modified-aggregate cost method:

$$\lambda_t = \frac{\lambda_{t-1}(PVFNC_{t-1} - NC_{t-1})(1+i) - G_t}{PVFNC_t} . \tag{7.3.23}$$

7.3.5 (a) Throughout this section we have used the term "gain" to refer to G_t, the gain under the ILP cost method. Now that we have (Table 7.3.1) separate definitions of accrued liability and normal cost under the two new cost methods, how would you define the gain under the individual-aggregate cost method? Under the modified-aggregate method? (Hint: Remember that "gain" means an unexpected decrease in the unfunded accrued liabiliIty, and take a look at equation (7.3.17).)

(b) Derive an expression for the total I/A normal cost at time t in terms of its value at $t-1$ and your expression for the I/A gain from part (a). Does your normal cost remain a level percentage of salary if actual experience equals expected?

(c) Repeat part (b) for the M/A cost method.

7.3.6 ***Numerical Example***

Consider a plan covering just two employees, employee A and employee B. The plan provides a pension of one-half the final year's salary and is established 1/1/83. On 1/1/84 the plan still covers only A and B, but on 1/1/85 you find that employee B has quit and been replaced by a new employee C. The pertinent data on the three individuals in question are as follows:

	Employee A	B	C
Date of Birth	1/1/33	1/1/43	1/1/53
S_0^j	$50,000	$20,000	--
S_1^j	60,000	25,000	--
S_2^j	70,000	--	$22,000

The actuarial assumptions are as follows:

Interest: 5%
Service table: none
Salary increases: none
Retirement age: 65
$\ddot{a}_{65}^{(12)} = 10.0$

The employer actually deposits each contribution (with one year's assumed interest) into the fund at the end of each year. The fund earns 10% the second year.

(a) Compute the costs of the plan as of 1/1/83, 1/1/84, and 1/1/85 using the ILP method with gains amortized over 15 years. (Answer: 13,029; 15,994; 16,952).

(b) Compute the costs for the three years under the individual-aggregate method using the gain-allocation method of equation (7.3.14). (Answer: 13,029; 15,994; 16,926).

(c) Compute the three costs under the modified-aggregate method. (Answer: 13,029; 15,994; 16,926).

7.3.7 Assume the same facts as in exercise 7.3.6, except (i) A was born in 1921, and (ii) the investment return is -25% in the second year and 5% in the third year. At the end of the third year, A retires and takes a lump-sum distribution of ten times his annual pension.

(a) What would be the fund balance on 1/1/86 if the I/A method were used, with gains allocated as in equation (7.3.14)? (Answer: $-\$1{,}149$)

(b) What would be the fund balance on 1/1/86 if the M/A method were used? (Answer: same as (a)).

(c) Can you think of a better gain-allocation procedure for use with the I/A cost method — one which would work even in this extreme case? Would it keep the individual unit normal costs level if there were no gains or losses?

Acknowledgements

It is well that I, as a first-time author, did not forsee the difficulty of writing and publishing a book like this one. Having now passed through the ordeal with more or less success, I must express my boundless gratitude to the persons and institutions who helped me do it.

Patricia E. Troy typed the first page and the last page of the manuscript, and everything between. She cut and pasted the handwritten formulas, made corrections as the author's mistakes were uncovered, retyped the manuscript, made more corrections, and retyped again — a monumental job for which I shall never be able to thank her enough.

The Society of Actuaries and the American Society of Pension Actuaries instigated my writing the book, and provided moral and logistical support during its creation. By exposing early versions of the manuscript to their students in the form of study notes, they provided the means by which many bugs were ironed out before the book went to press. A preface to the study notes invited written comments, and the response was gratifying. Not only were numerous errors corrected, but many respondents suggested alternative proofs or lines or reasoning which found their way into the book. With apologies to anyone whom I may have forgotten, I list below those persons who made significant contributions, by way of thanking them for their time and energy: William H. Aitken, Michael L. Bain, Mitchell L. Barlas, Richard L. Baum, Thomas E. Beresford, Steve Boger, Steven D. Bryson, Mark W. Campbell, Paul J. Cascio, Roy Arnott Chong-Kit, Linden N. Cole, Richard Daskais, Matthew G. Deckinger, Frank S. Derbak, Katherine L. Duguay, Samuel Eckler, Ralph M. Fecke, Jeff Furnish, Ruthann Hall, Carol M. Hasday, James H. Hughes, Michelle L. Kunzman, Farhad K. Minwalla, Ghislain Nadeau, D. Bruce Near, David R. Nelson, Charles A. Nichols, III, George D. Powell, Dale A. Rayman, Gerald Richmond, Paul Robitaille, Louis-Georges Simard, Mitchell I. Serota, William David Smith, Jerauld G. Spigal, Charles L. Thorne, Paulette Tino, Hungping Tsao, and Yang Soon Yim.

Index to Principal Notation

Listed below in approximately alphabetical order are the principal algebraic symbols used in the text. Symbols which were defined strictly for purposes of a localized discussion have been omitted. The page listed after each symbol is the page on which the symbol was first used, or first defined.

Symbol	*Page*	*Meaning*
$a_{\overline{n}\rceil}$	115	Present value of an annuity certain of one unit per year, payable at the end of each year for n years.
$a_{\overline{n}\rceil}^{(m)}$	106	Present value of an annuity certain of one per year, payable m times a year in installments of $1/m$, at the end of each $m$thly period for n years.
$\ddot{a}_{\overline{n}\rceil}$, $\ddot{a}_{\overline{n}\rceil}^{(m)}$	151	Same as above, but payable at the beginning of each period.
$\bar{a}_{\overline{n}\rceil}$	152	Present value of an annuity certain of one unit per year, payable continuously throughout each year.
$\ddot{a}_x$	50	Actuarial present value of a life annuity of one unit per year, payable annually at the beginning of each year as long as the recipient, aged x at commencement, survives (i.e., with the last payment on the first of the year in which the recipient dies).
$\ddot{a}_x^{(12)}$	8	Actuarial present value of a life annuity of one unit per year commencing at age x, payable in monthly installments of 1/12 at the beginning of each month, ending with the payment due in the month of death.
$\bar{a}_x$	74	Same as above, but payable continuously until the recipient dies.
$\bar{a}_{\overline{x:\overline{n}\rceil}}$	75	Actuarial present value of a life annuity of one unit per year, payable continuously for the life of the annuitant (aged x at commencement), but for at least n years in any case.

Symbol	*Page*	*Meaning*
${}_{n\|}\ddot{a}_x^{(12)}$	78	Actuarial present value of a life annuity of one unit per year, payable 12 times a year beginning at age $x+n$, to a recipient now aged x.
$\bar{A}_x$	152	Actuarial present value of a unit payable immediately upon death to a person now aged x.
$\mathbf{A}_t$	8	Set of active employees at time t.
AB_t^j	55	Accrued benefit of employee j at time t.
$\widetilde{AB}_{t+k}^j$	81	Accrued benefit of employee j at time $t+k$, projected using the data available at time t.
AC_t^j	54	Employee contributions accumulated to time t, with interest as specified by the plan.
AL_t^j	14	Accrued liability of employee j at time t.
AL_t	9	Total accrued liability at time t, for all employees.
$\widetilde{AL}_{t+k}^j$	18	Accrued liability of employee j at time $t+k$, projected on the basis of data available at time t.
B	48	Actual benefit payments made during a year.
$B^j(y)$	8	Actual pension payable to employee j commencing at age y.
C	11	Total contributions to the pension fund for a year (employee plus employer).
C_t^j	54	Contributions made by employee j at time t.
	196	Total contributions on behalf of employee j at time t.
C_x	58	Commutation function at age x based on all decrements in the service table: $C_x = d_x v^{x+1}$.
$C_x^{(k)}$	78	Commutation function at age x, based on decrement k only: $C_x^{(k)} = q_x^{(k)} l_x v^{x+1}$.
d	59	Annual discount rate associated with interest rate i: $d = i/(1+i)$.
δ	14	Annual interest rate compounded continuously, associated with rate i: $\delta = log(1+i)$.

Symbol	*Page*	*Meaning*
d_x	59	Component of service table: $d_x = l_x - l_{x+1}$.
D_x	8	Commutation function: $D_x = l_x v^x$.
${}^sD_x$	22	Commutation function: ${}^sD_x = s_x D_x$.
$\mathbf{D}$	47	Set of persons who die during the year.
$\mathring{e}_x$	152	Expected future life-span at age x: $$\mathring{e}_x = \int_0^\infty {}_tp_x\,dt\,.$$
F_t	11	Actuary's value of the fund balance at time t .
G_t^I	107	Interest gain for the year $t-1$ to t .
G_t	197	Total gain for the year $t-1$ to t .
i	10	Assumed rate of interest earned by the pension fund for all future years (compounded annually).
$i^{(m)}$	106	Nominal annual interest rate compounded m times a year: $$1 + \frac{i^{(m)}}{m} = (1+i)^{1/m}\,.$$
I	11	Investment return actually realized by the fund during a year.
I_B	48	Interest at assumed rate i on pension payments B from date of payment to the end of the year.
I_C	12	Interest on employer contributions at the assumed rate i from the date of deposit to the end of the year.
I_P	12	Interest on pension "premiums" P from the dates of retirement to the end of the year.
l_x	54	Number of survivors at age x in a service or mortality table (l_0 arbitrary).
μ_x	14	Force of decrement (hazard rate) at age x .
M_t	107	Market value of fund at time t .
M_x	57	Commutation function: $M_x = \sum_{z=x}^{\infty} C_z$.
$\overline{M}_x$	57	Commutation function: $\overline{M}_x = \int_0^\infty l_z \mu_z v^z dz$.
$\mathbf{M}_t$	177	Set of active employees who are plan members at time t .

Symbol	*Page*	*Meaning*
N	37	Set of new entrants into the set of active employees during a year.
N_x	16	Commutation function: $N_x = \sum_{z=x}^{\infty} D_z$.
$N_x^{(12)}$	73	Commutation function: $N_x^{(12)} = D_x \ddot{a}_x^{(12)} \approx \mathrm{N}_x - \frac{11}{24} D_x$.
$\bar{N}_x$	21	Commutation function: $\bar{N}_x = \int_x^{\infty} D_z dz$.
${}^sN_x$	22	Commutation function: ${}^sN_x = \sum_{z=x}^{\infty} {}^sD_z$.
NC_t	10	Normal cost of the plan as of time t .
NC_t^j	10	Portion of normal cost attributable to employee j .
P	11	Amount withdrawn during a year, from the pension fund, to "purchase" pensions.
$\mathbf{P}_t$	47	Set of pensioners at time t .
${}_tp_x$	50	Probability of a person now aged x surviving t years.
$PVFB_t^j$	30	Actuarial present value of future benefits for employee j , computed at time t .
$\widetilde{PVFB}_{t+k}^j$	33	Actuarial present value of future benefits for employee j computed at time $t+k$, assuming no changes in projected pension after time t .
$PVFBW_t^j$	40	Present value of hypothetical future benefits for employee j , computed at his entry age w using data as of time t .
$PVFCW_t^j$	69	Present value at entry age w of future employee contributions of employee j , based on data as of time t .
$PVFEC_t$	64	Present value at time t of future employee contributions for all active employees.
$PVFNC_t$	31	Present value of future (employer) normal costs for all active employees at time t .
$PVFNC_t^j$	31	Portion of the above attributable to employee j .
$PVFS_t$	39	Present value at time t of future salaries of active employees.
$PVFS_t^j$	30	Portion of above attributable to employee j .

Symbol	*Page*	*Meaning*
$\widetilde{PVFS}_{t+1}^{j}$	40	Present value at time $t+1$ of j's future salary, assuming salary increases occur as assumed.
$PVFSW_t^j$	40	Present value of j's future salary at entry age w, based on data available at time t.
q_x	10	Probability of a person aged x dying or terminating employment within one year.
${}_tq_x$	72	Probability of a person aged x dying or terminating within t years.
$q_x^{(k)}$	84	Portion of q_x attributable to cause k.
$q_x^{(k)\prime}$	83	Probability of a person aged x succumbing to decrement k within one year, assuming no other decrements are possible.
r	14	Assumed rate of salary increases.
R	56	Total refunds of employee contributions during a year.
$\mathbf{R}$	9	Set of employees who retire during a year.
$s_{\overline{n}\rceil}$	58	Accumulated value of an annuity certain of one unit payable at the end of each year for n years.
$\ddot{s}_{\overline{n}\rceil}$	59	Same as above, but payable at the beginning of each year.
s_x	22	Salary index (element of salary scale).
S_t^j	22	Annual rate of salary of employee j at time t.
$\mathbf{T}$	9	Set of employees who terminate employment during a year.
U_t	32	Normal cost as a fraction of covered payroll (or *per capita*) at time t.
U_t^j	22	Normal cost of employee j as a fraction of his own salary, at time t.
UAL_t	11	Unfunded accrued liability at time t.

Symbol	*Page*	*Meaning*
v	54	Present value of one unit payable for certain one year from now: $v = 1/(1 + i)$.
w	8	Entry age of employee j (subscript j usually omitted).
x	8	Age of j on valuation date (subscript j usually omitted).
y	8	Assumed age of employee j at commencement of his pension (subscript j usually omitted).

Index

A

B

C